*f*P

## Also by Touré

*Never Drank the Kool-Aid: Essays*

*Soul City: A Novel*

*The Portable Promised Land: Stories*

# WHO'S AFRAID

## — OF —

# POST-BLACKNESS?

## What It Means to Be Black Now

## Touré

Foreword by Michael Eric Dyson

Free Press

New York   London   Toronto   Sydney   New Delhi

Free Press
A Division of Simon & Schuster, Inc.
1230 Avenue of the Americas
New York, NY 10020

First Free Press hardcover edition September 2011

FREE PRESS and colophon are trademarks of Simon & Schuster, Inc.

For information about special discounts for bulk purchases,
please contact Simon & Schuster Special Sales at 1-866-506-1949
or business@simonandschuster.com.

The Simon & Schuster Speakers Bureau can bring authors to your live event.
For more information or to book an event contact the Simon & Schuster Speakers Bureau
at 1-866-248-3049 or visit our website at www.simonspeakers.com.

Designed by Carla Jayne Jones

Manufactured in the United States of America

10   9   8   7   6   5   4

Library of Congress Cataloging-in-Publication Data

Touré,
Who's afraid of post-blackness? : what it means to be black now / by
Touré ; foreword by Michael Eric Dyson.
p. cm.
Includes bibliographical references and index.
alk. paper)
1. African Americans—Race identity. 2. United States—Race
relations. 3. African Americans—Psychology. I. Title.
E185.625.T68 2011
305.896'073--dc22                              2010042788

ISBN 978-1-4391-7755-6
ISBN 978-1-4391-7757-0 (ebook)

Dedicated to everyone who
was ever made to feel
"not Black enough."
Whatever that means.

# Credits

Credit lines for images throughout the book:
"How Much is that Nigger in the Window" a.k.a "Tompkins Square
Crawl," 1991, New York, NY, by James Pruznick. Courtesy of James
Pruznick.
"World's Exposition," by Kara Walker, 1997. Cut paper on wall,
approx. 10 X 16 feet. Courtesy of the artist and Sikke Ma Jenkins & Co.
"Untitled from Runaways," by Glenn Ligon, 1993.
"Condition Report," by Glenn Ligon, 2000.
"I talk white," by Rashid Johnson, 2003.
"Signed Clarence Thomas 'Uncle Tom All-Stars' Judicial Robe Jersey," by
Rashid Johnson, 2006.
"Signed Angela Davis 'Civil Rights All-Stars' Throw-back Dashiki Jersey,"
by Rashid Johnson, 2003.
"Colonel Platoff," "Alexander the Great," and "Ice T" © Kehinde Wiley.
Used by permission.

# Author's Note

I have chosen to capitalize the word "Black" and lowercase "white" throughout this book. I believe "Black" constitutes a group, an ethnicity equivalent to African-American, Negro, or, in terms of a sense of ethnic cohesion, Irish, Polish, or Chinese. I don't believe that whiteness merits the same treatment. Most American whites think of themselves as Italian-American or Jewish or otherwise relating to other past connections that Blacks cannot make because of the familial and national disruptions of slavery. So to me, because Black speaks to an unknown familial/national past it deserves capitalization.

# Contents

# Tour(é)ing Blackness
# by Michael Eric Dyson

"**M**ichael, say that again so I really get your meaning," Oprah asked me. Fifteen hundred of us had gathered in 2007 on the grounds of her magnificent home in Santa Barbara for a swanky bash to raise money for Barack Obama's presidential campaign. As Barack peeled off slightly ahead of us from the private reception before the fundraiser where he and Oprah and Michelle had posed for pictures for the adoring throng, I walked arm-in-arm with Oprah on the way to the main event and repeated my standard defense of Obama within earshot of the future commander-in-chief.

"When it comes to defending Barack against the charge that he's not Black enough, I tell folk, 'Well, I've known him for over fifteen years, and what I've noticed is that he's proud of his race, but that doesn't capture the range of his identity. He's rooted in, but not restricted by, his Blackness.'"

"That's the phrase, Michael," Oprah enthused as she mouthed it back to me. "'Rooted in, but not restricted by, his Blackness.' Yes, that's it. Don't you think so, Barack?"

Barack nodded his assent, and in typically self-effacing fashion, deflected attention from his achievement and praised my idea with charming vernacular.

"Michael can come up with some words now," Obama let on as he flashed that famous megawatt smile. "That brother knows how to turn a phrase."

Perhaps the words resonated for Oprah because she'd used the same tack in her life and career. Decades before Obama seized the universe by its throat and spoke his way to the Oval Office, Oprah had to negotiate a white world that had little understanding or use for a Black woman who quickly became the globe's dominant media personality. She ruffled a lot of Black feathers by turning Blackness inside out and allowing it to breathe in the white world on its own with little explanation or apology.

Like most Black folk, Oprah found the batteries of Blackness included at birth, and ripped open the packaging and slid them in and started using the instrument of race before reading the manual—a long, historic, episodic, vastly complicated, genre-blending, shape-shifting, anatomy-defying, ramshackle, improvisational, antiphonal, allusive, radiant, dense, formal, informal, contradictory text composed from slavery forward in bits and pieces in essays, books, tracts, sermons and orations, in verses and stanzas, in solos and choruses, in blues bits and lingering lullabies, in dirges and ditties, in symphonic, orchestral sweep and staccato jazz strokes, in song and spoken word, in music and lyrics by writers and thinkers, poets and playwrights, preachers and pimps, vocalists and filmmakers, hustlers and Harvard-trained jurists, jive-talkers and juke-jointers, assholes and altruists, civil rights leaders and Black power advocates, beboppers and hip hoppers, fair-headed agitators and faint-hearted assimilators, Afrocentrists and integrationists, and a cast of millions. Oprah and Obama are the latest, if most visible, examples of how Blackness bends to the tongue it tumbles from at any given moment of time.

The sheer plasticity of Blackness, the way it conforms to such a bewildering array of identities and struggles, and defeats the attempt to bind its meanings to any one camp or creature, makes a lot of Black folk nervous and defensive. Sometimes the transfer of power to define Blackness is a bloodless affair where one meaning peacefully succeeds the next, as in the shift from colored to Negro to Black as a self-identifier among African Americans. Yes there were certainly some who got dragged kicking and screaming into the struggle to turn *Black* from a hated adjective into a prideful noun (and how some Negroes despised being called Black as if it underscored the dark mark of their natal misfortune). In cases where new perceptions of Blackness clashed with old receptions of Blackness, established definitions of race and their defenders often got the bum's rush and got trampled beneath the feet of new Blacks armed with new definitions of the not-same-old Blackness.

But the very malleability of Blackness permits Black folk to shape it into weapons to fight on all sides of the debate about what Blackness is or isn't. Republicans, gays and lesbians, scuba divers, Marxists, mathematicians, biracials, and Tea Party supporters alike are the odd men out in a Blackness they inherit and then make over, and before whose invisible court they are often compelled to argue about why they belong to a category that outsiders to Blackness have no problem putting them in. To sample Malcolm X, what do you call a Black person with a Ph.D.—or with membership in tony clubs and elite schools or marginal political groups or minority sexual orientations? You got it: they all share the dreaded epithet that condemns them to solidarity in derision even as they dramatically escape from traditional meanings of Blackness, and even as they trump the idea that a single gauge of oppression measures the full weight of their Black identities any longer, if it ever did. (After all, the suffering of poor Black folk is different from the suffering of rich Black folk, and even when wealthier Blacks suffer from persistent prejudice, it's hardly the same as the restrictive structural barriers faced by the working poor.) Sure it may help explain why they all get dissed; but it may not explain why the most salient features of their identities are no longer bound to a single idea of Blackness that can't account for them to begin with. In short, a lot of these folk aren't seen as genuinely and authentically Black by other Blacks, even as they get the kibosh from outsiders who "get" their Blackness even if they miss the other facets of their identity that throw up a challenge to narrow Blackness: their sexual orientation, their regional variety, their geographical diversity, their religious beliefs and practices, their class location and the like. A lot of

Blacks are silently excommunicated from Blackness inside the borders of race while being seen as only Black outside the race.

The truth is that the problems faced by those who are deemed insufficiently Black are a symbol of the problems all Black folk face in grappling with Blackness. In fact, the problems of not-Black-enough folk throw a bright light on how Blackness has always been more complicated and bigger than the Blackness we settled in and for. A single notion of Blackness was perilous from the start. The experiences of millions of Black souls could hardly be summarized in myths of unity aimed at freeing us from the vicious unanimity of identity imposed on us by ignorant racists. Black folk have historically fought the menace of the third-person pronoun *they*—referring to white power that initially had a name and face, such as Mr. Charlie and Ms. Anne, but which eventually became amorphous and disperse in systems of oppression that never seemed to lose the personal touch—with the equally elusive unity of the first person plural pronoun *we*.

Such an understandable strategy has had a whiplash effect: even as we lashed out against racists by proving in word and deed that we weren't the savages they said we were, our efforts to define who "we" are cut against the complexity of our Blackness and sacrificed the depth of variety for the breadth of unity. It made sense for Blacks to unify against oppressive forces as a strategy of racial combat, but it made less sense to adopt that strategy as a means to define the race. What it means to be Black will always be richer than our response to oppression at any point in our history. "We" can never helpfully define ourselves by our response to what "they" say or do.

The undeniable need to fight oppression can't overshadow the freedom to live and think Blackness just as we please. The point of fighting for freedom is for Black folk to define Blackness however we see fit. We can't reasonably expect each other to trade one sort of oppression for another. We can surely disagree with each other about what Blackness is and who best embodies it, and we can even call into question each other's morals and motivations, but not because we are the masters or architects of Blackness with the blueprint of authentic Blackness neatly folded in our Black pockets. We've got to make arguments based on how we see the past and the future, and we've got to offer compelling reasons for one action or another as Black folk based on good sense and sound judgment.

We can't argue from *a priori* Blackness, a Blackness that is given and remains steady despite the ebb and flow of history and struggle. We've got to do away with the notion that there's something that all Black folk have to believe in order to be Black. We've got to give ourselves permission to divide into subgroups, or out-groups, organized around what we like and dislike, and none of us is less or more Black for doing so. I think what Clarence Thomas has done on the Supreme Court is wholly destructive to Black folk, and I'm willing to root my arguments about his catastrophic performance in reasoned claims about politics and race. But he isn't any less Black than I am; he's got a different take on Blackness and race than I do. Whether his take on race is viewed as less or more helpful than mine should be judged, but not by reference to an unchanging, eternal idea of Blackness that is stuck in the Black sky as a North Star to shed light on our doings as a people.

That's why post-Black is so suggestive a term: It clearly doesn't signify the end of Blackness; it points, instead, to the end of the reign of a narrow, single notion of Blackness. It doesn't mean we're over Blackness; it means we're over our narrow understanding of what Blackness means. Post-Blackness has little patience for racial patriotism, racial fundamentalism and racial policing. Racial patriotism builds on the parallel between loyalty to the race and loyalty to the nation. Loyalty isn't the problem, but rather the sort of racial fidelity that often flies under the banner of Blackness. Black folk offered the nation a great gift by proving you are most loyal to your country when you're willing to accent its virtues and criticize its failures. Too often racial patriots are just as blind as other American patriots: my country right or wrong becomes my race right or wrong, and even more disturbing, racial patriots often identify their views of Blackness with the only acceptable views of Blackness, and are willing to railroad or expel all others who disagree.

Racial fundamentalism views race like religion, and true believers and ardent advocates for the race hold to narrow, literal tenets of racial identity and struggle. They often have little tolerance for more nuanced, less literal, more complicated readings of Black identity; who's in and who's out is determined by adherence to rigid tests of authentic Blackness. Gay folk are out, so to speak, because Africa didn't have any gay men or lesbian women before colonization by Europe; feminists need not apply for a Black card because they undermine the integrity of Black struggle unified around the implicit universality of Black masculinity. And racial policing desires to keep the borders and boundaries of Blackness safe from the criminal presence of inauthentic and subversive ideas. Racial policing aims to purge Blackness of ideological impurity and political instability by arresting the development of complex ideas of identity and struggle inside of Black minds and communities. In racial patriotism, racial fundamentalism, and racial policing, the weather is quite stormy and unvaried by season; it rains catechisms and dogmas all day long. If Black folk are ever to enjoy the sublime and raucous joys of Blackness, we've got to step into the sunshine of disobedient and complicated Blackness.

That's why I'm so glad that ingenious Black folk like Touré exist. He's free to be Black the way he sees it, and he feels no need to apologize for who he is or what he says or thinks. Ever see him on television? He's a riot of complicated Blackness: his handsome, chiseled face all aglow with mischievous ideas about the world we live in, delivered in an over-the-top style that dares the stereotype of the loud Black man to darken his reputation even as his mind races to put pop culture and politics into intelligent perspective. The brother is downright irreverent: a Black man who hosted a television series where, as the title suggests, he'll try anything once, which for him meant entering a demolition derby in Indiana, where, unless your name is Reggie Miller, Black men just aren't usually welcome or used to successfully treading (just ask Mike Tyson). He also tried bull-dodging as a rodeo clown in Wyoming, chasing a 15-foot boa constrictor, and shadowing a pest control official in Florida's panhandle to remove 60,000 bees!

Ever read his vibrant prose that pops off the page? He writes fiction and nonfiction with equal eloquence. Touré has written about Dale Earnhardt Jr. (now just how many Black men are involved in race-car driving, much less writing skillfully about the sport and one of its stars?), and he's proved that he could add color in more than one way to George Plimpton's knack for turning his journalistic observation into a sociological lab through direct participation in the lives of his subjects, taking to the basketball court with Prince, to the tennis court with Jennifer Capriati, and playing high-stakes poker with Jay-Z. And he's done all this while bucking the trend for young Black male writers of his generation: he dropped out of Emory in his junior year in 1992 to become an intern at *Rolling Stone*, where he's been a contributing editor since 1997, writing some of the most lucid, learned pieces on pop music and culture we've read. Maybe James Baldwin could get away with not going to college at all, and Ralph Ellison could leave Tuskegee after his third year to move to New York to study the visual arts, but that was way back when the opportunities for higher education weren't nearly as plentiful as they are now—and thus, the demand that such education be attained before opportunity is offered. Touré had that much swagger that he could trust his huge talents and his nose for what he needed to do to become who he wanted to be, to pull an Ellison-meets-Diddy and follow a path that took him from intern to impresario.

What's most important, and uplifting, about Touré is he just doesn't give a damn about what you think about him even as he cares deeply and writes beautifully about the human experience as a Black man free to marry outside his race, travel far beyond the limits of Blackness he forgot to acknowledge, speak about all sorts of issues that Black folk aren't supposed to speak about, and tell the truth about the Blackness he's lived his first 40 years robustly exploring. Touré's notion of post-Blackness is just what we need to move from exhaustive Blackness to expansive Blackness—from the idea that Blackness is one thing to a focus on the one thing that Black folk should never forget: that we are so many wonderful and terrible things all at once, and that we can live past the puny ideas and wan portraits of those who would hold us back to claim the birthright of enormous Blackness that is ours for the asking and doing. This brilliant book asks a lot, and does a lot more, like exploring how we are rooted in but not restricted by our Blackness. But above all, it makes us see ourselves in all our luminous and thrilling and complicated and splendid Blackness the way we are meant to be Black when we leave everything to our imagination.

# WHO'S AFRAID
## OF
# POST-BLACKNESS?

# Chapter 1

# Forty Million Ways to Be Black

**O**nce, I went skydiving. For about four minutes in 2007 I was above—and plummeting rapidly toward—a small town in the middle of the Florida panhandle. Jumped out of the plane solo at 14,000 feet. I did it for a TV show called "I'll Try Anything Once" in which every week I accepted fear-inducing challenges. On the way to the skydiving center the production team stopped for lunch at a restaurant where three middle-aged Black men who worked there recognized me from TV and came over to our table to say hi. We got to talking and they asked what I was doing there. I told them I was on my way to go skydiving. Their faces went cold. They were stunned. One of them said, in a conspiratorial tone and at a volume meant to slide under the sonic radar of the white people sitting right beside me, *"Brother, Black people don't do that."* The other two nodded in agreement. They quickly glanced at the rest of my team and then back at me as if that clinched their point: The only people doing this risk-your-life, crazy foolishness are some loony white boys and you. As they saw it I was breaking the rules of Blackness. I was afraid but not about breaking the invisible rule book.

The plane was old and small with only a seat for the pilot, barely enough room for five adults to sit on the floor, and not enough height to stand. There was one clear, thin, plastic, rickety door that didn't look strong enough to keep people from falling through it. The walls of the little plane were so thin that the sound of the engine permeated them

1

completely. In order to be heard you had to yell. The plane did not move with the efficiency and grace you want from a plane, it reminded me of an old dying car that sputters and wheezes and makes you pray it'll start and keep running until you get there. As it climbed into the sky it seemed to be saying, "I think I can, I think I can." If I hadn't been scheduled to jump out for the sake of television, I would've listened to the voice inside me yelling "Bail!"

At 14,000 feet the thin plastic door—which recalled a grandmother's couch protector—was pushed up and through the open maw you could feel the oppressively fast, hard, uninviting wind slashing by, daring you to play deadly games. You could barely see the Earth below, large buildings now smaller than ants, acre-sized fields tinier than a baby's palm. My eyes were saucer wide, my palms were soaked, my heart was banging in my chest as if looking for a way out, saying, "You can go, but I'm staying here in the plane." The breathless terror enveloping me as a jump virgin was not assuaged by my macho divemaster, Rick, a former cop and Marine with a military-style buzzcut who owns the drop zone, jumps twenty times a day, and finds the fear of newbies funny. Rick thought gallows humor was appropriate at that moment. With the door open he said, "Just remember, no matter what happens . . . I'm going to be all right." He laughed. I did not. He was going to jump out after me but he wasn't going to be on my back. I was going solo. Or as he put it, I was going to have the chance to save my own life.

As I scooted on my butt toward the open door—the wind vacuuming angrily like one of those horror movie vortices that'll suck you into another world—my mind said, "No! No! No!" I was directly violating my constitution as a human, which places a very high value on survival, minimization of physical risk, and not dying. Sliding toward the open door of a plane hovering at 14,000 feet was overriding the instinct in my reptilian brain. Still, I got in the doorway and grabbed hold of the sides of the plane. I could feel the wind smacking me in the face. I could barely see the ground. I could not imagine letting go. Then Rick began to count down from three. I told myself, "You will let go when he says go. You will not hesitate." I needed to tell myself those things because my body was semi-paralyzed. Rick said two. My frontal lobe tried to veto the whole thing. Can't we just wimp out and let the plane take us back to the ground? Then Rick said go. And I just let go. And I was falling.

Freefall does not feel like falling. It feels like floating but without the peace we associate with floating. Things are moving at supersonic speed and the virgin skydiver's mind can't keep up, can't process all that's going on, so it's a chaotic blur with the wind so loud you can't hear yourself think and can't hear yourself screaming. I think I was screaming for about ten seconds before I even realized it. And I kept trying to grab on to something, anything, but there was nothing, just air.

They tell you to keep your head bent upward and to not look down at the Earth because the view is awesome, and more important the weight of your head will send you into a spin or at least into the wrong dive position. But I looked down. Couldn't help it. And that sent me spinning heels over head and then hurtling down back first for a tumultuous forty-five seconds of twisting and turning and upside-down plunging, falling toward Earth with everything happening too fast to realize how screwed up everything was and how terrified I should've been. I pulled the cord but because I was in the wrong dive position—still falling on my back—part of the parachute coiled around my arm and did not unfurl. I looked up and saw this thread wrapped twice around my right forearm as I kept falling to the ground. If I did nothing I would've died eight or nine seconds later. But reader, I promise you, I was calm. I did not panic one bit. The voice in my mind was cool. With the same inner tone I might use to say to myself, "Hmm, we're out of pretzels," I said to myself, "Hmm, the chute's wrapped around my arm."

The day before my dive, during my eight-hour training class, Rick told me what to do if this happened: just shake your arm and the cord should come loose. So at about 5,000 feet from the ground—which skydivers know is next to nothing—I shook my arm as if shooing off a fly. The cord came loose and the chute went free and unfurled above me, breaking my fall.

Suddenly, the *sturm und drang* of freefall gave way to peace. I was floating gently, like a snowflake. All was quiet. I could look up and see the sun playing peekaboo amidst the clouds and below I saw tiny cars and buildings and fields. I felt like a speck of dust blowing in the cosmos at the whim of a much, much larger force conducting a massive, magnificent opera. And in that moment, the perspective I gained from being thousands of feet in the air made me fully grasp how small a part of this world I am. It made me as absolutely certain of the presence of God as I have ever been. That bird's eye view of Earth and the soul-stirring meditative quiet I was wrapped up in made me feel like a tiny dot in His awesomely sculpted world, a minute particle floating through a gigantic universe that will outlast me by a long ways. This is His world, not mine, I'm just a visitor and should be thankful for the few days I have. It was the most deeply spiritual experience of my life. I went skydiving and ended up in church. If I'd turned down the opportunity to skydive because "Black people don't do that" I would've robbed myself of an experience I needed to get closer to God. And who would deny me that? If I never go skydiving again I'll always carry with me the more tangible and concrete belief in Him that I got from that day. That's a profound gift. If I'd let being Black hold me back from skydiving I would've cheated myself out an opportunity to grow as a human.

To be born Black is an extraordinary gift bestowing access to an unbelievably rich legacy of joy. It'll lift you to ecstasy and give you pain that can make you stronger than you imagined possible. To experience the full possibilities of Blackness, you must break free of the strictures sometimes placed on Blackness from outside the African-American culture and also from within it. These attempts to conscript the potential complexity of Black humanity often fly in the face of the awesome breadth of Black history. If I'd believed that Blacks don't skydive I would perhaps have disrespected the courageous Black paratroopers of World War II—the 555th was an all-Black unit that valiantly jumped over twelve hundred times. Some Blacks may see the range of Black identity as something obvious but I know there are many who are unforgiving and intolerant of Black heterogeneity and still believe in concepts like "authentic" or "legitimate" Blackness. There is no such thing.

Henry Louis Gates Jr., the director of Harvard's DuBois Institute for African and African American Research, says there has always been a multiplicity of ways to be Black but now because of the economic and intellectual diversity in Black America there's "a multiplicity of multiplicities." There is no dogmatically narrow, authentic Blackness because the possibilities for Black identity are infinite. To say something or someone is not Black—or is inauthentically Black—is to sell Blackness short. To limit the potential of Blackness. To be a child of a lesser Blackness. "My first line in my class," Gates told me in an interview in his office at Harvard, "and the last line twelve weeks later is if there are forty million Black Americans then there are forty million ways to be Black. There are ten billion cultural artifacts of Blackness and if you add them up and put 'em in a pot and stew it, that's what Black culture is. Not one of those things is more authentic than the other."

Dr. Michael Eric Dyson, professor of sociology at Georgetown, agreed. "There's been an exponential increase in both the modes and methods of Blackness," he said in an interview at his apartment in D.C., "and the ways in which Black people are allowed to be legitimately Black. It used to be much more narrow. When I hear Black people tell me "Black people don't" fill in the blank—scuba dive or be gay in Africa or whatever—I think, you're ignorant. Because the beautiful diversity of Blackness is the most remarkable feature of a Blackness that we continue to try to quarantine. We'd rather quarantine Blackness but the beauty of Blackness is that it's a rash that breaks out everywhere. The moment we shatter those artificial encumberances of race—a stereotype from without or a rigid archetype from within—and feel no need to respond to either is the moment we are vastly improved, profoundly human, and therefore become the best Black people we can become. And we maximize our humanity. I mean, the irony is, the greater we maximize our humanity the greater our Blackness becomes."

I see a small-scale representation of Black collective identity expansion in hiphop. As a recorded medium it began in the late seventies and early eighties as a showcase for New York Black male working-class symbols, tropes, and signifiers. Almost all of the songs, clothes, attitudes, and purveyors of very early hiphop culture were about life in

5

the streets and clubs of New York City for Black men. Even when the Real Roxanne emerged she rhymed about her relationship, or refusal to have one, with Black men, rather than what she did with her girls when no men were around. There were many sorts of Black people around New York—and around America—but hiphop did not show them.

Modern hiphop does: its identity politics are much more complex. New York's hegemony has given way to a national culture, and the language and performance of Blackness of MCs from Atlanta, New Orleans, Houston, Detroit, Chicago, L.A., and other cities is different than that of New Yorkers. The expression of class mores has also broadened within hiphop: There are still many MCs playing exclusively with working-class signifiers, but in the wake of mid-eighties Black bohos like De La Soul and A Tribe Called Quest we now have Kanye West, André 3000, Common, Questlove, Lupe Fiasco, Kid Cudi, Drake, Pharrell and others whose personae are filled with middle-class and/or culturally avant-garde signifiers. There are also figures like Jay-Z and 50 Cent who grew up working class but joined the extreme upper class and now give us identities filled with a mixture of class signifiers. There are many women in hiphop expressing identity through their own point of view (as opposed to in relation to what men think). And, quiet as it's kept, there's a national gay and lesbian hiphop underground scene, showing us how far hiphop has come from being a site for Black, male, working-class, heteronormative identity. If hiphop were a person and you asked it what does it mean to be Black in 1983 and again in 2013, the answers would be far different. Still hiphop fails to capture the full complexity of Black America—there are many Black identities not represented in and by hiphop. But I think a similar broadening of the collective identity—and/or a broadening of the acceptance of it—has occurred within Black America. Blackness is a completely liquid shape-shifter that can take any form, just like the chameleonic agents in *The Matrix* or the T-1000 or the T-X in the *Terminator* sequels that are made of a mimetic polyalloy that allow them to take on any appearance. It's an unfortunate coincidence that both

6

of those memorable examples of infinitely mutable figures are villains because for the shape-shifter that power equals freedom: Be anyone you want at any time. As the artist William Pope.L says, "Blackness is limited only by the courage to imagine it differently."

Melissa Harris-Perry, a Princeton University professor of Politics and African-American Studies, believes Blacks are aware of and proud of our diversity. "We have a homogenizing media culture that makes all of us more alike than we might like to suggest," she told me. "That dominant discourse does present pretty limited possibilities of what it means to be a Black man or a Black woman. But in Black peoples' actual lives, in their families, in their churches, in their neighborhoods, they actually do know a lot of different kinds of Black people. And are not particularly surprised to encounter artsy Black people and gay Black people and, you know, perfect-English-speaking Black people, and hoodish. I mean, I think we are more aware of our fundamental humanity and the variation that goes along with it than we let on in public spaces. Now, do we have a way of saying to each other, 'This is an insufficiently Black or crazy thing that Black people don't do'? I mean, sure. But, we also go to poetry slams and are excited when one of us plays tennis and somebody else plays violin. I guess I'm just convinced that there's actually a lot more room in our conceptions of Blackness, particularly on a very interpersonal level, then we tend to let on. I'm saying I'm not yet convinced by the discourse or the evidence that I have out there that we really don't make room for each other."

Such is the intellectual diversity of Black people: We can't totally agree on whether or not Blacks have a collective awareness and acceptance of Black diversity. I know Professor Harris-Perry is correct that many of us are cognizant and tolerant of our diversity but I also know from personal experience that there are self-appointed identity cops in our community—people who are like Sergeant Waters in *A Soldier's Story*—policing the race and writing Authenticity Violations as if they were working for Internal Affairs making sure everyone does Blackness in the right way. But what is this right way? And who chose it?

"Sometimes Blackness is threatened," says Kehinde Wiley, the visual artist, "by a desire to go outside of a collective sense of deprivation and to engage education and opportunity. It feels good to all be down with one another. This notion of being authentically Black is comforting. To be down is to be with it, to be with your people, to be part of the collective. But I think it's time to grow out of that. The cult of the individual is something that is going to be a rescuing point for Black people. I think in order to do good for your community you have to do good for yourself and you have to stop thinking about being down and what everyone's gonna think about you. You have to see the whole field of options and professions and fields of inquiry that exist in the world like one big buffet court. You have to be able to say I'm gonna try something that my group has never tried before because in order for me to get somewhere I have to push myself outside of my limits and safe places. Because the white boys have always been given that free run to be individuals."

Dyson suggests that certain historical forces have motivated the identity expansion I'm suggesting. He gave me an analogy linking the romantic solidarity of the nationalistic sixties and seventies with a religious approach to Blackness while the post-Black rugged individualism of the new century and the future is more like a non-religious spirituality of Blackness. "When I was born in 1958," he said, "it was like the purpose of your life was to help further and advance the struggle for Black self-determination." I was born in 1971 and as a child in the seventies I got that same sense—that being Black meant being born into an army that you had to somehow contribute to. Not necessarily in an armed or violent way, just as not everyone in the army goes into combat. "At birth," Dyson said, "you were given a Black card that made you part of a group and you had to give to the group and be a good productive member. You had to sacrifice for the group and do everything in ultimate allegiance to that group. This is what I mean by religious Blackness. The ultimate spirit of the community was God. The Black leaders were the Holy Ghost. The martyrs of the movement were Jesus. So Martin Luther King Jr., Malcolm X—it doesn't matter their particular religious orientation—those who died, those are the martyrs, those are the Jesuses. As a result of that, any disagreement with the community was a disagreement with God, was a disagreement with your religious Blackness—any dissent was like apostasy."

But in the eighties and nineties Black America became more diverse in terms of education and profession and income, and no dominant Black leaders have arisen—perhaps because the community is too diverse to be led or maybe because deep down the community no longer wants to be led—and thus the sort of magnetic centrifugal force that once pulled the community together has faded away. That has led to a variety of approaches to Blackness. Says Dyson, "In the same way that many people say, 'Hey I'm spiritual but I'm not religious,' there are Blacks who dissent from the church of Blackness, from the religion of Blackness, but they're not sinners. They're good Protestants, they're just not Catholics. They don't think you have to pay obeisance to the pope or go to confession with the priest in order to get to God. They believe you can go to Him yourself. We have no pope so we can go to Blackness ourselves. It's an individual thing, it's a spiritual thing, not a religious thing. And I think that has made some Black people extremely insecure and extremely cautious. And I'm not suggesting that there are no legitimate reasons to be critical of the kind of willful individuality. It would be silly to believe that Black people are not still judged as a group even though we argue for this robust individualism. The fact is that we're still lumped together in many ways. But the civil rights struggle was about getting us to the point where we could be taken as human beings." Leading to a multiplicity of ways to be Black.

Dyson defines three primary dimensions of Blackness. He calls them accidental, incidental, and intentional but I prefer to call them introverted, ambiverted, and extroverted. The introverted (or accidental) mindset is about a perhaps more private relationship with Blackness. Dyson says it's "I'm an American, I'm a human being, I happen to be Black. By accident of my birth I am Black. It just happened that way." He gives Clarence Thomas and Condoleezza Rice as celebrity examples. Ambiverted (or incidental) Blackness refers to having a more fluid relationship with it: Blackness is an important part of them but does not necessarily dominate their persona. Dyson says it's "people who more completely embrace Blackness—they aren't trying to avoid it—but that ain't the whole of their existence. I love it but it doesn't exhaust me." In this group he places Barack Obama, Colin Powell, and Will Smith. "Then there's intentional [or extroverted] Blackness," Dyson said. "I be Black, that's what I do, that's what my struggles are about." This is Malcolm X, Dr. King, Jim Brown, Jay-Z.

But confining most people within one of these modes isn't easy. Different moments present different situations that demand that we modulate. "Here's the trick Black people always understand," Dyson said. "Depending on where we are, we're any one of those Blacknesses. This is the beauty of Blackness. When you're at your job and you're trying to get a raise in a predominantly white corporation, you're probably accidentally Black. You say, 'Hey, Bob, how are ya? Did you see "Modern Family" last night? Hysterical. All right, do I have the raise?'" Dyson and I agreed that you may also throw in a little extroverted Blackness to further your bond by bestowing a feeling of coolness on your audience. "You could say, 'Yo, you heard that new Jay-Z album? It's tight!' And you're saying it in a way that what you're really saying is 'I'm gonna give you temporary access to the Black card. This card will self-destruct in twenty-four seconds. But for a moment you'll feel cool and that'll help me build the relationship I need." I know some successful Black writers who go into the offices of stodgy white magazines calling everyone brother and sister, in a way that puts people at ease and makes them feel cool and respected and helps build a bond.

Then there's times you need to throw up Black signifiers like they're gang signs and be extroverted. "I think about Barack Obama when he was running for president," Dyson said. "He was down in South Carolina and he's talking about people saying he was a Muslim. Now, he's not gonna diss Muslims, he has Muslims in his family, but we know in the context of America that signifies negatively. So he says, 'You know I've been gone to the same church wit my bible in my hand'—'wit,' not 'with'—and they're laughing. It's a predominantly Black audience so he's talking directly to them. He says, 'You know, that's the okie doke, you know what the okie doke is?' They go, yeah. He says, 'Ya been bamboozled, ya been hoodwinked!' Now here's the genius of Barack Obama: because we know 'hoodwinked' and 'bamboozled' are from Malcolm X. So here's a guy using the language of the most famous Black Muslim there has been to deny that he's a Black Muslim, but still communicate an insider's connection with and understanding of Black culture. That is so Black!"

Dyson continued: "Black people have different modes of Blackness and when we need to be each of those varieties of Blackness, we exercise them. We vacillate among the modes depending on what we need. When you deal with multiple audiences you have to pivot around different presentations of Blackness."

The ability to maneuver within white society—and how high you can rise within white power structures—is often tied to your ability to modulate. Black success requires Black *multi-linguality*—the ability to know how and when to move among the different languages of Blackness. A prime example is Oprah Winfrey, who will switch modes in a matter of seconds and can sometimes convey multiple modes at one time. This is not selling out any more than cursing in front of your friends and not cursing in front of your grandmother is selling out: it's intelligently modulating among the various selves we all have inside. There are many ways to be Black in all Black people.

I would like, through this book, to attack and destroy the idea that there is a correct or legitimate way of doing Blackness. If there's a right way then there must be a wrong way, and that kind of thinking cuts us off from exploring the full potential of Black humanity. I wish for every Black-American to have the freedom to be Black however he or she chooses, and to banish from the collective mind the bankrupt, fraudulent concept of "authentic" Blackness. Some of us still cling to the myth of consensus, the idea that there is some agreement on how we should do Blackness—on what is and is not Black, a right path and a wrong one. We have no race-wide agreement and have never had one. "We want to think Blackness was a unified thing you could hold in your hand," Gates says, "but it was always like holding water in your hand. There was a core, like there still is a core—you could go to any Black church and feel at home. When you go to the barbershop, you know, it's like a warm bath, it's nice. There is a core, a recognizable Black culture, but out of that core it's splintered and fragmented and it goes off in ten thousand different directions."

In this book, I seek to legitimize and validate all those directions because we are in a post-Black era, which means simply that the definitions and boundaries of Blackness are expanding in forty million directions—or really, into infinity. It does not mean we are leaving Blackness behind, it means we're leaving behind the vision of Blackness as something narrowly definable and we're embracing every conception of Blackness as legitimate. Let me be clear: Post-Black does not mean "post-racial." Post-racial posits that race does not exist or that we're somehow beyond race and suggests colorblindness: It's a bankrupt concept that reflects a naïve understanding of race in America. Post-Black means we are like Obama: rooted in but not restricted by Blackness. It means we love Blackness but accept the fact that we do not all view or perform the culture the same way given the vast variety of realities of modern Blackness. It's not that some people are post-Black and some are not—and post-Black cannot be used as a replacement for Black or African-American—it's that we're in a post-Black era when our identity options are limitless. And there's no going back. Most terms have a confining aspect to them but post-Black is not a box, it's an unbox. It opens the door to everything. It's open-ended and open-source and endlessly customizable. It's whatever you want it to be. Such is the dynamic hyper-creative beauty of modern individualistic Blackness. Kara Walker, the great visual artist, told me it's hard to talk about an individualism movement, but that's what I see. Our community is too diverse, complex, imaginative, dynamic, fluid, creative, and beautiful to impose restraints on Blackness.

I am not here presenting myself as or claiming to be an "expert" on Blackness. I'm a Black person who loves Black culture and history and has been actively thinking and reading about what it means to be Black since I was a child. Because I am not a scholar, and because I thought it would be a fascinating research project, I decided to interview 105 prominent Black people about various aspects of contemporary Blackness. They include:

- politicians like Harold Ford Jr., the former Congressman from Tennessee; Sharon Pratt, the first female mayor of D.C., and Benjamin Jealous, the president of the NAACP.
- visual artists including: Kara Walker, Glenn Ligon, Lorna Simpson, Barkley L. Hendricks, William Pope.L, Gary Simmons, Julie Mehretu, Kehinde Wiley, and Carrie Mae Weems.
- recording artists: Chuck D of Public Enemy, Questlove of The Roots, Vernon Reid of Living Colour, Talib Kweli, Santigold, and Lupe Fiasco.
- writers: Malcolm Gladwell, Greg Tate, Stanley Crouch, Shelby Steele, Roland Martin, Nelson George, Juan Williams, dream hampton, Kristal Brent Zook, Jonathan Capehart from the *Washington Post*, and Charles Blow from the *New York Times*.
- academics: Dr. Beverly Tatum (president of Spelman), Henry Louis Gates Jr. (Harvard), Dr. Cornel West (Princeton), Michael Eric Dyson (Georgetown), Dr. Alvin Poussaint (Harvard), Patricia Williams (Columbia), Dr. Marc Lamont Hill (Columbia), Wahneema Lubiano (Duke), Dr. Jelani Cobb (Spelman), Dr. Elizabeth Alexander (Yale), Farah Griffen (Columbia), and Dr. Charles Mills (Northwestern).

I also spoke with Reverends Jackson and Sharpton, comedian Paul Mooney, filmmaker Reggie Hudlin, CNN host Soledad O'Brien, and "Mr. Boondocks," Aaron McGruder. I spoke to every significant member of the creative team of the television show that I think best epitomizes the post-Black ethos: "Chappelle's Show." That includes co-creator and co-writer Neal Brennan, who's white. I was not able to speak with Dave Chappelle for this project but I interviewed him when I was at BET—the interview took place after he'd left the show, when he was promoting *Dave Chappelle's Block Party*—and I pull from that interview here. That old Chappelle interview is also not counted toward the 105—these are all new interviews.

Toward the end of the process I decided it'd be interesting to include the perspective of Robert Farris Thompson, a white Yale history professor and a noted authority on African art and religion and Afro-Cuban dance, who knows and cares an extraordinary amount about Black culture. We had a nice long lunch at an Italian restaurant near Yale. I also had a psychiatrist interview me for two hours, hoping to unearth things I'd forgotten or not realized.

The people I spoke with challenged me, enlightened me, and helped me sharpen and deepen my ideas. I don't know if talking to a different 105 would have produced a totally different book, but this book would not be what it is without the amazing contributions of this 105.

I aimed to have the sort of deep, honest, intense conversations we have about race in private spaces—usually with smart or trusted friends after a glass of wine or two. None of these interviews were lubricated by alcohol but most had that level of candor and often the intensity of a therapy session. Reverend Jackson cried—not a sob but a single tear ran down his cheek—talking about a painful moment from his childhood.

Some questions I put to almost everyone, some questions I put to those in a specific field, and some questions I posed just to specific individuals. For the purpose of understanding the project, and so you can have a chance to think about how you would've answered, here are some of the questions I asked almost everyone:

- What does being Black mean to you?
- Does being Black mean something different now than it meant three or four decades ago? Has what it means to be Black changed over the last forty years and if so, how?
- Is there an authentic Black experience?
- What do you think about the concept of post-Blackness?
- Do you think Blacks have ways of imposing limits on Black identity?
- What does it mean when one is said to be "acting white" or is being "not Black"? What's the value to Blacks of attacking Blacks in that way?
- Do you think some Black people need to be more open-minded about what it means to be Black?
- Is Blackness at the center of your persona?
- Are there particular, necessary characteristics of Blackness? Is there a centrifugal force pulling Blackness together?

- What is the most racist thing to ever happen to you? What was its impact on you?
- What do you think of the words nigger and nigga?
- How is it certain Black politicians can make a silent deal with voters to be so-called "beyond race" and others can't? How is that deal made?
- Why are we still colorstruck? Are there advantages to being light? Are there disadvantages to being light? Are there advantages to being dark? Are there disadvantages to being dark?
- Would you be comfortable eating watermelon in a room full of white people?
- As a child in the seventies I was taught and I felt that Blackness was a movement, that being Black is like being part of an army that you must contribute to in some way. I'm not sure that we are involved in that same sort of a unified movement anymore. What do you think?
- Do you love America? Do you think Black people love America? Or are we conflicted, like a battered spouse?
- I believe that Black people correctly remain angry at America for the lack of rights and the oppression that we've experienced both as a collective and as individuals, but I wonder if we're giving ourselves enough credit for being key architects of America, especially in the twentieth century when, through Thurgood Marshall, Malcolm X, Dr. King, Huey P. Newton, and others, we forced the country to move toward being as democratic as it claimed to be. We're reluctant patriots but we're also critical shapers of this country—we've been molded by it but we've also molded it. What do you think about that?
- How do we create more Barack Obamas, by which I don't necessarily mean more Black presidents but more people who are proudly Black and intellectual, and are comfortable in Black and white spaces, and feel like they can set extraordinarily high goals without fearing that race will keep them from achieving those goals?

I talked to as many as possible in their homes or in offices or in restaurants—I met with Paul Mooney in a tiny dressing room at Caroline's after one a.m., following a show; with Kara Walker at her studio where

I glimpsed an extraordinary piece in progress; with Reverend Sharpton at a private, members-only cigar club while former Mayor Giuliani sat just a few feet away; with Reverend Jackson in the lobby of a hotel, then in his car as he was driven downtown, and then in a private room at Penn Station as he waited to board Amtrak. Some interviews had to be conducted over the phone. For obvious reasons I connected with Mumia Abu-Jamal by letter. Almost all of the conversations lasted exactly an hour, though Professors Gates, Dyson, and West talked to me for about 90 minutes while then–New York Governor Paterson could spare only fifteen minutes.

Some of those I interviewed I already knew personally, some I emailed cold, some were referrals from others I'd interviewed, and in some cases I met them through Twitter. I'm especially grateful to Thelma Golden, the curator of the Studio Museum of Harlem, for connecting me to so many in the art world. Golden, along with the artist Glenn Ligon, coined the term "post-Blackness" as a way of describing something they saw happening in art. I thought I saw the art movement they named traveling into and through the entire American culture. When I described my initial thoughts about this book to Golden—and asked if she felt I could apply her meme about Black artists to all Black people—it felt like I was asking her if I could take her magnificent, ultra-rare, expensive car for a drive on the highway. In essence, she said she wouldn't drive it on the highway but I could, if I dared.

Some will say, Hey, we're a society dealing with a growing jail population, AIDS, cancer and other health care problems, an education gap, widespread unemployment, predatory loans, foreclosure, rising poverty—how can you be talking about frilly issues like identity? Well, I believe that when the body is under attack—and I mean both the collective body and our specific bodies—then there's a need, or even an imperative, to check in on the soul. I will deal in depth and detail in this book with the impact of racism on our souls because I am in no way saying racism is over or has even lessened. In my research I found it remains a major shaper of Black identity—some of the people who spoke about the most racist thing that had ever happened to them, including Reverend Jackson, said it was a defining incident in their lives that led them to become who they are today. I do not discount or ignore the institutional and de facto forms of racism that continue to shape and oppress Black life in America. But I also think we can deal with those matters and these at once. One does not eclipse the other. As the painter Kehinde Wiley said, "People who say we can't afford poetry; we need to change lives, we need to feed people, people are dying of treatable diseases, people are starving, and you're talking about satisfying states of internal grace and being self-actualized authentically? I understand that. And I think that as adults we have to recognize the necessity for both. And as a mature society we are graced to be able to actualize both."

Who I am is indelibly shaped by Blackness, so I have to examine Blackness to know who I am. But I am much more than a repository for Blackness. If you are Black, you may be, too. I have been told, explicitly and implicitly, that there are borders to Blackness, and that sometimes I had strayed beyond them. Am I the fish that swam away from the school or did the school become as big as the ocean—so big you can't swim away from it? If Blackness is, like the ocean, too high to get over and too low to get under, then how could any Black person ever not be Black?

## Chapter 2

# Keep It Real Is a Prison

If words were people, "Post-Black" would not be a celebrity. Not yet. Few people know him and some of those who know him don't understand him. Some people are thrilled he's strolled into the collective mind but some are a little scared of him. Imagine a young, fresh-faced preacher with bright eyes arriving in town early one morning, bursting with presence and radiating pride and positive energy. But he has the air of a radical who wants to shake things up. His first name alone tells you he's got new ideas. That he's here to do things in a new way. And when someone arrives proposing major changes to your world, that can be frightening. But relax. His mission is spiritual liberation.

"To me, the instruction 'keep it real' is a sort of prison cell, two feet by five," wrote Zadie Smith in "Speaking in Tongues," a 2008 essay in the *New York Review of Books*. "The fact is, it's too narrow. I just can't live comfortably in there. 'Keep it real' replaced the blessed and solid genetic fact of Blackness with a flimsy imperative. It made Blackness a quality each individual Black person was constantly in danger of losing. And almost anything could trigger the loss of one's Blackness: attending certain universities, an impressive variety of jobs, a fondness for opera, a white girlfriend, an interest in golf. And of course, any change in the voice. There was a popular school of thought that maintained the voice was at the very heart of the thing; fail to keep it real there and you'd never see your Blackness again.

19

"How absurd that all seems now," Smith wrote. "And not because we live in a post-racial world. It's Black people who talk like me, and Black people who talk like Lil Wayne. It's Black conservatives and Black liberals, Black sportsmen and Black lawyers, Black computer technicians and Black ballet dancers and Black truck drivers and Black presidents. We're all Black and we all love to be Black and we all sing from our own hymn sheet."

If there are forty million Black people in America then there are forty million ways to be Black, as Skip Gates says. That's forty million hymn sheets. What an amazingly vibrant chorus we make up. We are in a post-Black era where the number of ways of being Black is infinite. Where the possibilities for an authentic Black identity are boundless. Where what it means to be Black has grown so staggeringly broad, so unpredictable, so diffuse that Blackness itself is undefinable. What it means to be Black is different for each Black person and every answer to the question "How do you do Blackness?" is valid. One cannot honestly say some person is not Black for doing Blackness "incorrectly" or for some crime against the race, like the way they talk or who they are, because every way of being Black is legitimate: we are Allen Iverson and Grant Hill, Michelle Obama and Mo'Nique, Serena and Tiger, Mary J. and Santigold, Lenny Kravitz and Jay-Z, Cornel West and 50 Cent, Denzel and Andre 3000, Nas and Kanye, Toni Morrison and Lil' Kim, Bill T. Jones and Q-Tip, Judith Jamison and Mike Tyson, Beyoncé and Minister Farrakhan, Justice Thomas and General Powell, and Dr. Rice and President Obama.

In the post–Civil Rights generation the largest Black middle class in history has developed thanks to greater educational opportunities and increased access to professional, technical, and managerial professions. This is not to say all is well with Black America, far from it, but a larger slice of Black America has been able to enjoy the spoils of America than ever before and that has led to a fundamental change in Blackness itself. Black America has become more economically, academically, and intellectually diverse and thus the varied experiences of Black Americans has led to innumerable ways to embody or wield Blackness to the extent that Blackness has become so vast that it's impossible to hold it in your mind. "There was an expansion," says Professor Bambi Haggins of Arizona State University, "for people who came of age after those barriers had been legally brought down. People could vote, there was integration, there was affirmative action, there were some systematic things that had been changed so as they grew up things started being different for both the Black middle class and the Black lower class. Plus we got images of Black success and wealth and privilege that hadn't been there before, like Cosby, Oprah, Eddie Murphy, Michael Jackson, Michael Jordan."

I also think there has been a critical generational break from that part of Black history in which to be Black meant a near-constant, warlike struggle for de jure and de facto rights. Several interviewees spoke of the sense of Black trauma that attended previous generations but does not visit my generation in quite the same way. My parents grew up in segregation with laws and society arrayed to attempt to keep them boxed in to niggerdom. Blacks had to fight a civil war—which, in many battles, was an armed insurrection—in order to become full citizens. Through the Civil Rights and Black Power struggles many—not all but many—of those visible and invisible chains were broken. I grew up in an integrated world without racist laws holding me back. When I was old enough to hold a gun there wasn't much to take up arms about. The battles had to be fought in a more nuanced way. The fight for equality is not over but that shift from living amid segregation and civil war to integration and affirmative action and multiculturalism—and also glass ceilings, racial profiling, stereotype threat, microaggression, redlining, predatory lending, and other forms of modern racism—has led many to a very different perspective on Blackness than the previous generations had.

The warlike conditions that previous generations lived under led to a more compactly constructed sense of identity because the enemy was clear and the life possibilities felt constrained. The post-warlike conditions of my generation have led to a broadening of identity and, in many, a laying aside of the sense of Black trauma that attended previous generations. Duke Law Professor Wahneema Lubiano said, "Post-Black is what it looks like when you're no longer caught by your own trauma about racism and the history of Black people in the United States. Then everything is up for grabs as a possibility. Because you're not wearing the trauma anymore. You get to use something that produced all that trauma and do something else with it. So that's how I'm thinking about how post-Blackness can operate. It's not a disavowal of history, it's just the determination that you're not wearing all that trauma anymore and you're not waiting for the world to be different to live your life in more interesting ways. And it doesn't mean that you can't snap to a moment when you want to make a comment about racism, when you want to take on a particular kind of political battle."

"Both my parents grew up in segregation and there was a dogmatic transference of trauma," said UC Santa Cruz professor Derek Conrad Murray. "Like they had this experience and it was my obligation to take that trauma that they experienced and basically keep that flame alive. It reminds me of some of my Jewish friends talking about being indoctrinated into this kind of trauma narrative of survivorship and thinking of themselves as survivors of the Holocaust. I think that happens in a lot of Black households. There's this mandate that we have to feel this kind of trauma and then carry that with us through our lives. And we honor the history of the struggle of Black people in America but we still want to construct our own notion of Blackness that is separate from that of our parents and grandparents."

Shelby Steele, a celebrated author and research fellow at Stanford, has noticed the same generational disconnect. "I grew up in the fifties and the sixties, during the era of segregation in Chicago and what we had in common as Blacks in those days was victimization. The fact that we shared this oppression, and so you know it really was the center of the Black American identity. How do you deal with this absurd fact that you are oppressed because of the color of your skin? So, you know, oddly it gave us a bond and we sort of knew each other in that. This is no longer a segregated society so that old core identity that we shared just doesn't have the solid footing that it once had. So I think that there is no longer a real centrifugal force to the Black identity and this becomes, I think, more the case as time goes on rather than less the case. And so that's one of the things it means to be Black today, that we don't really know what the hell it means, certainly not with the kind of certainty that we did in the past." Steele says ethnic groups can cohere around a common enemy but what happens when the enemy leaves the field? It's too simplistic to say the enemy of Black America has left the field but given that racism was a binding force in many respects, the changed nature and function of racism leads to a very different Black identity.

Wait, who does Touré think put limits on Blackness? What is he talking about? We've had bold, original thinkers who took Black identity to new places and challenged the traditional identity boundaries for decades—Prince, Basquiat, Pryor, Hendrix, Sly, Baldwin, Ellison, Miles, George Clinton, Octavia Butler, Nina Simone, Ornette Coleman, Thelonious Monk, Zora Neale Hurston, and on and on. Well, call them our identity liberals and I contend that in the post-Black era their ranks are multiplying, maybe even exponentializing. And that they're in a cold war of sorts with our identity conservatives who are convinced Blackness is this and not that and certain people who are judged to be unprogressive or inauthentic or "not Black" need to be shaped up or weeded out by any means necessary. We've all heard and felt the Blackness police among us judging and convicting and sentencing and verbally or mentally casting people out of the race for large and small offenses. Maybe you have thought about writing an Authenticity Violation because someone's not Black enough. But that is completely unproductive.

The legendary photographer Carrie Mae Weems told me, "Black people can be very limiting for themselves. I don't feel as though I'm being confined by anybody other than myself, you know. And that goes across everything that I do in my life. To the extent that I am confined, I'm confined only in my own head. So my responsibility to myself is to figure out ways to break through to new territory. The great freedom, you see, would be for Black people to say, 'You know what? Fuck y'all. I'm just gonna do what I do.' That would be the great step forward. I just do what I do and sometimes it's about Blackness and sometimes it's about Israelis and sometimes it's just about shit." Weems concedes this is not a fault of Black people, it stems from constantly being reminded of our status as other. "For the most part Black people don't really move through the world in that way," she says, "because there are always these reminders that you are from a very particular social space that the world has not completely embraced yet."

Another legendary photographer, Lorna Simpson, echoed Weems. "People have opportunities in the way they construct themselves and if you're not reliant on the society around you to provide you with that construction then you can make yourself or construct yourself any way you'd like. So it's the idea that individuals can build communities but in such a way that they are not reliant on a status quo to confirm for them who they are."

Simpson continues: "I find within the Black community we can be so striated in expectations of how you're supposed to live, who you're supposed to date, how you're supposed to operate, what kind of job you're supposed to have, how you wear you hair, and I never felt that I wanted to play by those rules because that's not what I wanted out of life. So to make my life the way that I wanted I had to make a lot of independent choices about how I would live my life. It's kind of about having the audacity to be able to live one's life within the way that they want to live it without feeling the need to conform."

There is no consensus on what it means to be Black and never has been. Answers to the question of what it means to be Black that are contrary to your own are not incorrect answers. The fact that you don't like how someone else is doing Blackness doesn't mean they aren't Black. Blackness is not a club you can be expelled from. And just because someone gets "expelled" from the race the way, say, Clarence Thomas has, it doesn't mean they don't continue to battle racism on a daily basis, so what does expulsion really mean?

In Thomas's case it seems the jury is looking only at certain pieces of evidence. Juan Williams is close with Thomas. "I know him personally," Williams said. "When I think about Clarence Thomas I think about the kid at Holy Cross who studied Malcolm X speeches to the point that he can recite Malcolm X from memory to this day. You don't want to get into it with him about Malcolm X. This is a guy who was running breakfast programs for kids and just about to become a Panther at Holy Cross. A guy who went to Yale and would not let his professors view him as anything but Black. I mean, he wore coveralls at times just to say I'm a Black country boy, now you deal with that. I'm not going to pretend to be something, to dress up in a white shirt and try to look preppy. No, he dressed like a country Southern Black bumpkin in order to clearly define himself. This, to me, is a very strong sense of a Black person taking control. And if you talk about the most authentic Black experience I would say his is up there among them. I get very suspicious whenever I hear about authenticity but to me this was an authentic Black experience: Clarence Thomas grew up a few steps from the slave experience, in Pinpoint, Georgia, under harsh, punishing segregation. Blatant racial division and people who still spoke Geechee and that kind of stuff. That's one of the prime slave markets in the nation, down in the Carolinas and Georgia, those are entry points for Black people coming in, and in many ways it's not far removed from that experience." When you consider the totality of his life it becomes harder to say he isn't Black.

We've been arguing for decades about identity and authenticity and who's Black and who's not and I want to yell above the din—Truce! We're all Black! We all win! Because Blackness has boundless possibilities. Especially in the post-Black era. "Post-Black means," says visual artist Glenn Ligon, who's co-credited with coining the term, "a more individualized notion of Blackness. I just think we're getting beyond the collective notion of what Blackness was. Blackness was about group definitions so there could be Black leaders who spoke for Black people in total. And I think we've moved beyond that and we're entering the space where more individualized conceptions of Blackness will be the rule and not the exception. I think that's where we're headed."

It's critical, in a world with highly individualized notions of Blackness, that we allow each other latitude, freedom, and the benefit of the doubt.

Sometimes you think you're seeing a Black person be regressively Black but the opposite is happening even though you can't see it. Take, for example, William Pope.L, a mind-blowing performance artist who calls himself "a fisherman of social absurdity." He once stood outside of an ATM giving away money, thus turning on its head the relationship of ATM withdrawers and the panhandlers who orbit ATMs hoping for a spare dollar. He sometimes travels the country in a truck he calls the Black Factory, setting up shop in some town and asking people to bring in objects that represent Blackness to them. Then Pope.L and his team use the objects in skits meant to spark dialogue. He's addressed/attacked the commodification of Black bodies by sitting in the window of an art gallery wearing just underwear while smeared with mayonnaise. The title of the piece is a killer punchline: "How Much Is That Nigger in the Window?" He's great for titles dripping with irony that make mincemeat of gigantic memes in the Black collective mind. He titled one of his books *William Pope.L: The Friendliest Black Artist in America*, which, to me, is hysterical.

Some of Pope.L's best-known projects are his crawls, where he dons a business suit and crawls on hands and knees through miles of Manhattan, moving a foot or less at a time. Pope.L has several close family members who are homeless, or have been in and out of homelessness, including a brother, so the issue has great personal resonance for him. His crawls investigate what it means to lose horizontality—the habit of walking upright. When you become vertical what happens to you, how do people respond differently? Artists do not usually bring attention to the issue of homelessness. This is politically electric art. Also, as Professor Paul Gilroy of the London School of Economics points out, Pope.L is "lowering the Black body's center of gravity, taking it closer to the low-down and dirty," so there's an interesting racial aspect, too. Mistake Pope.L during his crawl for a hobo or a detriment to the race and it's your intellectual loss. But that can sometimes be hard to see up close.

William Pope.L during his Tompkins Square Park Crawl.

In one of Pope.L's crawls, the Tompkins Square Park Crawl, he moves through lower Manhattan's Tompkins Square Park, or attempts to. Pope.L has not crawled very far when an older Black male resident leaps up to protest. Pope.L has his crawls videotaped and in this instance the videographer was white, which led the resident to think he was perhaps a news cameraman shooting a Black homeless man. The resident goes to Pope.L and says, "Are you all right, brother?" Then he interrogates the cameraman, saying, "What are you doing showing Black people like this?" Right there he throws down his gauntlet: Attempts to create negative, regressive images of Blacks will not be tolerated here. The videographer says, "We're working together," and Pope.L confirms that. This throws the resident's understanding of the moment into chaos—he is standing over a Black man who is complicit in creating and perpetuating negative, regressive images of Blacks. Oh, hells no! The brotherly allegiance he'd expressed a moment earlier is instantly erased, replaced by indignation. Pope.L tries to mollify the resident by saying he's working and will come back in half an hour and discuss the work over a Coke, trying to move forward and not have this interaction become the focus of this crawl (even though this tense argument about portrayals of Blackness will lead to an illuminating interaction). The man refuses to end the conversation and rejects Pope.L's promise of a future discussion and the vague explanation "I'm working." He threatens to break the camera—i.e., violence will be used to halt the apparatus of your derogatory image-making—thus forcing Pope.L to get more specific about his strange work that looks a lot like homelessness.

Pope.L says, "I create symbolic acts." The resident does not understand. He says, "What is a symbolic act? Crawling up to the white man, or what?!" There the resident makes visible the elephant in the virtual room—"the white man" doesn't just mean the specific white videographer, it means white people in general. So this isn't truly a conversation between two people. There is also the silent, imagined audience of white people whom the resident, and Pope.L, know will eventually be receiving these images. But where the resident is afraid of the whites' reaction, Pope.L is not. Eventually the resident gets to his real point: "You make me look like a jerk!" Because, he feels, any denigratory images of Blacks would denigrate him, too. Because all Black people have a shared responsibility for the way Blacks are seen, because all Black people are representative of all other Black people. But in who's eyes?

I see all Blacks as individuals. No Black person could do anything that would make me think less of all Black people. Seeing a Black person behave repugnantly or regressively—be it the social ruination of a homeless person or the intellectual embarrassment that is Clarence Thomas or the ridiculously childish behavior of some spoiled athlete—does not make me think less of Black people in total. I suspect most Black people think the same. (If a Black person's view of Black people is so fragile that one act could make them think less of all Blacks, they need to see a therapist, posthaste.) So that notion of anxiety over what will befall you if other Blacks are seen in an adverse light comes from a fear of the white gaze. When we say, "bringing down the race" we mean "bringing down the race in white eyes." So the man is saying, "Whites will see you looking ramshackle and think less of me." I understand his point but I refuse to live my life in fear of the white gaze.

If, on a scorching day in July, you just happened to have a taste for watermelon to quench your burning tongue, and you happened to be in a room full of Black people, you would order and eat it without concern. But if, on that same sizzling summer day, you just happened to be in a room full of white people—in a restaurant where you were the

28

only Black or one of two or three Blacks scattered throughout the dining room—would you still order that watermelon you desire? Or would you not order it because you don't want to fulfill some stereotype? What about fried chicken, another stereotype-fulfilling, though less politically weighted, symbol-heavy food? Would you be comfortable to eat that in front of whites you don't know? Questlove, for one, told me he is not. "I'll be the first to order fish instead of chicken," he said. "If I'm on the Acela train, no, I'm not bringing no fried chicken on the train. I'll eat fish. I don't know why I still think that but it's just like that. I hate to say this, but no, I will not eat fried chicken in front of white people." He's not alone. Reverend Jackson said, "Eating watermelon in public? We're not that free. 'Cause the stereotype was that deep. We're still overcoming the burden of a four-hundred-year journey and the beneficiaries of that journey must honor the integrity of that journey."

Cornel West told me, "When you really get at the Black normative gaze, what you find is that oftentimes the white supremacy inside of Black minds is so deep that the white normative gaze and the Black normative gaze are not that different." I hope that more of us can get to a place where we don't make personal decisions based on the white gaze. It's quite a heavy invisible chain to lug around. I can't live like that. For example, I love me some fried chicken and I don't care what white person knows it. Good fried chicken is the bomb. It's not the healthiest thing you can eat but that's a different conversation. The point is, I refuse to curtail my life because of a fear of the white gaze. And that relates to way more than eating fried chicken and watermelon at the Ritz.

Many of the visual artists I talked to spoke of the liberating value in tossing off the immense burden of race-wide representation, the idea that everything they do must speak to or for or about the entire race. That's a heavy thing to carry around and it can stunt your spiritual and artistic growth quite badly. "The first obligation of art is to represent the truth as the individual sees it," Michael Eric Dyson said. "Whereas in Black communities the artist has often been burdened with what James Baldwin called the 'obligation of representation.' But now part of what it means to be Black is I can be true to what I believe. The reason why

Black artists have the leisure not to be obsessed with what kind of Blackness is authentic or legitimate is because people who were obsessed with Blackness as legitimate or authentic paved the way." Throwing off the burden of representation can give an artist the space to discover who they really are apart from the dictates of the community and the past and the confining strictures of worrying about the white gaze. "Artists are saying I'm gonna just do what I wanna do, how I wanna do it," said artist Gary Simmons. "And that is a very positive thing. You're not carrying a certain kind of, I don't want to say baggage 'cause that's a very heavy-handed term, but they're not carrying a burden with them that they have to address certain issues because of who they are, they're like I'm just going to make my stuff and that's the way I'm gonna roll." Not that distancing oneself from the groupthink is ever easy. Kara Walker told me, "Not representing the entirety and having this sort of push and pull against the group mentality is kind of fraught. I have those moments sometimes in the studio like no matter where you go there you are. And it's like you sort of push against the grain. There's a generation coming up that's less conflicted, I hope." Pope.L is older than Walker but you know he refuses to compromise to the white gaze because his crawls are videotaped to be shown to the art world, which is overwhelmingly white.

Back at Tompkins Square Park, the resident has summoned a police officer, escalating his attempt to halt the horrible image-making and bringing the imagined white audience onto the stage. He argues that Pope.L needs a permit to make a movie. The officer rejects that claim, saying, "All he's doing is making a video." It's fascinating that in his battle against Pope.L's alleged transgression against Blacks via the creation of negative imagery, the resident breaks the unwritten Black male law that a Black man should never call the cops on another Black man if physical violence is not involved. But I guess the visual or image crime against the race he perceived Pope.L to be committing is so egregious that it's acceptable to him to commit a different crime against the race and gender by involving the police. To the resident, Pope.L's attempt to create images that would degrade the race—and him in particular—require immediate action by any means necessary. Of course, he can't see that in the grander scheme Pope.L is playing a role and essentially agrees with the resident that Black degradation and homelessness are abhorrent. But where the resident wants new images of Black degradation to not be made, Pope.L wants to push artistic images of homelessness into people's faces. The resident judged Pope.L a race traitor for creating repugnant images without realizing that Pope.L was creating repugnant images as the opposite of a race traitor. As D'Arby English wrote in his brilliant book about contemporary Black art, *How to See a Work of Art in Total Darkness,* "If Pope.L's action breached an implicit Black middle-class unity in upward striving, it also exposed that unity is a form of social control." The resident was using the idea of unity and the ethos of "we must do right by Black people" in an attempt to control Pope.L and force him to abandon his actions. The imperative to unity is sometimes a disguised weapon that someone can use to try to enforce social control. The moment gives us two men with opposing conceptions of how to uplift the race coming into conflict, and because one did not understand the other's method, he incorrectly judged him a race traitor. This highlights how we need to give each other the freedom to be Black in the way we see fit. The brother or sister you think is being regressive could be being progressive in a way you can't yet understand.

The concept of post-Blackness originated in the art world, articulated in the late nineties by Ligon and his close friend Thelma Golden, the curator of the Studio Museum of Harlem. They felt a new chapter in Black visual arts had been entered, a generational shift had occurred, but didn't know what to call it. "Post-Black started," Golden told me, "as a sort of shorthand between Glenn and me to talk about how artists understood their content as it related to their identity and to how they lived their lives as Black people. It seemed to us that what was a set of somewhat simple but incredibly freighted choices in the past were now sort of broken up in so many different ways. And for us that became a way to define things as being post-Black art. And the truth is, it was wildly misunderstood."

Golden attempted to crystallize post-Black art in a 2001 show at the Studio Museum of Harlem called "Freestyle." It included Julie Mehretu, Rashid Johnson, Deborah Grant, Laylah Ali, Sanford Biggers, Mark Bradford, Kojo Griffin, Adia Millett, and Kori Newkirk. Curator and author Okwui Enwezor called "Freestyle," "One of the most important shows of the decade not only because of the articulation of this generational transformation where the work of Black artists is no longer absolutely bound by the image or the idea of race, but also its anticipation of that possibility that made Barack Obama the president of the United States." Derek Conrad Murray, professor of the history of art and visual culture at UC Santa Cruz, agrees that "Freestyle" was "one of the most important exhibitions that have ever happened in the United States" because it advanced the concept of post-Blackness.

In the catalog Golden wrote that post-Black artists were "adamant about not being labeled Black artists though their work was steeped, in fact deeply interested, in redefining complex notions of Blackness." This is a critical notion: They wanted to be defined as artists with the freedom that entails, rather than Black artists, which boxes them in, but they also wanted to retain the liberty to talk about Black subject matter when and where they pleased. They wanted to have it both ways at once. Why not? "They are both post-Basquiat and post-Biggie," Golden wrote. "They embrace the dichotomies of high and low, inside and outside, tradition and innovation, with a great ease and facility. . . . Their work speaks to an individual freedom that is a result of this transitional moment in the quest to define ongoing changes in the evolution of African-American art and ultimately to ongoing redefinition of Blackness in contemporary culture. . . . At the end of the nineties Glenn and I began, more and more, to see evidence of art and ideas that could only be labeled (both ironically and seriously) in this way—post-Black. . . . In the beginning there were only a few marked instances of such an outlook, but at the end of the 1990s it seemed that post-Black had fully entered into the art world's consciousness. Post-Black was the new Black."

Of course there was an antecedent in the paintings of Jean-Michel Basquiat. He was generally not descriptive of Blackness and Black life as many brilliant Black painting stars before him had been. Romare Bearden, Jacob Lawrence, Horace Pippin, and William Johnson they often painted Black people and our tropes in ways meant to ennoble Blacks and tell our stories, and that was valuable and necessary for their time. Basquiat rejected the burden of representation and the need to ennobilize Blacks and much of the time didn't give his figures any clear visual raciality. His obsession with anatomy and seeing the inside of the body suggests a vision of humans as deeper than race. But Basquiat was no oreo—he did not reject Blackness. Occasionally he discussed Black heroes from jazz and boxing or talked about the African slave trade or critiqued Black policemen, but this was just a part of his vocabulary and far from a dominant part. His style included all sorts of Black-American and Black diasporic influences as well as many references to European masters. His paintings discussed African art, European art, and modern art: He embraced high and low, inside and outside, and flaunting influences from Black and white culture because he was rooted in but not restricted by Blackness. "Jean-Michel represented this freedom in this way of wielding Blackness," Professor Murray said. "He was the quintessential post-Black artist in that he could move between the Black world and the white world on so many levels. Now it's more acceptable for people like him to be in the public eye and be out there."

Kara Walker was not in the "Freestyle" show but Golden considers her a major influence on it, one of the artists who, Golden wrote in the catalog, "reinvented the debate on culture and identity in contemporary art and . . . set the platform for this new post-Black existence in contemporary art." Professor Murray calls Walker one of the two major figures of post-Black art. (The other, he says, is Kehinde Wiley.) Walker is massively respected by critics, influential to fellow artists, and revered by the intellectual establishment—she is one of the youngest people to ever receive a MacArthur genius grant. She is also reviled by many artists, some of whom have conducted campaigns to have her work kept out of museums and published books filled with fiery essays damning her work. This seems to me the Pope.L Tompkins Square Park argument writ large—a battle over whether certain complex images are progressive or regressive for Blackness. A demand, from an artist, to take great liberty with potentially derogatory images in order to express something complex is met by a negative reply to that demand from others who nominate themselves as the keepers of Blackness.

"After Kara won the MacArthur," said Professor Murray, "I attended several major conferences about African-American art and saw some of the most volatile exchanges from the elder statesmen in the Black arts community and the younger generation that I've ever seen. It was like shouting matches. A total breakdown in communication between the generations. It was an extremely important moment. When I think about post-Black I think about Kara Walker because that was the moment when the younger generation developed the courage to say, listen, mom and dad, I'm gonna do this my own way. I'm gonna live my life the way I wanna live it, unapologetically. I'm going to embody Blackness in a manner of my choosing."

Walker cuts and pastes onto walls large black silhouettes of fantasy and nightmare slave narratives with Black and white characters of all ages interacting in hyperviolent and hypersexual ways—orgiastic scenes that can evoke horror, anger, laughter, tears, sometimes all at once. Her work is highly confrontational, pushing harsh visions of slavery into your face. She makes artistically gorgeous renderings of subject matter that is grotesque. She does not present slaves and massas and their families in typically heroic and villainous roles, and that in and of itself is challenging to viewers. And because she's not painting but pasting gigantic cycloramas to the wall and filling large rooms with these intense scenes that can barely be seen all at once, they can feel very real and tangible, as if you're behind some shrubs, wandering into a horrific moment from slavery in the dark of night with only the moon to illuminate it and can only make out the scene via darkened silhouettes. They're all black and all you can see are shapes but you're never confused about who's Black and who's not. Walker's dramas are literally drained of dimension and color as they're all about race and the multiple dimensions in which it operates. And her silhouettes are sharply and expertly cut with X-Acto knives so there's a violence implicit in the form and what it says: This

Black woman has taken a knife to history and recast it in her own vision. Walker says she sees herself as the master, her figures as her slaves, and her canvas as the plantation, which is an interesting juxtaposition: Instead of seeking to end the cycle she embraces it and grabs the mantle of the master, i.e., the villain. But interestingly, even as master of a world filled with masters and slaves she does not free her slaves and they're not snatching the revenge modern descendents wish to give them. Walker gives us moments where slaves are seen overcome by penises as large as their bodies or sucking on each other's breasts or hiding under a white woman's huge skirt—tragicomic moments that can make you cry or make you laugh to keep from crying. Who wants to be taken back to slavery and to brutally honest or wildly fantasized moments of rape and sex and power and violence and moral corruption? Walker is clearly not toeing the party line. "She's not trying to make you feel good about who you are when you're looking at the work," Professor Murray said. "The pressure of being a Black person who's a cultural producer is there's this kind of demand placed on you to create uplifting imagery. That's how you show your love for Blackness. You perform your part in the struggle for Black uplift. But Kara's not trying to validate you and make you feel good about being Black. She looks at power relationships in very complex ways, she moves away from this simplistic binary between good and evil in terms of the way she recalls slavery. Even among slaves there are power relations. There were abuses taking place and there's multiplicities of forms of abuse that are occurring all the time, and power struggles, and that's a postmodern way of looking at it. She's not interested in that simple binary of who's good and who's bad and I think that's really post-Black."

Carrie Mae Weems said, "Kara's work is really great because it implicates everybody. Everybody is implicated and everybody is a victim. You know, it's perverse, it's masochism, it's sadism, it's all there in this sort of twisted thing that our forefathers went through. And I think that Kara takes it one step further, and I think that this is the thing that's so great about her, is that she also implicates herself in the work. And that, I think, is the great, great, great, great, great strength of the work. You know, that I'm willing to peel back all the layers and expose my filthy self in my perversions, in my angst as well in relationship to this Black body and its relationship to whiteness."

Kara Walker's 1997 piece "World's Exposition" gives us the sort of wild slavery scene she's known for.

Kehinde Wiley said Walker's work "shoots radically through Blackness by virtue of perversion. She looks at the deeper sides of our psyches, including the more lascivious natures. When you feel like I'm going too far, maybe I shouldn't say that, that's when the utterance needs to happen. Kara Walker's work is like a great painting in which everyone is so absurdly outside of themselves that it becomes carnivalesque. It's perfect provocation to see race at that tipping point at which it becomes absurd. It's almost like Kara allows race to become so heavy that it folds in upon itself and starts to decay upon its own sweet stink and it liberates it. It becomes post-Black by running directly toward Blackness."

Wiley continued: "To be effective as an artist or a cultural practitioner we have to rise above immediate circumstances—immediate identity, immediate communities—but also to engage those communities as the foundation points for our practices." This, perhaps, is another way of saying, being rooted in but not restricted by Blackness. "You see this conundrum," Wiley said, "illustrated so beautifully and succinctly in the work of Kara Walker in which she goes so decidedly toward the individual by virtue of revealing the contours of her most inner, deepest psyche and shoots through the rubric of minstrelsy and her basic notions of child slavery."

When I asked Walker to define post-Blackness she immediately said, "individualism." She discussed how that impulse existed at the earliest moments of her artistic career, which lays bare why she moved so far away from the party line. "I've been on my own internal project here," Walker told me, sitting on a couch in her studio. "When I was a teenager, well, even as a younger kid but also especially as a teenager when we lived in Atlanta, there were one or two really sort of pivotal moments when I was kind of thinking about this Black art thing. Sometimes my dad [Larry Walker, an accomplished artist and art professor] was jurying shows like the Black arts invitationals or juried art shows and things like that. And I just remember going to a few of them with him and there was a sort of pomp and circumstance around them, you know. It was very Black. I mean, Coretta Scott King was at one of these openings, you know, not talking to people, and you sang the Black national anthem and we looked at the artworks submitted by mostly amateurish artists, but there was a kind of a feeling of, you know, the kind of racial pride that felt to me a little passé maybe. Like, for me, I think it was that I was just so ambivalent about learning how to be devout about Blackness. I just had like this churning sense of anxiety and ambivalence and disappointment and a kind of individualism."

It's difficult for me to imagine an artist from a previous generation presenting images from slavery with the crude, in-your-face irreverence that Walker brings to them. But one of the generational shifts that the post-Black era brings us is the impact of emotional distance from the past struggles: These are not Blacks who grew up in a time of organized battles for rights in the street and that leads to a different perspective on Blackness. Walker's freedom to immerse us in difficult slavery images and to inject into them the comedic force of a madcap

Andy Kaufmanesque carnival at which you're not sure if you're supposed to laugh comes only with the distance of time. She's leaning hard on the math of tragedy plus time equals comedy. And yet we know she is not irreverent or disrespectful of slaves and slavery. She is diving into our subconscious blood memories and fears and mixed-up dreams about slavery.

Walker said, "A lot of the work isn't really even about slavery. It's just kind of using it as a way into a conversation that nobody would have in any other context. The conversation is about power. It's not divorced from history and slavery and race and miscegenation, it is really kind of crucial that those things also be there, but it's like we want to keep the skeletons in the closet and keep looking at them and talking about them and not really acknowledge the sort of perversity of that activity, you know? And I'm really interested in acknowledging the perversity of that activity."

Walker said she imagined herself as the master of the images on her canvases and I said I thought it was interesting that she saw herself as a master, creating and in control of slaves (and massas) but not freeing the slaves she created. She left them enslaved and on the plantation. To not free the slaves she controls says something about her. "They can't go anywhere 'cause they're tied up in the world of being images," she said. "I mean, that's sort of my thing right now relative to painting, and it's not unrelated to my earliest thoughts about my earliest problems with painting, there's sort of no place for me to enter into that imperialistic kind of ownership place where the white male artist can say, 'This is my canvas, this is my world, and I'm going to do whatever the hell I want with it 'cause I'm free to do that.' My position was always a little bit more ambivalent and sort of reactionary. Like, 'No, wait, I'm the body unto whom things are done, so how can I actually do things to the body of the canvas?' So I'm trying to see if there's a way to continue to have this conversation about the position of power that an artist occupies relative to images and objects and the viewer—I'm trying to see if that's as interesting as talking about it through slavery."

Dave Chappelle similarly mines modern visions of slavery for comedy without disrespecting slaves. In one sketch from "Chappelle's Show" he presents a series of outtakes from *Roots* in which the sacred drama is sent up. In one vignette we see Chappelle as Kunta Kinte getting whipped by a massa who demands he call himself Toby—that classic, heartbreaking scene where the African's proud spirit is broken and he accepts his new life as a slave. But then Chappelle turns and says to the actor playing Massa, "Yo, Steve, I told you to stop hittin so hard!" The actor apologizes and Chappelle turns to face him as if to fight and we see the pad he's wearing on his back. Suddenly he's flipped from playing Kunta to his real self: the boss of the show. He leaps down off the wooden stage and runs up on the white actor playing Massa, who falls to the ground, scared of Chappelle's wrath. As if to underscore the joke that "We have shattered the fourth wall," the sound man runs into the shot, following Chappelle. The actors playing slaves laugh as Chappelle physically menaces the cowering white actor. Chappelle says, "I told you he was scared of me." This is a brilliant line because it opens up another layer—Chappelle is now utilizing the stereotype of Black male fearsomeness to frighten this white man even though Chappelle himself knows this is fake: He's no tough guy, he's a comic from a middle-class background. Then, just to twist our head around once more, Chappelle runs back onto the whipping stage and slips back into Kunta, his face worn out as if he's in pain from being whipped. Like Walker's work, this is art rooted in discussions of slavery but it's really about a TV show and modern visions of slavery that have been shaped by historical distance, thus allowing for a certain irreverence to seep in. No artist would be similarly irreverent about a more recent Black American catastrophe like Hurricane Katrina. Several artists pointed out that modern creators as diverse as Walker and Chappelle approach slavery with a bit of impudence or even cheekiness that would not have been previously possible, because they have a general sense of removal from the sacredness of history that inspires a feeling of independence and individuality. This is work that is emblematic of this post-Black era.

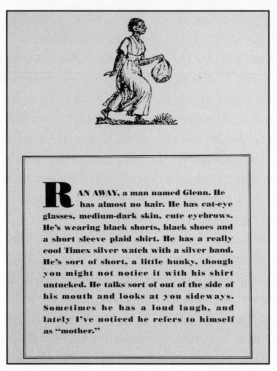

RAN AWAY, a man named Glenn. He has almost no hair. He has cat-eye glasses, medium-dark skin, cute eyebrows. He's wearing black shorts, black shoes and a short sleeve plaid shirt. He has a really cool Timex silver watch with a silver band. He's sort of short, a little hunky, though you might not notice it with his shirt untucked. He talks sort of out of the side of his mouth and looks at you sideways. Sometimes he has a loud laugh, and lately I've noticed he refers to himself as "mother."

Glenn Ligon's 1993 piece "Untitled from Runaways" employs the tropes of slavery in a playful way, not laughing at slavery, but comically imagining his modern self as discussed by a runaway slave poster.

"We all make work that comes out of our time," says visual artist Fred Wilson. "It's all wrapped up in who we are and where we are, and the time period in which we're living. And Kara and Dave's work—it just seems completely apparent that that work could not be done in previous generations and it really speaks to how different, what different times we are in. There's understanding about this work that would not have existed for the mainstream prior to now because there's a certain amount of African-American history being used as the lingua franca for the country at this point. And I believe it's not something that could have occurred at any time before this moment."

Golden told me, "If one had seen the 'Freestyle' exhibition, one would see a generation of young people who grew up in a moment where all aspects of Blackness were truly pop culture. This was not marginal culture but pop culture." Black culture was once coded and culturally distant, like the secluded juke joint off the beaten path where Blacks rollicked and explored their artistic and aesthetic souls and intrepid whites trekked out to it as if into the uncharted forest, to see something exotic. Now Black culture is more like Starbucks: located on every corner in every major city and available to anyone who wants in. It is the lingua franca—the common language. Now the minutiae of Black culture is on wide display and Black artists and people can no longer honestly think Black culture is some private space that we alone know about. Glenn Ligon said, "A friend of mine said, 'Oh isn't it great that you have Blackness as this subject matter that you can dip into, where I'm not Black so I don't have that.' And I was like, What country did we grow up in? What do your children listen to? We have to get past this notion that Black culture is separate and apart from America, that it's this object that can be studied but is so alien and foreign that only Black people can understand it and white people have no relationship to it. We have to move beyond these clear binaries about where culture is imagined to reside and who has ownership of it." I recall some Blacks encountering the 1980 film *The Big Chill* and being surprised to discover whites feeling that Motown was very much their legacy. There will never be a hiphop *Big Chill* moment. Everyone knows hiphop's legacy is shared. The mainstreaming of Black culture has led to many whites seeing Black culture as a palette they can draw from—as if Black culture is theirs, too—a shocking and off-putting development for many Blacks. Even "nigga," despite its power to offend, has spilled out of Black culture.

"You know what really bothers me?" Santigold says. "How it's become such hiphop slang that now you have white kids going around calling each other 'nigga.' And that's really dumb. At that point you're like, see what you did? Now the word's totally stupid. When I hear two little baggy-pantsed white kids calling each other 'nigga' I'm just like, All right, that's crazy." These are not simply intra-American issues. Talib Kweli says: "When you go to Africa and Africans say, 'my nigga' and that's the way to relate to you, that's a fucked-up feeling. I'm not gonna lie. South Africa, Tanzania, every place I've been in Africa they say it. Why wouldn't they think that's the thing to say? 50 Cent told me the same story. He's like, 'I show up and they're like Fifty, you my nigga!'" Sure, Africans are Black so they don't offend Black American sensibilities the way white nigga-users do, but Africans do not have a direct connection to the Black American experience that nigga comes from and speaks to, so for Africans to feel ownership over nigga feels a bit peculiar. But much of the world feels Black culture is available to them. So what impact does that have on Black culture and its producers? How does that transform Black culture and, with it, Black identity?

The mainstreaming of Black culture has had a transformative impact on the culture producers—instead of Blackness as a private world they share, explain, and defend, Blackness becomes something they can explore and redefine as they wish. One of the stars of "Freestyle" was Rashid Johnson. "There's a generation of Black artists before me who made work specifically about the Black experience," Johnson says. "But I think for my generation, having grown up in the age of hiphop and Black Entertainment Television, there's less of a need to define the Black experience so aggressively to a white audience. I think it gives us a different type of opportunity to have a more complex conversation around race and identity. It's not a weapon for me, it's more of an interest." He can deal with the Black experience as an interest, not an obsession—not an all-consuming aspect but one part of his persona, one of the things he thinks about—because in his lifetime the thirty-two-year-old Johnson has seen Black culture become pop culture.

That demands something new. Thelma Golden said post-Black artists "have an attitude that embraces Black culture as a subject matter that's not specific to them, not autobiographical. With Black artists there's always the issue of are they an artist who happens to be Black or are they a Black artist? But the younger generation of artists, they really don't care so much. That used to be a problematic division—to say 'I'm an artist who happens to be Black' seems to indicate some level of distancing oneself from identity but to say 'I'm a Black artist' seems to put politics and identity at the forefront of an aesthetic practice. This post-Black generation of artists saw themselves working with Black subject matter as the generations before but they were working in a world that understood that subject matter as being cultural in a general way. I feel like it has to do with the shift in the way that hiphop became a dominant cultural form so that would make it easier for a generation of artists to be working with certain kinds of Black symbolism and have a general audience read it with some fluency." So when an artist like Johnson approaches Black culture he knows he doesn't need to deconstruct it for white audiences because they arrive at his art with as much understanding of Black culture as they want to have. Certainly, there are levels of spiritual understanding of Black culture that are nearly impossible for white people to reach—I mean, almost always a Black joke or trope or reference will be understood differently by Black and white audiences. But for most white people, if they choose to immerse themselves with open minds and watch certain movies and shows, read certain books, listen to certain singers and MCs, and talk honestly with the Blacks they encounter at work or school or in their social lives, then they can come to be, as Golden put it, relatively fluent in Black culture. These are not assumptions that Romare Bearden or Jacob Lawrence could have made and it necessarily shifts the post-Black generation's relationship with Black cultural production.

This is why post-Black artists have approached race in ways that are far less expository of the Black experience and less reverential about sacrosanct tropes or ideas from the past. They're more willing to discuss Blackness at an in-group level of intimacy and to challenge self-definitions of Blackness because they understand Black culture as shared culture rather than something that is private or must be preserved in a glass case. Rashid Johnson's photograph "I talk white" shows the words "*I TALK WHiTE*" written in white on a mirror, thus bringing into the open the intra-Black dialogue about what Blackness is and when, in some eyes, it shifts to oreoness or whiteness. Zadie Smith, recall, put tremendous weight on voice in establishing authenticity—"The voice was at the very heart of the thing," she wrote. "Fail to keep it real there and you'd never see your Blackness again." So Johnson is getting at a seminal issue. To be said to talk like a white person (generally an issue of how your voice sounds, what words you choose, and how you pronounce them as opposed to what you say) is among the more biting in-group insults, something one would never say about themselves, which makes Johnson's self-identification as someone who talks white shocking and maybe scandalous. Yet Johnson doesn't accept the felony uncritically—the phrase "I talk white" feels grammatically awkward and it fits with Black English's purposeful skewering of grammar. So as Johnson asserts that he talks like a white person he does it in a way that respects Black grammatical norms—he does it in Black English—thus challenging his own assertion, or melding the two ways of talking by bringing a linguistic sense of Blackness into the discussion of him talking like a white person. So is he actually talking white? It seems the brother's pleading guilty in the slyest way possible.

Rashid Johnson's 2003 piece "I talk white."

Glenn Ligon's piece "Condition Report" makes plain the post-Black impulse to critique the Civil Rights movement and reject reverentiality toward it. Ligon acquired some of the iconic "I Am a Man" signs that striking Black sanitation workers in Memphis held in 1968 and took one to a painting conservator who put tiny marks all over it, indicating what needed to be addressed in order to conserve the print. Ligon presents two signs, one as he found it and one with the conservators' marks on it, thus investigating the sign as a visual document rather than an historical artifact and saying Black history is a thing or a product or an interest to be deconstructed or improved, not something to be worshipped. "My relationship to the Civil Rights movement is not my parents' relationship to it," Ligon told me. "So I understand the political necessity of Black men carrying signs that say I am a man, but I also understand we're in a different moment. The ideas of masculinity that circulated around the Civil Rights movement are not the ideas of masculinity that circle through me and my friends. I think you see the aging of our ideas, the marking of our change, the change in our ideas about the Civil Rights movement, the change in our ideas about masculinity. Like, can you imagine someone carrying a sign like that now? No. One can call that post-Black but each generation redefines the previous ones and looks at the same material and interprets it in different ways. But I think maybe that's what post-Black means. Sort of, people inventing things from what they have."

A similar Ligon painting, 1988's "Untitled (I Am a Man)" presents the words *I Am a Man* in black on a white background but the words are presented with none of the bravado of the original signs carried in 1968. D'Arby English, in *How to See a Work of Art in Total Darkness,* writes, "Ligon was an eight year old in the Bronx when [the Memphis sanitation workers' strike] took place, and thus estranged from the marchers by at least a generation. This distance is registered within the painting: Ligon's version, in relation to the original in which the thickly printed slogan reaches nearly to the sign's edge with "am" in boldface and underlined, presents the letters as shrunken in size and withdrawn from the edge—a recession we might read as a kind of historical distance that interrupts the clarity as well as the politics of the image." The historical distance from the struggles make the old battles into something foreign and disconnected and less tangible than they are for our parents. Consequently, we interact with them very differently. "Ligon's taking these sacred images," Professor Murray says, "and chipping away at them and critiquing them and that's very post-Black because he has the courage to take these images that are beloved, these untouchable images of Blackness that are tied to the struggle for equality for Black people in this country, and somehow tear them down in a way that illustrates that for people of his generation they don't have the same meaning. Maybe for him they're not symbols of uplift, they're symbols of something that is confining or somehow degrading and alienating or they're denying him recognition. I think there's something very post-Black in that."

Glenn Ligon's 2000 piece, "Condition Report"

I did not attend the "Freestyle" show Thelma Golden curated but the show created unavoidable waves that eventually reached me. I began to hear about post-Blackness as an art world idea that could have broader implications and revolutionary potential. Then one afternoon, casting about online, flowing from link to link, I stumbled on Rashid Johnson's piece "Signed Clarence Thomas 'Uncle Tom All-Stars' Judicial Robe Jersey," which shows a black Supreme Court judicial robe with the name Thomas, and above his signature, the number '91, the year Thomas joined the Court. By adding some tropes from a sports jersey Johnson posits Thomas as a member of a fictional team: the Uncle Tom All-Stars. Hysterical. Not laugh-out-loud funny, no, something far deeper. In my mind I was rolling on the floor. But Johnson had picked on a particularly divisive figure whose ultra-conservative—some would say self-hating—policies and positions have forced many Blacks to confront the reasons why we feel a connection to certain Blacks and not to others, and how that connection goes deeper than skin color because Blackness is about far more than color. Ligon said, "I heard Angela Davis talk about Clarence Thomas and say she could not have imagined a situation where there was a Black nominee for the Supreme Court who she'd be virulently opposed to. She said race is an anchor but not a sufficient anchor, there are other kinds of considerations that she brought to the table so she could not support Clarence Thomas just because he was a Black person. That wasn't enough. I think that in some ways is what post-Black is about."

 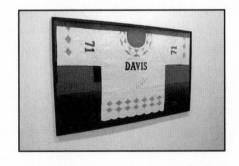

Rashid Johnson's 2006 piece "Signed Clarence Thomas 'Uncle Tom All-Stars' Judicial Robe Jersey" and his 2003 "Signed Angela Davis 'Civil Rights All-Stars' Throw-back Dashiki Jersey."

I wondered who else would be among the Uncle Tom All-Stars? I could imagine a few people I'd put on the team, but who else would the joke's creator nominate? A little Googling led me to a similar Johnson piece, "Signed Angela Davis 'Civil Rights All-Stars' Throw-back Dashiki

Jersey," which was a white dashiki with on the back the name Davis and the number 71, for when she was imprisoned. This was also funny, though less sarcastic and sardonic, but immediately I visualized the hallways of one of Jay-Z's 40/40 clubs, which are filled with framed and signed jerseys from stars of every sport, redone to commemorate the Civil Rights All-Stars, the Black Power All-Stars, the Slavery All-Stars, and more. Young Black men used to wear throwback sports jerseys as fashion and I could see the Angela Davis jersey being worn on the street alongside the inevitable jerseys commemorating Malcolm X, Huey P. Newton, Marcus Garvey, Frederick Douglass, Harriet Tubman, Nat Turner . . .

Johnson's pieces unlocked a door for me, pointing me toward something I hadn't known I'd wanted. It was like seeing a brother sass our parents in an intelligent way and realizing that I'd needed to do that and if he could I could, too. Johnson had broken through some holy reverence that my generation was supposed to have but didn't want. We'd studied the Civil Rights and Black Power movements and respected their advances and achievements and sacrifices but, from the vantage point of decades later, the long term, we could also see their limitations, the places where they'd fallen short, the ways Blacks were still suffering with some of the same problems, the places where the old heroes hadn't delivered. Johnson was speaking to all that with his jerseys, giving these Black historical icons a certain reverence—he called them all-stars, although Thomas ended up on an all-star squad no one would want to be on—while poking fun not at those individuals as much as at the reverence we have for them. The jerseys say these people are our history, so honor them, but also, these people are history, so let's move on.

These thoughts were possible only because Johnson sees Blackness not as a weapon but as an interest. Post-Black art presents Blackness not as an assault weapon—there's more to Blackness than bludgeoning people with memories of past atrocities and injustices or the discussion of how difficult it is to be Black and deal with whites. Blackness is also something to investigate, enjoy, and ponder on its own terms. Kori

Newkirk, an artist who was in the "Freestyle" show, says, "We're all making work that doesn't hit people over the head with the race conversation anymore."

The word "interest" also indicates it's not an all-consuming aspect but a part of a person, one of the many things that makes up who you are. Post-Black art takes for granted that Black culture is pop culture as well as shared culture, that Blackness is something everyone is interested in and somewhat knowledgeable about and something that is available to anyone to pull from. As one of Pope.L's pieces says, "Black people are crossover."

Not only is Black culture available to whites and others, but white culture, or any culture, is available for Blacks to use, deconstruct, and recontextualize at will. Multi-culturalism destroyed the idea that certain cultural legacies belong to certain cultural groups and art in the post-Black era takes that freedom to the nth degree.

Golden once told the *Village Voice*, "The great promise of the multicultural rhetoric of the eighties is true. These artists very easily cite references across very huge lines with no need for justification on any side; one artist the other day cited Robert Colescott [an important Black painter] and Sigmar Polke [an important German painter] in the same sentence and it wasn't about one being better than the other, or the need for one more than the other—like, I need to cite Polke so you'll know I'm a serious artist working in the Western tradition or I need to cite Colescott so you'll know I'm down. No, it was like, 'Polke-colescott.'" The post-Black era is filled with these sorts of cross-cultural mashups—from *The Grey Album* where Jay-Z's vocals are mixed with Beatles music; to white singer-songwriter Nina Gordon's cover of N.W.A.'s "Straight Outta Compton," slowly singing their vulgar autobiographical rhymes over sweet acoustic guitar to Chappelle's "Clayton Bigsby" sketch where a blind Black man believes himself a Klansman, to the cultural schizophrenia of a world where Eminem is an elite MC and Tiger Woods and the Williams sisters dominate overwhelmingly white endeavors. In this mashed-up world the work of Kehinde Wiley fits very well.

Kehinde Wiley's 2008 painting "Colonel Platoff on His Charger."

His 2005 painting "Ice-T."

His 2007 painting "Alexander the Great."

Wiley makes portraits of modern Black men drenched in hiphop tropes—the prominently branded clothing, the hi-tech accessories, the powerful poses—positioned to replicate specific paintings from the Renaissance as if to make it a form of visual sampling. If he were a music producer he'd give you hardcore New York MCs rhyming over Beethoven. Greg Tate said it's like "the lush classical strings on a Wu-Tang record with street brothers in the middle repping' tude." Those Renaissance paintings were a form of reportage: The subject was saying, "Look how rich I am," and showing off his possessions. Wiley gives us the same sort of reportage by including all the branding that modern consumers use to define themselves to the world. Wiley's mashing of modern Black images and aesthetics with centuries-old European ones makes plain the wide breadth of cultures he feels is his to access. His work is emblematic of the multiculturalism and cross-cultural mashups that inform post-Blackness. Wiley described himself as double-dutching with "one foot in the history of art and another in street as it lives and evolves and seeing how those two can have a relationship with each other."

Wiley, who says he's inspired as much by Versace as by Vermeer, has been described by Professor Murray as "the most prominent of Thelma Golden's stable of post-Black artists . . . a prototypical exemplar of this new post-Black avant-garde in his envisioning of Blackness beyond abjection and racial trauma. He expresses little desire to engage the identity politics birthed in the 1980s and 1990s, thus forgoing the crushing weight of group belongingness and the compulsory essentialized Blackness demanded of him."

It's no accident that Wiley's beginnings in painting are not about searching for a way to express himself as a Black person, but about literally escaping the violence of South Central Los Angeles in the eighties. His mother sent him to art programs as a small child to keep him off the streets. The classes took him to view some of the greatest art collections in Southern California, which inspired him but also created massive class conflicts. "We went to places such as the Huntington Library and Gardens," Wiley said, "in which there's an extraordinary collection of eighteenth and nineteenth-century British portraiture. And in those paintings you saw the trappings of class and wealth and power and the vocabulary of the leisure class, all refined down to a distinct way of looking at the world and that was ridiculously alienating coming from my class. What the hell are these people doing with these powdered wigs and these pearls and these lap dogs? But at the same time as a young painter I had a very strong desire to participate in masterful painting and to be able to make that sort of mimetic presence." He's saying he wanted to make paintings that were crisply accurate and realistic even while the subjects of the paintings he saw offended him—and surely the lack of Black faces in that canon bothered him, too. "My later understanding of what those paintings said about how bodies displayed in public space had a lot to do with bodies controlling other bodies, controlling colored bodies, empire, colonialism—all of those things being in those paintings is something that I both critique and engage at once in my work." It's almost like he's now making work for the boy who went to the Huntington Library and Gardens and said, "Who the hell are these old, rich white men and why should I care about them, and where are the people who look like me?" Like he's remixing those old paintings by sliding in hypermodern Black street figures clad in gear and accessories so up-to-the-minute and culturally accurate that as soon as the paint is dry the painting is dated. But still, there's a message about a Black man's love of the history of painting and the Black place in that history.

There's also a conversation about visualizing Black physical power. Wiley puts his models in authoritative, alpha poses and presents them in a heroic light. "When you're looking at my paintings you're looking at, sure, high-priced luxury objects for wealthy consumers," Wiley said. "And you're looking at something that tries to embrace the absence of people of color in the major museums and gallery spaces throughout the world. But you're looking at the negotiation of conflicting moral sets, value sets, and in that sense it goes beyond the simplistic, just-add-water political corrective that we oftentimes see when thinking of people of color in art creative processes."

In a world where these sorts of collisions are commonplace, something new had to develop. Artists, particularly visual artists and recording artists, are the embodiment of the collective imagination. In the Black American community especially, our artists have an extremely important post in our collective mind as an element that helps us define who we are and who we want to be. Because visual artists aren't tied to the same rat-racey commercial apparatus as recording artists—i.e., visual artists are not trying to quickly sell many inexpensive units to a large mass of people—they can take chances with identity and aesthetics that even other artists can't. So they're in their own laboratory of the future, studying identity and aesthetics. And like engineers on the Apple campus in Cupertino, California, working on a secret new revolutionary product, it would eventually end up at the ubiquitous Apple stores throughout the country. And, like the iPod, post-Blackness has ended up in the White House.

I've never lived a typical Black experience. My father did—he grew up in the projects in Brooklyn rooting for Jackie Robinson and the Dodgers, and in the slums of Harlem, sometimes eating at the church of the legendary minister Daddy Grace. He married a Black woman and spent his life working in Mattapan, one of Boston's Black working-class neighborhoods. I grew up in a middle-class neighborhood where we were the only Black family. I attended prep school where I was usually the only or one of very few Black kids in the class, and rooted for Larry Bird and the Celtics. I played tennis, though my base was a Black tennis club that served the working-class families from the surrounding areas: Imagine the YMCA but with tennis and a mission to create scholarship opportunities and show the tony white clubs that Blacks could beat them at their own game. I played tennis into my thirties but now I practice yoga. I married outside the race. I live in Fort Greene, Brooklyn, where there's a vibrant and historic Black artistic community as well as lots of interracial families. For these "offenses," and others, I've been told I talk or act white by both Blacks and whites. I've been called an oreo by Blacks and once had a white person say, "You're not, like, a real Black guy." I think he wanted it to be a compliment.

I am very much a real Black guy. I am not what some expect a Black man to be because my life has been lived with wider boundaries. I'm not alone in that. "TV on the Radio and Santigold are generational bellwethers," said Greg Tate. "They're doin things in ways that are completely in sync with the opportunity to define yourself outside of the record company paradigms of Black music or the BET paradigm or the Essence Festival paradigm. But if you sit down with them you're like, yeah, they some Black folks. They look like Black folks, smell like Black folks, sound like Black folks. But I think that there's just no way, given the complexity of their minds and their range of influences, they gonna try to squeeze all that into this box called 'neo-soul' or 'contemporary R&B' or 'radio-friendly hiphop.'"

Santigold's given name is Santi White and she's one of the most interesting sonic artists working today. Her debut album, *Santogold*, made her the hottest new artist to emerge in 2008. Her music is nothing like what's traditionally considered Black music. It's a difficult-to-classify stew drawing from rock, electronica, new wave, punk, and post-disco—sounds Black people rarely make, forget listen to—as well as traditionally Black genres like dub and reggae. I asked Santigold, "Can we call your music Black music?"

"Of course you can call it Black music," she said. "'Cause I'm Black."

That alone makes it Black music?

"Hell yeah. That's all. I'm Black and I'm making it, so it's Black music."

That's the post-Black attitude at play.

"The concept of post-Blackness is the only thing that makes sense to me," Santigold said. "I can't imagine living in America and not being exposed to everything. It's not a conscious decision; post-Black is, to me, just reality. It's the only intelligent way to live. It's just human. I don't think that anybody could have every single thing that they are defined by the fact that their skin is Black. It doesn't make any sense for me to entertain the idea that because I'm Black I'm supposed to be exactly one way. I don't understand how a human being who has a brain and thinks for themself could actually exist in that way. For me to put that on myself as a spirit growing up in the world, I disagree with that as much as I disagree with prejudice." What Santigold and so many others understand, perhaps intuitively, is that now is a time for post-Blackness, as if we're computers that have been working with personas powered by an operating system called Blackness 9.0 that has amazing creativity but still has some limits on what you can do. Then post-Blackness comes along, offering a revolutionary OS called Person 10.0, which allows you to customize everything, even the operating system itself. It allows you to do anything you can think of.

It takes one sort of courage to ignore and defy the white gaze but another kind of courage entirely for a Black person to ignore and defy the Black gaze, and to, say, stride boldly and guiltlessly into Harlem with your white girlfriend or boyfriend to eat sushi and deconstruct the ballet you just attended while silently refusing to be cowed by the judging eyes of those around you. You know there's nothing justifying the idea that this kind of Black person isn't really Black. It's not that they're not Black, it's that they took their Blackness to the ballet because they like it and because Blackness is like a Visa card—accepted everywhere you want to be. It's strange that Black people are so creative, innovative, and improvisational with our personal style and our cultural productions but don't always support each other in being equally creative with our conception of Blackness, our identity. It's like some Black central consciousness says, "You can and should get funky with anything you can get your hands on, anything except your mask." Post-Blackness is saying, "Go ahead, get funky with your mask."

NYU professor Jason King said, "Black people are now exploring their freedom in ways they haven't been able to in the past because of certain kinds of Civil Rights pride issues. One of the more negative legacies of the Civil Rights movement was that all Black people were expected to be monolithic in terms of how to express pride. Like there's only one way to express it and I think that what you're seeing is a rejection of that monolithic model. People are trying to personalize things."

The novelist Colson Whitehead said, "What was called oreoness ten to twenty years ago is being who you are and being comfortable with doing what you want and not caring about what other people think.

Being called an oreo was stupid then and it's stupid now. People are just more aware that those categories are dumb. If you're an authentic person, true to who you are and how you're wired, then like what you like, whether it's Led Zeppelin or 'Happy Days.'"

Harold Ford, the former Tennessee Congressman, told me, "Post-Blackness means being an American. Being as broad and as full an American as you can be."

# Chapter 3

# The Rise and Fall of a Post-Black King

On the first episode of "Chappelle's Show," Dave stuck a flag in the ground and declared his allegiance. He was onstage introducing "Frontline: Clayton Bigsby," a sketch about a blind Black man who believes he's white and who's a white supremacist—one of the most incendiary, complex, and hysterical discussions of race ever aired. Before the sketch, Chappelle told his studio audience, "This is probably the wildest thing I've ever done in my career. And I showed it to a Black friend of mine. He looked at me like I had set Black people back with a comedy sketch." Then Chappelle shrugged as if to say, "Oh well," flicking away whatever responsibility to the race the friend thought he should have, like dirt off his shoulder. Then he said, "Sorry." But it was a non-apology that made it clear he felt he had nothing to apologize for. And with those lines Chappelle did something as aggressive as anything in the controversial sketch: He publicly declared his allegiance to his comedic and artistic vision and, more importantly, his independence from a need to advance the race with his work. He admitted he was aware of the possibility or perception of setting the race back with a sketch—though a certain edge in his voice suggests he finds dubious the potential to set the race back with a comedy sketch—but he plows ahead anyway, almost spitting in the eye of the Black gaze. His goal was comedy, his North Star was his mind. He would not allow himself to be constrained by a directive to do good for Black people at all times. He was independent from the need to do work that necessarily and overtly "advanced" the race. But Chappelle was no race traitor, quite the opposite: Being free from the need—the burden—to advance the race is in itself an advance for the race.

Artists have a special place in the collective mind of the groups that claim them: They are the embodiment of the group's imagination. The great ones push at the edges of what it's permissible to say and think and do and thus shape how the group sees itself as well as how outsiders see the group. Artists must work with dangerous truths the way scientists who don protective gear work with dangerous chemicals. But my truth is not necessarily yours. To demand that artists conform to a sort of group-think is to reduce them to being propagandists and to put chains on the collective imagination. Only through complete artistic freedom can any artist discover and present his or her own truth. They cannot embody our collective imagination with censors hanging over their shoulders. Black comedians have long held a special place in the Black commu-nity as truth-tellers and philosophers—people who could say things that were true but were too subversive for sober political discourse. They can only explore the truth with the freedom to report whatever it is they see. In the end the audience will vote with their wallets and their minds. In Dave's case they voted for him in a landslide: Two years after declar-ing himself separate from the need to uplift the race he was the most popular and most thought-provoking and thesis-inspiring comedian of his generation. DVD sales of "Chappelle's Show" sold in the millions, shattering records.

"Chappelle's Show" is the clearest example of post-Blackness ever seen on television. A show like "Grey's Anatomy" gives us post-racialism: It's filled with characters who are Black (as well as Asian and Latina) but race is almost always of no importance. Any of the characters could be switched to another race with little or no change to the character or the storyline. In that world, race does not matter. "Chappelle's Show" gives us post-Blackness: a vision of race that is as complex and messy and fluid as it is in modern America. Sure, many of the sketches are pure comedy with no political thought behind them, but much of the show is the product of deep political thought and a clear-eyed vision of the modern racial landscape. Questlove was the show's musical coordinator and a friend of Chappelle's. "I know that he wants his impact to be about him holding a big-ass mirror up to America," Questlove said.

Chappelle's realistic image of modern America—as seen through the prism of comedic caricature—confronts the complexity of racial identity in a multiracial and multicultural society, explores the joys and pitfalls of having multiple ways of performing Blackness at your fingertips, and dives into the cross-pollinization of contemporary Black and white culture, i.e., the ways that cultural Blackness and whiteness are fungible and fluid. In Chappelle's world we see Blacks mentally transitioning into whiteness, we see whites happily being mistaken for Black, we see a multiplicity of ways of being Black, and we see a DuBoisian double-consciousness actively at work. And we see Chappelle using history and historical Black trauma like a toy. Wahneema Lubiano says, "One of the things I associate with what people are calling post-Black is the determination not to have history weigh on our individual shoulders as something that's only and always serious, right. So I found his willingness to mess around, to play with history, not only entertaining but smart. It's as though he was unwilling to pledge allegiance to the fact that Black history had so crippled us that there was no possibility that we could even play with the things that were used as stereotypes and caricatures against us. It's like he fully inhabited the possibility that you don't only wear history, you get to comment on it, to talk back to it. So I would watch his humor just to watch him refuse to be intimidated by the seriousness of racism.

"This probably sounds like therapy speak," said Wahneema Lubiano, "and I probably have spent too many years in therapy, but there's a moment when you're doing therapy and you're venting for the fiftieth fucking time about some trauma and you suddenly realize that you're really not venting anymore, you're just telling the story as it happened. You're no longer tearing up every time you think about it. You're no longer shredding yourself for what's happened to you. You're just saying yes, so then this thing happened, and you hear it in your voice. You're really bored with the trauma. So for me watching Chappelle I thought, 'This is what it looks like when you're no longer caught by your own trauma about racism and the history of Black people in the United States.' Then everything is up for grabs as a possibility of art and performance art. Because you're not wearing the trauma anymore. You get to use something that produced all that trauma and do something else with it. So maybe that's how I'm thinking about how post-Blackness can operate. It's not a disavowal of history, it's just the determination that you're not wearing all that trauma anymore and you're not waiting for the world to be different to live your life in more interesting ways."

Was Chappelle aware of all this? Of course. When I interviewed him for BET in 2005 he said, "I'm just tryin' to be funny, man. But sometimes what's funny to me, just 'cause of how I was raised or where I'm comin' from, might have a message."

The "Clayton Bigsby" sketch is about the topsy-turvyness of race today speaking about a world where a Black Harvard professor gets arrested for allegedly being racist toward a white cop who teaches other cops about the wrongness of racial profiling, and then both go to the White House to discuss it with the Black president and ultimately the professor becomes friendly enough with the cop that the officer gives him the handcuffs used to arrest him, which promptly end up in the Smithsonian. The Professor Gates and Officer Crowley incident seemed like something that leapt off "Chappelle's Show" and into the newspapers but that's because Chappelle and Neal Brennan, the white co-creator and co-writer of "Chappelle's Show" and a close friend of Dave's until the sudden end of the show, were good at studying modern life and putting that on screen. Sure, they put everything through a comedy machine that added enough exaggeration to make it funny but underneath the comedic caricature the show was a sharp discussion of modern race.

Clayton Bigsby was born blind and was told by the teachers at the school for the blind where he grew up that he was white. He believed it and thus became white in his mind, echoing the intellectual selling out many Blacks think Clarence Thomas and Condoleezza Rice and others have undergone. Bigsby is not a creature dreamed up in the imagination of Chappelle but a remix of his grandfather. On the DVD commentary

Chappelle says, "My grandfather looked like a white person and probably was a white person. He was born in a white hospital in 1911, when
it was impossible for a Black woman to have a baby in a white hospital
under any circumstances. . . . He went to a school for the blind but they
had to tell kids he was white so he wouldn't get in any trouble. The day
after Martin Luther King got shot he was on a bus in D.C. and heard
some brothers harassing a white dude. "Get off the bus, you honky! We
should kill you for being around here." And my grandfather's thinking,
'Man, what white person would be crazy enough to ride a bus in D.C.
the day after King got shot?' And at a certain point he realized they were
talking to him."

During the sketch a shift from white to Black occurs in miniature:
As Bigsby is driven past a car from which hiphop is blaring he yells,
"Why don't you jungle bunnies turn that music down! Niggers make me
sick!" Of course the car holds four young white men, highlighting that
in a world where cultural segregation is long dead and many whites feel
hiphop is part of their cultural legacy—and the dominant music culture
of their generation—the sounds someone's booming give no clue as to
who they are. The boys in the car digest what Bigsby has said—"Did he
just call us niggers?"—and they are thrilled. They slap five ecstatically,
celebrating someone mistaking them for Black, joyous about their racial shapeshift. If Bigsby is a reimagining of Clarence Thomas then they
stand for the hiphop-obsessed wiggers in America today, people who
don't simply love hiphop but wish to be Black, though their wish includes no understanding of the downsides of being Black. This moment,
too, is rooted in something literal. "Paul Mooney had referred to me as
a nigger in some way," Brennan said, "and I was so flattered by it. . . . It
felt like some sort of acceptance, you know what I mean? It really felt
like acceptance. Like it felt like whatever being a nigger means to Paul
Mooney, he sees me somehow as similar." Brennan recognized that this
interaction is particular and endemic to this era: "Only in the hiphop
generation," he said, "could a Black guy call a white guy nigger and the
white guy's heart soar."

That sort of frank racial interplay in which both sides feel smart about the other's race is more common in this generation than ever before, and it's the reason why racial interactions in this generation are sometimes different and why "Chappelle's Show" was able to be so smart about modern race. Both Chapelle and Brennan, in separate interviews, said the reason why the show was so smart about race was because it generated from a Black and a white mind. Brennan says, "We were both pretty racially ambidextrous. Like, I know a lot of shit about Black people and he knows a lot of shit about white people. Just from pure exposure and interest. I'm as inspired by Spike Lee as Dave is by Kurt Cobain." That sort of racial ambidexterity is widespread in this generation and a major source of the sociocultural energy powering post-Blackness. If post-Blackness were a shining light bulb then this generation's racial ambidexterity would be part of the electrical current making it shine.

In the midst of all the racial shape-shifting going on in the Bigsby sketch, one interesting character seems to fly under the radar: Clayton's friend Jasper. He's a white supremacist who takes care of Clayton, protecting him from racists when they threaten Clayton with harm and helping to hide his identity. When Clayton arrives at the hall where he's scheduled to speak Jasper gently reminds him to put on his Klan hood. He could use Clayton's blindness against him by letting his fellow white supremacists see Clayton's race as evidence of how stupid Blacks are and thus how correct the supremacists' racist ideology is. But instead Jasper puts interracial friendship ahead of racist ideology, helping a Black man and thus violating his own core beliefs in service of a friend. Rusty Cundieff, who directed the Bigsby sketch and directed more episodes of "Chappelle's Show" than anyone else, says, "That's a reality today. People espousing a belief while at the same time ignoring or excusing their belief in favor of another belief. So Clayton's handler knows he's Black, but is like, you know, that's fine, 'cause he's my friend and we see eye to eye on this." (At the end of the sketch, after Bigsby learns he's Black, he leaves his blind white wife of many years because "she's a nigger-lover." I wonder if he exiled Jasper from his life for the same reason.)

Chappelle knew they'd created something not just funny but brilliant and politically accurate in spite of the exaggerations. So when his bosses at Comedy Central pushed back and tried to shove the sketch off the first episode a major battle ensued. "Dave was willing to walk away if they didn't put that sketch on," Cundieff said. "He felt that strongly about it. Comedy Central felt it would scare people but Dave and Neal, very rightly, were smart enough to know that it had to be in the first episode because it really was what they were trying to do with the show: this kind of mash-up of hiphop culture with current attitudes and being smart." Brennan said, "We had a vicious argument with Comedy Central about it. Vicious. Screaming. They said they didn't feel the sketch was representative of the show. We argued the opposite. But I'll say this for Comedy Central, after about six episodes they came to us and said, 'We don't really know what we're talking about when it comes to your show,' and gave us relatively free rein. After the first season one of the execs apologized to Dave for the awfulness of their note on the Bigsby sketch."

The hiphop generation's games with the word "nigga/nigger" and the topsy-turvyness of modern race are embedded in the "Niggar Family" sketch. A white family in the 1950s with the surname Niggar—and the halcyon placidity and aw-shucks naivete of "Leave It to Beaver" or a Norman Rockwell painting—has the gamut of Black stereotypes flung at them by Clifton, their Black milkman, who's having a ball because of the recontextualization of race inspired by their name. It's no surprise that he says they're his favorite family to deliver milk to. Thus again whites in a sense become Black—or at least the victim of Black stereotypes—and a Black becomes white in that Clifton, dressed all in white to deliver milk, is the one with the stereotyping gaze.

The Niggar family starts the recontextualizing before Clifton arrives onstage, remarking that their late-sleeping teenage son "sure is one lazy Niggar." But Clifton plays the game with a much more devilish edge. He pops in while they're having breakfast and when he's offered a slice of bacon he says, "I know better than to get between a Niggar and their pork! Might get my fingers bit!" A moment later he reminds the father, "You didn't pay your bill last week and I know how forgetful you Niggars are when it comes to paying your bills." When it's time to leave, Clifton walks out of the frame then pops his head back in and ecstatically yelps, "Niggars!" as if he couldn't miss one last chance to call some white folks "niggers." Clifton moves through the sketch with knowledge the family lacks, as if only he is aware of the word "nigger" and the constellation of racist thoughts that typically accompany it. As he spits stereotypes at the family they're largely reactionless while he's clearly enjoying the subtext. This is an interesting portrait of racial knowledge: The white fifties' TV family for whom race is never an issue remains unaware even when the Black milkman rubs it in their face because in his life race is everywhere, like the weather. The pain of all this racial awareness is brought home toward the sketch's end. Clifton runs into Timmy, the teenage Niggar, at a nice restaurant. Momentary confusion ensues when the maître d' announces, "Niggar, party of two," which Clifton thinks is a reference to him and his wife. He approaches the podium to politely complain—"Just because we're colored didn't mean we came out here to be disrespected," he says—then finds the maître d' was actually talking about Timmy. Clifton says, "I bet you'll get the finest table a nigger's ever got in this restaurant," and then laughs a long, hearty, bluesy laugh at the thought that this teenager's social rank outstrips his by so much. Then comes the line that turns the sketch from a recontextualization into deep social commentary. Clifton says, "Oh, Lord, this racism is killin' me inside!" And with that the tone of the sketch changes drastically. He's been having a blast at the Niggars' expense but his fun on their turf is merely a vacation, a stop in his day where he can step into bizzaroworld. Once they all step outside the Niggar home, the Niggars continue living their blissful existence, soaking up the benefits of white supremacy, while Clifton resumes his subservient position under the heel of white supremacy. And this is not merely figurative pain—he says racism is killing him to underline how racism is sometimes felt as physical pain. So teasing the Niggars was fun but, in terms of social power not unlike a toddler shoving a bodybuilder. Thus Clifton's laughing at the Niggars has been bluesy laughter—laughing to keep from crying. Brennan said that last line was improvised.

The Niggars sketch is hysterically irreverent about the subservient position Blacks of that era were forced into in life and in media. Chappelle is consciously imitating Rochester and having fun with that controversial coon figure, giving him a vicious edge. The Rochester figure demands the sketch live in the fifties while another of Chappelle's sketches, the Racial Draft, is a scenario that could only take place in contemporary America as it sends up the widespread genetic biracialism and multiracialism of today as well as the ubiquity of cultural multiracialism (i.e., people who are racially ambidextrous). The sketch gives us a series of races and ethnic groups as if they're at an athletic league's draft, choosing new members from the pool of individuals considered diverse. The sketch suggests that this event will create racial clarity but the audience knows the racial complexity of the modern world is so great that achieving clarity is impossible, which is why the idea of even attempting it is hysterical.

The Black delegation chooses first and selects Tiger Woods. Graphics on the screen say TIGER WOODS: NOW 100% BLACK. The Asians grouped together in the draft's audience are visibly devastated to "lose" him (though it's unclear exactly what they have lost). In the moments after the selection is made Tiger's Blackness is said and shown to be in motion as if he's morphing in front of our eyes into someone Blacker. Chappelle, playing a commentator, says, "If you ask me he seems Blacker already." And Chappelle, playing Tiger, says, "So long, fried rice; hello, fried chicken." Later in the sketch the Asian delegation takes the Wu-Tang Clan, which, in the sketch's logic, makes sense because there's a strong cultural connection even though there's no genetic one. The audience knows the idea of someone's cultural tie being strong enough to forge a genetic connection is funny because it's ridiculous.

In two sketches Chappelle deals with the multiplicity of ways to be Black and what it means to have several ways of being Black—or multiple ways of performing Blackness—available to you. We don't change the way we perform Blackness the way we change our clothes, but consciously or subconsciously we all have subtle identity choices and we adjust depending on the situation. Brady is a well-known talk show host and comedian who many Blacks find corny or deeply filled with the countenance, tones, and tropes reminiscent of whiteness. If you imagine Blackness as a continuum of identity tropes able to be plotted along a horizontal line then perhaps Jim Brown, Richard Pryor, Malcolm X, Jesse Jackson, Angela Davis, Pam Grier, Lauryn Hill, and Michelle Obama would be at one end while Brady would be at the other end with Byron Allen, Condoleezza Rice, and Bryant Gumbel.

The Wayne Brady episode arrived a season after a sketch in which Paul Mooney said, "Wayne Brady makes Bryant Gumbel look like Malcolm X." For years many Blacks have thought of Gumbel as being at the end of the line, so for Mooney to place Brady so far past Gumbel is shocking. But is any of that fair? Obviously Brady did not think so. Questlove, who was "Chappelle's Show's" music coordinator, said they were in Beverly Hills shooting when Dave ran into Brady who pulled Dave aside and said, "You know, that really hurt my feelings when I saw that sketch." Because Brady knows Blackness is fluid. "The show actually became the lesson that they wanted to teach America," Questlove said.

In the sketch, which takes up an entire episode, Chappelle has been fired from his own show and replaced by Brady. This interacts with the perception of Brady as a vulturous sellout on two levels. First, difficult, prickly, controversial Chappelle—who forces whites to think about things they'd rather not—has been replaced by Comedy Central's white executives with Brady, a white-appeasing Black man who's much easier for whites to deal with, thus confirming Black fears that white-appeasers, who are of no value to the Black community, will be used to replace and silence Black performers or leaders who are valuable and helpful to the Black community partly because they make life for whites uncomfortable. Second, sellouts like Brady can be relied upon to steal those positions. So Brady the sellout is available to the white power structure as a tool to muzzle a progressive voice and he is selfishly willing to be that tool and take another Black actor's job.

We see Brady happily delivering the show's opening monologue by himself while holding flowers someone in the audience has given him. Meanwhile, behind the scenes, Chappelle is moving in to recapture his show, wearing a camouflage winter bubble jacket that establishes him as synchronous with Black sartorial trends and also militant. He's like a righteous revolutionary staging a violent coup: Dave Guevara! He chloroforms two white execs and knocks out a third, clinching his thug bona fides, then struts into view onstage, seeming hypermasculine as Brady stands there holding flowers like a ballerina or an opera singer at the end of her performance. At this point they seem to be standing on opposite ends of the Blackness continuum and the masculinity continuum. Chappelle points this out, saying, "You do your thing, I do my thing." But a moment later, Chappelle tosses to a filmed sketch where their performance of Blackness shifts radically.

Brady, playing himself, is driving Chappelle, who's also playing himself, as they talk about the need for unity among Black actors, a counterpoint to the lack of unity Brady shows in the prelude. Then Brady stops the car beside a small nightclub and begins firing an AK-47, killing someone. He then goes to check on his stable of prostitutes, collects money from them, and threatens to choke one of them. The Brady we see now is thuggish, studly, hypermasculine—someone who'd fit on the Jim Brown/Richard Pryor side of the continuum. This is further reinforced when Brady manipulates Chappelle into smoking angel dust, thus linking Brady with Denzel Washington's devilish cop from *Training Day*. Washington is someone who would sit on the superBlack side of the continuum, and his Detective Alonzo Harris would sit even closer to the end of the line than Washington himself, so Brady is doubly (or triply) linked to the superBlackness Chappelle had denied him. It's critical Brady is playing himself in the sketch, which should force you to rethink who you think Brady is. Is he merely acting oreo-ish when he's onstage acting or hosting a talk show and perhaps he's superBlack when he's offstage? Or is he someone with multiple ways of performing Blackness at his beck and call? (Or is he just good at laughing at himself?)

Brady shows how incredibly fluid his ability to alter his performance of Blackness is when his car is pulled over by the police. As soon as the white officer walks up, Brady goes into oreo mode, leaping to the non-threatening end of the continuum. When the cop recognizes him, Brady smiles sweetly, pulls a microphone out from inside his jacket—confirming the hoary stereotype that Blacks are always ready to perform—and begins singing a Dionne Warwick song. This is no accidental choice: Warwick is widely known to the hiphop generation as one of its loudest enemies, a woman who testified against hiphop to Congress and infamously stumbled over the name of hiphop legend and global icon Snoop Doggy Dogg. Also, her music lacks the edge found in most of the soul music of her generation, so it has not aged as well for most Blacks. If Brady had sung Aretha or Al Green or Stevie Wonder this moment of performance as an expression of his non-threatening nature would not be as razor sharp. In singing Warwick, Brady is again positioning himself as a Black person who knows how to pacify whites. But as the cop dances along with Brady's singing, Brady stops abruptly, twists the cop's neck, and lets him drop to the ground. Then he drops the mic in a way that recalls Michael Corleone dropping a gun after a murder in *The Godfather*. In a matter of seconds, Brady has leapt from one end of the Blackness continuum to the other and back. If you thought he was just a whitey-loving Tom, you've gotta rethink him because he's just shown you the breadth of Blacknesses available to him is as wide as the continuum itself and his control over his performance of Blackness rivals the physical agility of an NFL wide receiver. After this sketch, to label Brady a Tom would seem too simplistic because he's clearly deeper than that. And underestimating him could be dangerous: At the end of the sketch Chappelle gets shot. At one point in *Training Day* Washington's Alonzo threatens someone by saying he's surgical with his gun. It would appear that Brady is equally surgical with his performance of Blackness.

Of course this is not simply a Wayne Brady issue. The ability and need to mediate between different ways of performing Blackness exists in all Black people, especially in the modern era where we typically work, party, and/or reside in a racially mixed world. And the choice of how you perform Blackness in one moment versus another can mean all the difference between getting ahead or not, as well as the difference between feeling good about yourself or not. Chappelle's characters make these choices consciously to heighten the comedic potential but these are choices many of us make subconsciously on a constant basis. The sketch "When Keepin It Real Goes Wrong" presents Chappelle as Vernon Franklin, a vice president at the fictional Viacorp as well as the first in his family to attend college, thus ending the cycle of drug addiction and violence plaguing his family for generations. But in a meeting where he's the only Black person in the room, Franklin's white mentor, celebrating some business victory, turns to Franklin and says, "You da man, gimme some skin!" It's a hamfisted caricature of Black slang.

This is a moment many Blacks who work in predominantly white spaces have experienced: white person offends by misappropriating Blackness and reducing you to a stereotype and less of an individual than everyone else in the office. When this happens in the workplace the attendant power dynamics make it much more complicated. Do you swallow it and continue receiving a paycheck at the risk of feeling like a sellout, or do you speak your mind and maintain your self-respect while risking the loss of your revenue stream? The conundrum runs deep: If you forcefully push back against your mentor's insult you'll probably feel a surge of Black pride. You protected the race and your own racial dignity when someone disrespected. If the entire race were watching on a hidden camera, you'd get a purple heart. If you do nothing and allow the disrespect to go unchecked you may feel like you've betrayed the race and abandoned your principles and ideals, still you're getting paid. But too many moments like that can lead to a debilitating identity crisis or soul-eating depression. So how do you maintain a positive self-image and a job in a world where you feel torn between making nice so you can get money and putting your foot in whitey's ass so you can feel good about yourself?

The voiceover in the sketch says, "Vernon got along with everyone he worked with, which in his heart of hearts made him feel like an Uncle Tom." So Franklin's already been waging an internal struggle between doing the social work necessary to stay at Viacorp and respecting himself as a Black person. He's been told at some point that a Black person who gets along with whites too easily is probably a sellout and a real Black person—one who's on the Jim Brown/Malcolm X side of the continuum—is discomforting whites at some level. So Franklin's mentor's assault is the last straw that forces him to confront the challenge of what it means to do right by himself and to do right by the Black community when those two desires diverge.

So what's Franklin to do? Just take it, the way he imagines a sell-out would, or pull out his street tropes and violently retort? He's got to choose which among his various identities is the appropriate one to respond with: Should he keep it Gumbel or get Malcolm X on this man? He makes the best choice—for the comedy sketch. He gets street and curses his mentor out. If the entire Black community was watching via hidden camera the audience would burst into ecstatic applause. Alas, in the next scene Franklin is wiping a windshield at a gas station. It's unclear if he's just washing cars or is allowed to pump gas, too. Either way his professional career has been derailed and he seems on his way to continuing the cycle of drug abuse that's plagued his family for so long. But there's a consolation prize: He kept it real. The trophy that goes with it has a few cubic zirconias on it.

I suspect the modern dilemma that Franklin went through—how to mediate between an individual's professional needs and what the individual thinks community wants from him as well as how to maintain self-respect—was also thrust onto Chappelle himself, leading to his abrupt and shocking exit. In the midst of taping "Chappelle's Show's" third season, shortly after signing a contract that would pay him a reported $50 million, he heard a white person laugh at a joke in a way that rankled him. And that was the trigger to make him walk away from his show. Questlove said, "He felt as though the interns weren't laughing with him, they were laughing at him. And he just caught himself and he walked off the set. When I called Brennan I was like, okay, what's up? And he was like, Dave's gone. And we found out in *TIME* magazine that he just went straight to Africa."

But what really happened? No one but Dave knows for certain. Surely there must be several reasons. Chappelle repeatedly blamed "the large corporate monster," but that rings false: Comedy Central had just agreed to pay him double-digit millions and had grown less and less controlling of his material over time. (Brennan and Cundieff talked about how there was a fight to get Season One's "nigger"-filled "Clayton Bigsby" sketch on, but there was no editing of Season Two's "nigger"-filled "Niggar Family" sketch.) Surely Chappelle had the corporate freedom to say what he wanted to say—when he left he was working on a sketch about his racial conscience and how he struggled with whether or not to order and eat fried chicken in front of white people even though he loved it. The sketch included similarly biting jabs at other races. Does that seem like someone who's being reined in?

But did Chappelle continue to feel the spiritual and political freedom to speak his mind? Was the burden of representation beginning to weigh on him? Did he feel that the gigantic multiracial audience he'd attracted was correctly reading his sophisticated race comedy or was he somehow perpetuating racism and stereotypes? In the "Clayton Bigsby" sketch's intro he'd thrown down his gauntlet—I'm going to do what I believe is funny and I don't care if you think it sets the race back. But that was episode one of a new show on a relatively small network that no one thought would become a cultural phenomenon that would sell more DVDs than any other comedy show in history. By the third season, Brennan says Chappelle was writing sketches and then later calling them racist and demanding they be cut. When the show grew to a gigantic size did he struggle with the Anxiety of Black Public Success—am I enriching myself at a detriment to the community? As a public person if I put smiles on white faces is that evidence that I'm an Uncle Tom? Chappelle's character Vernon Franklin had a meltdown because his getting along with all the whites in the office makes him feel Tommish. When Dave had become the favorite Black comedian of most young white Americans, what did he feel?

In all histories of "Chappelle's Show" the ill-toned laugh is the epiphany that leads to the end of the show. But insiders say the ill-toned laugh was not truly the beginning of the problem. There was blood in the water—or doubt in Dave's mind—before that. "It wasn't really a day—it was over, like, a week," said Donnell Rawlings, who played several characters. "You felt something was wrong. Last time I saw him before he took off, he was a werewolf, I was a mummy, and Charlie [Murphy] was Frankenstein, and he said, 'I guess fifty-two million ain't enough.' He was kind of like talking to himself. That's when I knew something wasn't registering right because fifty-two million is way enough for me."

When I interviewed Chappelle for BET I asked him why he left the show and he blamed Comedy Central, which gave him room to be vague because, as he said, he couldn't afford litigation for slandering them. I didn't buy it. He was one of their greatest revenue generators. There was no value to them in rocking the boat. But there were some things he said that perhaps offer some sort of answer, a place where he talked about self-respect and risking the loss of it and pushing back against that.

"It's like, you know, you've seen this happen to people before," Chappelle said. "Mariah Carey's departure from her latest deal. Didn't that happen right after she made a highly publicized one-hundred-million-dollar deal?" In 2001 Carey signed an $80 million deal with Virgin Records and soon after had a nervous breakdown that led to a stint in a hospital and a break from public appearances. "And what did she say about it? She said, 'I found myself micromanaging my career.' Same way I'm doin'. And she said, 'It was as if everybody was working against me.' Which is damn near exactly what I ended up sayin'. So this is not an unusual thing. You see these things happen all the time. . . . So, you know, I didn't like the way things were goin', so I left. . . . Listen, man, I will say this: Walkin' away from fifty million, not the easiest thing in the world to do. But I did it, and I really, really want to put it behind me and focus on the many good things that I hope to have happen in the future."

I asked, "The happiness you feel now is worth it?"

"Yeah, man," he said. "Listen, at the end of the day you want to be able to respect yourself. You know? You don't want to do anything that—that makes it hard for you to do that. We all do in some fashion or another at some point in our life. But the quicker or the faster we can correct ourselves, I think the easier your life will be. You know, at the end of the day you don't want to regret things. So that's how I'm tryin' to live. It's not easy, but . . ."

"And now you respect yourself?"

"I respect the shit out of myself. If you're goin' into an environment every day that you don't feel good about yourself in, you start to ask yourself, 'Well, why am I going here?' And if you don't like the answers, or you don't think these are respectable answers, if they don't somehow make you sit well with yourself, then I don't think it's wrong to take a look at that."

Months after the show ended, Chappelle went on a nationwide stand-up tour and talked about why he left. He told a story that he said would explain everything. It was from Iceberg Slim's book *Pimp*, in which a prostitute who's been with Slim for many years says she wants to leave. The pimp says okay but she must turn one last trick for him. She goes to a hotel but in the midst of having sex with a man he dies. Distraught, she calls Slim, who rushes over to the hotel room and comforts her. He tells her he's going to take care of this for her but he's doing her a gigantic favor and putting himself at great risk to do so, meaning she's going to have to continue working for him for many more years to pay off her new debt. She's sad but agrees and goes back to the street to work. And once she's gone, the dead man wakes up. He was a plant meant to help Slim entrap her.

Chappelle presents himself as the prostitute, suggesting that Comedy Central is the pimp entrapping him. But I believe, as Donnell Rawlings does, that in the story Chappelle is both the prostitute and the pimp. "Who you upset with?" Rawlings said of Chappelle. "Be real with it. You not upset with the white man. You upset with yourself." The pimp and prostitute are separate sides of himself—either his writer self and his performer self, or his old, audacious, barely famous self and his new, national-phenomenon-and-scared-of-it self or some other psychological dichotomy. Either way, it's Chappelle who's put himself in a position he doesn't want to be in, a place that makes him feel like a prostitute because he's questioning whether he's bringing down the race with work that's too subtle for a massive audience, including many white people who don't understand Black comedy and culture. The audience is the john in the joke pretending, seeming, to be dead—when the comic does his job well the audience is killed—but they are not. He thinks maybe they are laughing at him and helping to trap him and keep him prostituting. Chappelle's comic mouth has written checks that his body is afraid to cash. And the abundance of whites at the party that is his edgy cultural production makes him wonder if he's gone from brilliant cultural commentator to a culture-damaging sellout. Telling abrasive jokes about your family when it's just family in the room can feel cathartic but telling them to a massive audience of outsiders is treason. The freedom of the post-Black era has scared him to death. So he picks up the gauntlet he threw down at the beginning of the show and he runs.

# Chapter 4

# "Shut Up, Touré! You Ain't Black!"

I am a real and authentic Black man, even though once, in a room full
of Black people, I was loudly and angrily told by a linebacker-sized
brother: "Shut up, Touré! You ain't Black!" It was the most humiliating
moment of my life but also one of the best moments of my life, because
it forced me to take a searingly painful look inside and figure out exactly
what it means to me to be Black. It led to a liberating epiphany and
being at peace with who I am. That moment started me inching down
the mental road that would lead to this book. The world had before that
told me I wasn't Black, or wasn't their vision of Black, but subtly, never
that bluntly. It was for me a sort of nigga wake-up call.

The fight to figure out who I am has long been intertwined with
an internal discussion of what it means to be Black, similar to how
others struggle with what it means to be Catholic or Jewish, because
there is an almost religious aspect to Blackness. But in a time when
the definitions and parameters of Blackness were in flux as radically
and rapidly as ever in history, I had to learn to shake free of both the
white gaze and the Black gaze so I could define myself for myself. We
are all a product of the times we live in and so I have been shaped by
the eras of affirmative action, Buppie-ism, multiculturalism, and post-
Blackness as well as living in the shadow of what might be considered
Black America's Greatest Generation: those who fought in the streets
and the courts to desegregate and force America to give Blacks greater

access to the American dream. Because of their struggles and successes my generation had new opportunities as well as a certain survivor's guilt: We wanted to fight but there were no longer battles as fierce and overt as those they'd already confronted. I had a sense of arriving at the battlefield at the moment most of the hard work has already been completed, able to benefit without having had to fight. So I had greater academic, professional, and personal opportunities than most Blacks of previous generations and a conscious sense of wanting to make the most of those opportunities because people had died for me to have them. I would never be hosed or have to sit in, but racism had not retired, it just got more subtle, so I had different challenges to contend with. I've had to learn how not to be manipulated by modern racism or the cultural bullying that is identity fascism. I also had to keep my self-esteem intact against a plethora of messages that I was of lesser value or ability. Or lesser Blackness. Racism doesn't often come with a machete these days but the death of your self-esteem by a thousand cuts can still lead to the murder of your soul.

On the morning of my first day of first grade, as I was about to leave for the private school where I would spend the next twelve years, Mom zipped up my jacket and pulled me close and said, "Remember, you have to be twice as good as those white kids!" I took it to mean that I had to work harder and be smarter to get my due, as in, they're going to discount my ability because I'm Black so I have to be better in order to get ahead. Yes, I thought like that as a child, because my parents taught my sister and me that being Black meant hard work and having to fight to get what was ours. (Decades later Mom explained that she'd meant I had to behave better because she thought the teacher would be expecting the Black kid to act out.)

My parents were ascensionists, determined to take advantage of the new opportunities that were opening up for Blacks in the seventies. After growing up in working-class homes, my father started his own accounting business, bought a house with a yard and a picket fence in a nice middle-class suburban community, and sent the kids to a private school. They didn't care about being the only Black family in the neighborhood or theirs being the only Black kids in their classes. My parents were insistent on ascending to the middle class and having my sister and me go even higher than they had, and they were not about to let anything stop them. After they bought their house on Hart Circle in Randolph, Massachusetts, but before they moved in, one of the families on the cul-de-sac started a petition to keep the Black family from moving in. None of our other neighbors signed the petition and my parents didn't let it deter them from moving in. I recall once a small rock flying through one of our windows. My parents did not get all that upset about it, as if refusing to flinch.

My parents were also big enough to let the petition roll off their backs. The neighbors who started it had a son my age and I was always invited to his birthday parties. I always went and every time his parents were super nice to me. When I was four and five and six I was the sort of kid who would go to a birthday party and spend half the afternoon chatting up the parents. I recall sitting beside their son in the front seat of their car talking with his mom as she drove a carful of boys to some birthday adventure. It wasn't until years later that I learned of the petition they'd launched before I was born. And it shocked me: They'd been so nice. They'd treated me with respect even as a little kid. They didn't seem at all like racists.

Getting my sister and me into a storied private school—Milton Academy, where Robert and Ted Kennedy and T.S. Eliot had gone—was a source of great pride and a fantastic omen for a bright future. It also came with great responsibility. We repeatedly got stern admonishments against embarrassing the race in any way, as if we were personally responsible for the image of every other Black person. My parents told us whites expected us to be late, slovenly, and subpar. We were to be articulate, smart, and never, ever play the fool. We were instilled with a fear of fulfilling stereotypes. It was not incumbent on others to open their minds, it was our burden to live down the stereotypes. To fulfill them would be a shameful crime.

Back then my parents were quite taken with white approval. If we acted out in public they'd say things like, "Don't confirm what those white people think." Or "They expect you to behave like buffoons! Trick 'em!" They loved it when white strangers came up to us in restaurants and complimented the manners and behavior of their children. If that happened now I'd find it patronizing and offensive. So you were expecting buffoonery? Did you also tell the white family over there that their kids are well behaved, or was that not a shock? But my parents appreciated those moments. They didn't look down their noses at traditionally white activities, and we took lessons in tennis, piano, and skiing, so that, they said, we could one day more easily socialize with our white peers. There were a small piano and Picasso prints in our house. As role models they pointed to Arthur Ashe, Bill Cosby, Marvin Gaye, and Ed Bradley—men who were classy, articulate, intelligent, and dignified. My parents were very proud to be Black but weren't the sort to march in the streets; they preferred being inside players. They preferred Motown to Stax, preferred Ernie Barnes to Jean-Michel Basquiat. They often had lobster dinners for their friends, who included Black politicians, lawyers, developers, and painters. To me there was nothing abnormal about a Black person going to MIT, becoming an architect, speaking a little French, and knowing about fine wine while strutting through life with a persona filled with Black tropes because my favorite faux uncle did all those things.

Still, it was impossible for me as a small child in Boston to not notice the racism around me. In the third grade there was talk of a class trip to Bunker Hill, a place made famous during the Revolutionary War. But it was in an area—Charlestown—my parents felt was dangerously racist. When my mother heard about the trip, she told me in a dismissive tone to not even bother bringing the consent form home. There was no way she'd let me go to Bunker Hill. I didn't need to ask her why. By that point I already knew there were some parts of Boston that we would not go to for any reason. It was as if nigger-eating dragons lived there and there was nothing you could do to stop them so you just avoided them. But there were no supernatural creatures, just people who had automatic hatred for us. They had not met us but had already decided to hate us so much that we wouldn't risk driving through their towns. As a small kid I knew not to go to West Roxbury, Lynn, Southie, and a few other places. The knowledge that automatic hatred of you existed just up the road sent a shiver down the spine. And it was depressing. Why did they hate us? Why is it nothing could be done about this? Why was no one challenging or protesting this? But at least all that was up the road in an avoidable place.

At school everyone dealt with race and racism in an upfront and candid way. We talked about it in and out of class, and almost all of my classmates and teachers were respectful, open-minded, and non-racist almost all of the time. It seemed utopian. I was slapped out of my comfort zone forever in the eighth grade. Students who were in grades nine through twelve were required to meet each morning en masse for Morning Assembly. Back then they separated assembly by gender so four hundred boys met together in one auditorium while four hundred girls convened in a separate one. Late in the school year all the eighth graders were taken to Morning Assembly, to introduce them to the next year's routine. The first morning that I went with my class of eighth-grade boys to sample the assembly I sat with rapt attention, excited to be among the older boys (as opposed to the semi-slumber you brought to the exercise as an older kid). The assembly consisted of the headmonitor—our term for the student-elected school president—shepherding us through announcements from teachers and administrators regarding schoolwide business, and skits from varsity teams or drama club productions trying to drum up audiences.

Randall Dunn was then the headmonitor. He was the school's first Black headmonitor, a brother from Jamaica who did well in the classroom; was on the varsity football, basketball, and track teams; and had tons of charisma. He was respected by teachers and students on the field, in the classroom, and on the quad. Everyone seemed to love him, including the admissions department at Brown, which had accepted him. But a few days before my first assembly a group of students sat around in the dorm talking about what colleges they'd gotten into and questioning how it was these monumental decisions were made, and someone said to Dunn, with a matter of fact, this-is-obvious tone, "I know you're headmonitor and you got all this other stuff going for you but when it comes down to it, it's really 'cause you're Black."

Dunn was shocked. Here was someone saying to his face that even though he had a fantastic academic profile, one of the best in his class, the bottom-line reason he'd gotten into an Ivy was affirmative action. Dunn told me that sucked some of the excitement out of his accomplishment. He couldn't help but feel this was a sentiment felt by much of the school community. He said he felt he deserved the emotional equivalent of balloons but got shrugs.

So that morning in the assembly Dunn spoke to his classmates in a calm, even voice that betrayed no anger and made no demand but wasn't self-pitying, either. He was strong without being attacking, standing his ground and shining a light on some ugliness that was not his fault. He said he knew some students thought he'd gotten into Brown because he was Black and that wasn't right. He'd worked hard and he'd earned it. And then, after his brief address, he moved on, but not without casting a pall over the room.

I got chills. If this popular, charismatic, athletic, brilliant guy couldn't win the total respect of his classmates then what chance did any Black student have? No matter how great you became—even if you were a headmonitor with stellar grades and three varsity letters they'd still think you couldn't have earned your way into a good school. Was Black skin a cloak of inferiority? Who knew how many people smiled in your face but privately thought, "You're Black so you're not that smart and without the helping hand of affirmative action you wouldn't even be here." As if affirmative action was proof of your lack of ability rather than proof that when the playing field was leveled you could excel. When I walked out of that assembly I felt I had a lot to prove. I knew there was a minefield ahead of me and no way to avoid the bombs, and even if you didn't actually step on the bombs, you were already transformed by constantly looking out for them.

—Dunn, who is now the headmaster of a progressive Michigan private school, experienced what social scientists call a "microaggression." NYU Professor Peggy Davis defines them as "subtle, stunning, often automatic, sometimes non-verbal exchanges that are put-downs of Blacks by whites." They serve as reminders of purported Black inferiority. They include making stereotypical assumptions, being culturally insensitive, and questioning whether racism exists. One common subset of these microaggressions is something I call the "resume check," which is like a descendent of the free papers check that free Blacks dealt with during slavery—a white person basically assumes you do not belong and checks to see if you do. In 2002 I went to Italy to work on my second book at a two-month writer's retreat that was attended by several college professors. You had to apply to be a part of the retreat, and you had to show how serious you were about the project you'd be working on while you were there by getting recommendations to confirm your importance in your field. They only took about twenty people per session.

Halfway through my session several of the professors became nervous, like birds squawking hours before the storm arrives. A new person was coming: Helen Vendler, a famous Harvard poetry professor whose imminent arrival made the professors there nervous. They told me she was brilliant and brusque. They made her sound like a peacock with technicolor plumage who would eschew humility and not only show off the extreme beauty of her feathers but also point out the lesser beauty of everyone else's plumage.

Helen arrived and during her first few days had informal introductory conversations with the others at the retreat. One morning she and I happened to find ourselves alone on a veranda and the second question she asked me, with a note of confusion in her tone, was, "How did *you* get here?" She was clearly asking, "How did you earn the right to be here? How did you qualify? Because the demographic evidence doesn't spell it out for me." She was asking about my credentials, as if she could not comprehend how a late twentysomething Black man could get accepted to the same august writer's retreat as her. I felt she was resume checking me. I know she didn't ask all the others that question, no doubt because she assumed they belonged (and because she certainly hadn't asked anyone I polled). But she was curious to glance at my free papers to make sure that I was supposed to be there. By then I was experienced in being resume checked and all too aware that submitting to it would only suggest that I tacitly agreed that she had valid reason to check me. And later, a tangible wave of shame would come washing down over me. So after she said, "How did *you* get here?" I paused and said, "By plane." I didn't have to prove my worth to her even if she was a Harvard professor. Just because she had a master's didn't make her my master.

But it took a long time for me to develop the ability to completely dissociate someone else's vision of me from *my* vision of me. Being a Harvard professor immediately established her as an important person and we all naturally want the respect of people we deem important. So it takes some hard work long before then and considerable inner strength to have a settled sense of self that would not internalize her message that I may not have belonged. It's easy to think we are in control of defining ourselves for ourselves, but social psychology has long understood that the self-image is constructed in part by how you are viewed by others. George Herbert Mead, one of the founders of social psychology, called this the "looking-glass self." You see yourself as the world sees you. This is why the constant bombardment of microaggressions can be so pernicious: They bring society's inferior view of Blacks to our face and can chisel away at our self-esteem.

Microaggressions can also serve as triggers for "stereotype threat," the idea that when you fear being judged by or living down to a stereotype, that alone is disruptive enough to negatively impact your performance. Claude Steele, the provost of Columbia University and a professor of psychology there, has done extensive study on stereotype threat and wrote an excellent book about it called *Whistling Vivaldi*. The concept states that we're all aware of the stereotypes about our identities, so in situations where you do something that your identity group is negatively stereotyped for, you will fear proving those stereotypes true and that will cause you to freeze and fail, or work harder to disprove them. But that means it's more challenging for you to succeed because you're doing two jobs at once: attempting to solve a difficult task while also battling a stereotype, using extra mental and spiritual energy, fueled by your determination to not fulfill it. Dr. Steele told me, "People say, why not use the stereotype as motivation to disprove it and perform better? Well, that's exactly what they're doing. They're trying really hard to disprove the stereotype. But when you have to do that all the time it makes being in an area where you have to do that a lot of work because you're multitasking. You're trying to do the task and trying to disprove the stereotype and in a lot of situations that will backfire and you'll perform worse. You think you're multitasking but study after study shows you can't. You're not multitasking, you're alternating your attention between the two things. So now your performance is going down. And that starts to be frustrating and that makes the whole thing worse and it gets to be a feverish situation.

"I don't think it's something we 'let' ourselves feel," Dr. Steele said. "It's something any human being in this situation would feel. I don't think it bespeaks any kind of predisposition on our part or weakness on our part to be open to this sense of threat. It's just a rational assessment of the probabilities of the situation. You don't have to have a special weakness to be thinking, 'They could be thinking something about me.' It's natural. People think about stereotype threat as an in-the-air, ephemeral thing but it's tangible. It takes a physical toll. Pain is there."

This is something that Black people encounter often—the list of negative stereotypes about us is long—and it touches anyone in a situation where they are aware of a negative stereotype about their group. Malcolm Gladwell talked about a scientific test where he gave Black kids the SAT and then, before giving it to them a second time, he subtly reminded them they're Black, simply activating in the moment their knowledge of their Blackness—or that they're being looked at as Black people rather than just as people. After that they scored far worse. "Just reminding people activates these kind of unconscious internalized prejudices," Gladwell said. "And it changes the way you do the SAT. It can make you incredibly cautious, like, 'Oh shit, I got this burden I'm dealing with. I've gotta make sure I . . . ' and that's of course the exact wrong attitude for doing an SAT." And stereotype threat runs across racial and gender lines. "This is my favorite one of all time," Gladwell said. "You take rich white kids and you have them jump. You measure how far they can jump and then you bring in a new instructor to do the measuring. The instructor's Black. They jump way less, 15 or 20 percent less. They kind of freeze up." The Black coach need not say anything to activate the stereotype of whites' inability to jump, the kids already know it. Of course, the athletic ability of white children being diminished by stereotype threat is nothing compared to, say, the impact on Black children fighting an uphill war to prove they're intelligent.

Even Dr. King felt the sting of stereotype threat and was obsessed with not fulfilling certain negative expectations he anticipated. As a young man he was obsessed with being early, arriving at his classes fifteen minutes before they began, and with being clean, inoffensive, and articulate. "This is Claude Steele writ large in arguably the greatest American ever," Dyson said. "Stereotype threat resonant! Maybe one of the reasons why he plagiarized is because he felt, 'No matter how good I am they're not going to accept it,' 'cause clearly King is brilliant, clearly King is a genius, even then he's extraordinarily, rhetorically sophisticated, but still he's got self-doubt and that self-doubt is the product of his vulnerability in a society that doesn't acknowledge Black genius."

I've felt stereotype threat acutely many times, when the whites around me have subtly let me know they're not sure if I'm intellectually up to a certain level of performance expected in a given situation. So then you adopt an "I'll show them" attitude and you work harder to prove them wrong. But that added fuel isn't always helpful in an intellectual endeavor and the pressure to disprove a stereotype—moments where you have the identity of the entire race on your back—can make you feel like Atlas holding the world on your shoulders. That feeling makes me admire so much more all those historic Black forerunners like Jackie Robinson, Althea Gibson, the Tuskegee Airmen, Thurgood Marshall, and all those who were the first to go to a given college or graduate school. I cannot imagine the pressures they battled.

So what do you do? Ignore your eyes and ears and pay attention only to the voice inside. You need an unshakeable self-esteem, an unchangeable self-image, and an impenetrable self-confidence that can withstand the attacks you see coming and those you can't see because they seep in like gas. You know you're smart and you belong at Milton or Brown or Harvard or *Rolling Stone* or Goldman Sachs or wherever it is you've reached, and anything anyone else says to the contrary is a comment on them, not on you. Racist attitudes speak volumes about their holders and say nothing about their targets. But detaching yourself from society's view of you is very hard work; it's a lesson I learned—or, an attitude I installed—over many years.

At Milton I was painfully aware of being different than everyone, of being other, and sometimes I felt I was walking around with a giant red marker-drawn circle around me, orbiting my body. That was an all but tangible way of feeling racialized after years of experiencing and witnessing microaggressions and racial differences and perhaps even stereotype threat, even though almost everyone around me seemed to be going out of their way to try to be non-racist. But still I was hyperaware of race. Whites were maybe underaware of race but they were still able to be hurt by race. I learned that the hard way.

In my eleventh-grade American History class we sat at a large round table that was meant to encourage group discussion rather than having the teacher just tell us what to think. Because we dealt with contemporary issues that many of us talked about outside of class, some kids came to the room like intellectual gunslingers, eager to fight. We were young, independent thinkers dealing with hot-button issues, like baby chemists handling pyrotechnic chemicals. It's surprising that feelings didn't get hurt all the time. Of course the most emotional moment of the year involved race and I was in the middle of it.

Reverend Jesse Jackson was then running for president and twenty years before Obama's victory, to have a well-respected Black man be part of the race meant the world to Blacks and to me. Years earlier, when I was six, seven, and eight, my dream was to be the first Black president and everywhere I went I told everyone. I was fascinated with politics at an early age and studied the history of the presidency so well I could name every president in order, along with when and how long they served and several pertinent facts about them. As a kid I read Theodore White's *The Making of the President 1960*, thinking about how to use

85

JFK's strategic lessons to my advantage. But at some point the dream faded away. I think around age ten I came to believe that it was impossible for a Black person to become president and drifted into thinking about what else I might try to do with my life. No other dream replaced it, that dream just faded away. And now that I see I was wrong it's sad for me to look back at the Black boy who dreamed of being president and came to believe the lie that a Black commander-in-chief was impossible. It's tragic he thought that he was dreaming too high. When I applied to colleges I wrote several essays about wanting to be a political advisor. Dream downsizing.

So for Jackson to have taken up my dream and run so far with it was deeply inspiring and meaningful. For Blacks to feel as though becoming president was out of the question means an important part of the American dream is off-limits. It is American to feel that anything is possible—we have no caste system, meaning anyone can start at any place and reach any level. But before Obama most Blacks felt as if there was a national glass ceiling. We could get rich but we could not, we thought, become president. And if a crucial part of the American dream is off-limits then we are not full Americans. Jackson's candidacy was doing nothing less than helping to show it was possible for a Black candidate to one day win. Jackson was in the collective mind, working at the far edges, where dreams of becoming a Black president had died and the soil was barren and hostile, and he was preparing the land for seeds.

So, one day the class discussion flowed away from the lesson plan and onto the subject of Jackson, and I ended up in an intense, emotional debate about Jackson's political relevance with Sam Williamson. Sam was a whip-smart, egotistical Manhattanite, and a national squash champ with all the swagger that dominion over that little world could grant. If there was a Young Republicans club at Milton he would've been president. Sam argued that Jackson was an irrelevant part of the race, because he had no chance to win, while I argued that he was relevant, because he was bringing issues to the table that would not otherwise be discussed (like poverty and race) and because he was opening avenues for Black people to be in the presidential race, which meant further inclusion for

Blacks in what it meant to be fully American. We jousted, each unwilling to give an inch in front of our classmates, tensions rising as we shot back and forth, locked in verbal combat. It was an intellectual game to him, where to me Jackson's candidacy was wrapped up in all sorts of racial baggage, partly because I was a boy who had given up on my dream of becoming the first Black president.

This is where race can function like a dog whistle. Call it a Black whistle: The reverberations emanating from certain names or words or symbols or tropes can be heard only by Blacks because of our intimate relationship with the culture. Whites don't hear the same sounds. Sam, unable to hear the Black whistle, didn't know he was pushing buttons deep inside me by asserting that this extraordinary Black man was politically irrelevant. By saying that about Jackson I was hearing him all but say Black people were irrelevant. And as we went on verbally punching each other I felt the sting of racism, though I knew deep down Sam was not consciously being racist and was not meaning to be. Finally, in disgust, but not intending to hurt him, I said, "That's what a racist would say." I was not calling him a racist, just saying that he was sounding like one. But I did not then realize that for many white people being called racist is the absolute worst insult possible. And Sam—the brilliant, arrogant, swaggering kid from Manhattan—began to cry. He bent over into himself and started trembling and tears spat from his eyes. The room fell dead silent. The combustible chemicals had exploded and if emotions were visible, you would've seen them splattered all over the walls. The teacher leaned over—she happened to be sitting next to him—and put her arm over his shoulder to comfort him. She looked at me with raised eyebrows, a face that said, See, you need to be careful where you point that gun.

During my grade school and high school years every day was a multicultural day for me. If I wasn't at school I was almost certainly at the tennis club that was my second home. But this was like no tennis club you've ever seen: Sportsmen's Tennis Club was a not-for-profit in Dorchester owned by Blacks and aimed at serving the working-class kids in the neighboring areas. There were a few middle-class families and a few non-Black ones in the club's large extended family, but it was undeniably a culturally Black and ghetto tennis club. There were cracks in some of the courts, holes in some of the nets, and the kinetic, propulsive energy and high theater of a Watts backyard BBQ or a late-night Harlem street corner. The overtly stated mission of the club was to teach tennis to working-class kids so they could develop skills good enough to earn them scholarships to colleges they would not otherwise be able to attend or afford, and thus change their lives. So I saw two Black socio-political ethos fused together: the sixties "I'm Black and I'm Proud" sense of a nationalistic us vs. them movement (we went to junior tournaments as if to racialized Davis Cup ties, ready to battle whitey) and the seventies "Movin On Up" sense of going after your piece of the pie in the Affirmative Action era.

The place taught me to play tennis and gave me all the Black cultural nutrients I needed. That was where I studied Black culture in impromptu classes about Black cool and the dozens and the Smurf and "Soul Train" and "The Message" and "La Di Da Di." And my daily movement from the preppy school to the ghetto club did not give me vertigo, it meant that doing rapid cultural 180s became second nature to me and code-switching on a dime became the norm. I saw there were many ways to be American as well as many ways to be Black and I noted the different ways others were performing Blackness in varying situations. I learned how to become malleable, how to do the shape-shifting I would need for my life: how to do the twoness-step.

At the club I learned all about that particularly resilient strain of Black self-confidence that lives in spite of the unending attempts to crush it. It's a steely, resolute self-assurance that goes to war to preserve itself every day, a necessarily unshakeable self-esteem that, when functioning properly, laughs at the efforts to break it down. The ineluctably over-sized Black ego is not self-indulgence, it's self-preservation—it's armor against a world that seems to have a nefarious, well-funded multimedia PR campaign working against it around the clock. Columbia Law Professor Patricia Williams says racism is "so deeply painful and assaultive as to constitute spirit-murder." Society is attempting to assassinate our souls. Without an impregnable defense—a steely Black ego unable to be shaped by the onslaught of negativity—you were doomed to succumb. Without the ability to divorce yourself from society's view of you, from the white gaze and its negative vision of Blacks, then the mind virus of Black inferiority would seep in, eroding the value of your achievement and your self-worth—because you may be class president and stuff but really, you only got ahead because you're Black. I needed to take that sort of spiritual armor with me into school every day to shield me from those who might try to degrade me as they'd tried Randall. Because sticks and stones may break your bones but words can cause permanent damage. But it took years to build the sort of impenetrable shield I would need. Titanium is strong but the sort of shield I had in mind required Teflon.

The need for a Teflon self-esteem shield became crystal clear in the summer of 1980 when the nation realized that in Atlanta, Black boys and girls my age were disappearing and turning up dead. The killings had been going on for about a year when the nation began looking at it as a phenomenon and began collectively freaking out. The way the story developed was in and of itself frightening—for a year Black children were being killed systematically by some person or group and not only had no one been caught, but the pattern hadn't even been noticed. That only doubled the sense that Black children's bodies were worthless— they could be slaughtered like veal and dumped like garbage and the authorities weren't concerned enough to even pick up a pattern. The kids were stabbed or bludgeoned or shot or strangled. Most were strangled, or violently asphyxiated, as in a lynching. This, in the hometown of Dr. King. A city that had a Black mayor, Maynard Jackson. A place that called itself the city too busy to hate. If microaggressions were sending a subtle but clear message that the Black mind was inferior, then the Atlanta Child Murders were bullhorns yelling that Black bodies were so irrelevant they were killable in bulk quantities.

Between July 1979 and March 1981 in Atlanta, twenty-nine Black boys and girls between the ages of nine and fifteen were executed. The summer of 1980 was called the Summer of Death. In Black households across the nation it was a terrifying period. Atlanta seemed powerless to protect its Black children from the invisible hand snuffing kids out one by one, and no one knew how far across the nation the problem would spread. I was about ten, and Black ten-year-olds were being hunted and killed. That meant my parents keeping me on a short leash and enforcing an absurdly early curfew. I was locked in the house long before it got dark.

I remember lying alone in bed when I should've been outside, my heart pounding, thinking, what if some killer comes through the window tonight? What will I do? It was like living in a horror movie. And deep down I sensed that this was a symbol for how race operated in America: Black people were like lambs living among wolves. We could be snatched away at any time. We were powerless.

Barry Michael Cooper, the screenwriter of *New Jack City*, interviewed several mothers of murdered boys for a movie project. He says the child murders—both living through them and interviewing the families victims—gave him years of nightmares. He got emotional as he talked about the child murders as a parent of two boys. "I'm sorry I'm raising my voice," Cooper said. "I get too amped on this, man, forgive me. It's just that it did a lot to hurt the psyche of Black America for a long, long time. There was a tragic sense of loss. There was a sense of national bewilderment, like, what in the world is going on? Now they're touching our kids?"

He recalls some people blaming the parents, as if the abductions were the result of poor supervision, but talking to the families revealed a much more frightening reality. "The women I met, they weren't bad parents, man. These weren't negligent parents. No, these people came under the cover of darkness, man. Going in childrens' bedroom windows and snatching them in the middle of the night. They weren't always outside playing and running around, ten o'clock, eleven o'clock at night. They were home. They were home. Parents talked about going into the room in the morning to get their kids up to take 'em to school and a kid is not there. Could you imagine that? You talkin' about *Amityville Horror*, but real. That was vampires, ghosts, ghouls, goblins coming into your house, into your kids' bedroom, in the thick of the night and snatching your kids."

The child murders changed Cooper as a parent as they surely changed many Black parents. "At the time my sons were like one and two years old," he said. "I would get up in the middle of the night and just watch them, man, just make sure they were okay. I would damn near have OCD. Go downstairs, check my locks, make sure the windows are locked, you understand what I'm saying? And I'm in Baltimore. But I don't want this happening to my family, man. In an odd way it made me a better parent. It made me more vigilant with my sons and almost damn near overprotective."

Cooper also interviewed a boy named Stanley Parker who'd been abducted, raped, and left for dead, but somehow survived. "He was raped so savagely that his, his spine was twisted. He was mentally challenged and the actual attack he was very foggy about but he sat and remembered that it was some Black people that abducted him but it was also some white people there. The story that I heard—I didn't go to sleep for two weeks, man. I had nightmares."

Eventually there was a break in the case and an arrest—Wayne Williams, a mentally unstable Black man. He was convicted of two murders—but of adults, not children. He was believed to have committed many of the murders but few people thought he'd committed all of them. And that conclusion left a certain turmoil. Had the serial killer stalking and slaughtering Black children been caught or not? Had the culprit really been a Black man and not the Klan? Had we just lived through a bizarre embodiment of self-hatred? Was a Black man framed to hide a much more sinister truth? And if you did not accept the idea of Wayne Williams as the lone killer, and many do not to this day, then did the government cover up a strange tragedy and let the real killer or killers get away? And perhaps some day more Black boys would disappear. Thus for some Blacks old enough to remember the child murders, Atlanta remains a loaded symbol, a Black whistle with an ominous sound. "Atlanta's a place that really frightens me to this day," Cooper said.

Eight years after the last boy was killed, I went to college: to Emory in Atlanta. It brought back some of the senses that I'd dumped into the word "Atlanta" as a kid; of the helplessness of Black people and the worthlessness of Black bodies. But I was determined to be no one's victim and to forge my own path. My freshman-year social world revolved around a clique I formed with my white hallmates, an outgrowth of friendships I made in my first days at school when you're grabbing for any anchor you can get. I was no oreo, I got along with my Black classmates, but spent way more time with my white friends. That was an offense I would pay for later.

In the spring of my freshman year a Black freshman pre-med major named Sabrina Collins, a woman I'd never met—very few Black students could say they knew her well—made an announcement that rocked the campus. Collins's dorm room had been vandalized. Someone had slashed her teddy bear, soaked her clothes with bleach, and taken a tube of lipstick and written on the wall: NIGGER HANG. Cut to mayhem.

Next thing you knew the campus was crowded with newsmedia from around the country who lined the sidewalks trying to interview students, members of the New Black Panther Party marching around, and both the Georgia Bureau of Investigation and the FBI patrolling and snooping everywhere. But the group that made the most noise were the Black students who banded together in a way that would've made Dr. King, Malcolm X, and Huey Newton proud, putting what we'd learned in our African-American political science classes to work—protesting the incident, the administration, the South, the past, the future, whiteness, everything. We were angry and militant and skipping class to have sit-ins where we took over the student center or the lobby in front of the president's office. Day after day we kept on protesting because nothing was happening. And even though the whole world was watching, things kept happening to Collins. She got a death threat through the mail. Then she lifted the rug in her room to find DIE NIGGER DIE written on the floor in nail polish. That's when she collapsed and was hospitalized for emotional trauma. She was said to have gone mute. We kept on protesting because we saw her as a symbol of all of us—a racist attack against her was an attack on everyone. If she wasn't safe on campus none of us were. We were fighting back against the same sort of blatant racism our parents had told us about, rather than the more subtle strains we encountered more often in our generation. We knew we had to roar back because this was hardcore racism in the heart of the South. The Klan had a headquarters down the road in Stone Mountain. The child murders . . .

Almost all of the white students were sympathetic to our cause, but we were so politically immature we barely valued their support. Once during the weeks-long hullabaloo the leaders of the various Black student groups held a meeting about what to do next. There was confusion and dissent about how to respond because this overt event seemed merely the most visible example of all the racism festering on campus: the Black professor who hadn't gotten tenure, the omission of an African-American Studies requirement from the core curriculum, the Public Safety officers who policed us rather than protecting us. The meeting that was scheduled to last an hour went on for three. Meanwhile, a large group of white students sat outside, waiting for their turn to join and their chance to show solidarity. But the Blacks-only meeting went on so long that eventually the white students felt alienated and unwanted and they left. They remained sympathetic to the cause but offended by the people behind it. The Black students, feeling militant, angry, and righteous, refused to apologize.

A new campus group was formed called Students Against Racial Inequality that labeled Emory "a hostile environment for people of African descent." A rally was held at which two hundred students and faculty showed up and SARI's leaders presented Emory's president with a list of demands. They included building two new centers for studying Black culture, increasing the numbers of Black students and professors, adding courses from the African-American Studies department to the core curriculum, and dismissing the director of Public Safety. We were asking for the moon but we felt we had the political capital to do it—the racist attacks on Collins were attacks on all of us that showed how insignificant the Black presence at Emory truly was.

Meanwhile, detectives were working on the case, examining finger-prints and microscoping fibers and reading her letters. Then someone noticed that in a death threat sent to Collins the author had misspelled "you're" as "your." In letters Collins wrote she had a habit of misspelling "you're" as "your." And right there her story began unraveling. Finger-print analysis on the slurs written in her room and other hints pointed to her. "There certainly is some direct evidence," said the county solici-tor, "and a great deal of circumstantial evidence, that would cause one to believe that Collins was the only person involved in these matters."

That conclusion came like an unexpected punch to the gut. We'd had the chair pulled out from under us by our own Tawana Brawley. This contradicted the script I'd learned about Black lambs and white wolves. This was a Black person manipulating racism for evil, selfish reasons. It was said that just before the initial incident Collins had been sus-pected of cheating in chemistry class and an honors code investigation was being considered. And just like Wayne Williams being convicted of the child murders, once again a serious charge of horrific racism was officially concluded to have been carried out by a Black hand. Again we were told the enemy was not coming from outside the community but inside it. To me it seemed that in my generation racial matters were going to be far more nuanced and slippery than they'd been for my par-ents. For me racism was not always a matter of clearly defined lambs and wolves, but was more of a double-sided gun.

The summer after my freshman year, as I caught my mental breath from a turbulent moment, something led me to pick up *The Autobiogra-phy of Malcolm X*. He was a central icon for hiphop and Black men of my generation at that point so it wasn't some obscure tome I was reaching for, it was more like, "let me go deep into what it is exactly that makes him so powerful and so widely admired." A few pages in I could see it. Here was a man with a Teflon shield. I had to know how he'd built it and what he could do for the one I was beginning to construct. Reading that book that summer felt like a religious experience. His strength of mind, his laser focus, his Black power ideas, his iconoclastic brilliance, his rock-solid self-assuredness that was coupled with an ability to be open-minded enough to change his mind when necessary, and his total lack of concern for the white gaze—this was the role model I craved. Reading about Malcolm was amazingly liberating. He changed me radically and instantly. I switched from majoring in psychology to African and African-American studies and made a 180-degree shift in my social life. I left behind my white friends from freshman year and inserted myself into the Black community.

Now I spent all my social time with Black students, always sat at the Black table in the lunchroom, and got involved in Black student organizations. I went to step shows and started trekking over to Spelman and Morehouse to attend their parties. At first some Black students were surprised to see me choose them over my white friends after I'd spent freshman year doing the opposite but most accepted me without issue. I knew some were whispering behind my back, saying cruel things, calling me an oreo because I'd socialized with white kids freshman year. It hurt to know that word was slinking around in the shadows behind me but as long as most of the Black students accepted me I could ignore it. I founded and ran a Black nationalist editorial-filled newspaper called *The Fire This Time*, arranged for Chuck D to come speak on campus, and fought for and won a coveted spot to live in the Black Students Association's small private building that we called the Black House.

Junior year I lived in the Black House; ran *The Fire This Time*; was an African-American studies major; was a regular at every Black Students Association meeting and at every party or step show thrown by the Qs, the Alphas, or the AKAs; and was close friends with the two unquestioned student leaders of the Black community. I also wrote a column in the main school newspaper called "40 Inches and a Pen." And my girlfriend was a Black med school student. But at Emory, where the Black community was perhaps still recovering from the traumatic Sabrina Collins debacle, people were very sensitive about what was considered traitorous behavior. So the whisper was still slithering around behind me until the night someone forced me to deal with it.

It was around 2:30 a.m. and the party at the Black House was winding down. The music was off and the last twenty people at the party were seconds away from filing out the door. The two other Black House residents and I had previously complained about the aftermath of Black House parties, when we were left to clean up, and once again it appeared that other students were about to leave us with a mess to shovel. I had a momentary and not-very-heated argument with another student about it being unfair that again the janitorial work was being dumped in the laps of the Black House residents. And then the linebacker-sized Black man from Alabama, who wasn't even in the conversation, who spoke so rarely in public I was unsure what his voice sounded like before then, silenced the room by loudly and angrily saying, "Shut up, Touré! You ain't Black!"

I felt as though time had stopped and I was falling through space. I couldn't hear a thing as all the sound around me suddenly died. I felt the skin melting off my skull as if I was beginning to evaporate from the heat of the embarrassment. I felt like a machete was slicing through my mind. I was miniscule, deflated, worthless, nothing. No one came to my aid. No one said, "That's not right." No one moved to comfort me. They all just stood there gawking as if at a horrific car accident. They all just watched me drowning.

I didn't say anything. I just turned and walked away and went into my room as if I could get away from the memory if I just got away from the scene of the crime. I closed the door and vowed to never again think about that moment. It was far too painful to contemplate. This was a memory I had to put in a box. But it wouldn't leave me alone. On the screen in my mind it replayed in an endless loop. Five a.m. came and went as I lay there trying to escape, praying for sleep as that memory ate at me. At six I got out of bed, went to my desk, and began writing. It was just for me, to help me make sense of what had happened and process the moment so I could put it behind me. I had to ask myself if what he had said was true. It must have been true if it hurt so much, right? It was true by his definition of Blackness and of me but he didn't know me, we'd never even spoken. And giving him the power to define me was no different than giving Randall Dunn's microaggressive dorm-mate the power to define him. Why was I working to reject being defined by the white gaze but not also working to reject definition by the Black gaze? Was I going to demand I be defined by me or not? Was I going to build a Teflon shield and reject all external definitions and truly control my own self-image or not? Because I knew that I was no oreo. I made social mistakes as a freshman but I had always loved Blackness.

So I wrote about how pathetic his accusation actually was. Who gave him the right to determine what is and is not Blackness for me? Who made him the judge of Blackness? To say I'm not Black is to accuse me of apostasy as if Blackness were a religion that could be escaped. But we cannot abandon Blackness even if we commit treason against it. It's permanent. Even an Uncle Tom must suffer beneath the boot of white supremacy. And I'm not a Tom just because you don't understand me. I may be a work in progress but I will always be Black. The only things in life that I am obligated to do are pay taxes, be Black, and die.

When I finished writing I realized it was the most honest thing I'd ever written. I said, "Wow, I'd be embarrassed to publish this." I'd have to hand it in with my eyes closed while the rest of my mind said, "No way, don't put that out, you can't!" And that's when the provocateur in me said, "If you're scared to publish it, then you absolutely must publish it! Yes, it's embarrassing to you as a person but that makes it great for you as a writer!" He had tried to kill me and failed and when I decided to own the moment, no matter how embarrassing to me, he lost all power to hurt me.

I decided to use the piece in my column in the main school paper rather than the paper I'd founded so that it would have maximum visibility. If I was going to put it out, I had to put it out on the biggest stage I had access to.

That was the first time I saw what it was like to write something that seemed to set the world on fire. It felt like every single student and professor on campus read the piece and said something about it to me. Almost all of them were impressed. Most of the Black students were shocked that I'd put myself on the line like that. I heard the linebacker was mad and embarrassed and wanted to beat me up. I hadn't put any identifiers in my piece but everyone knew whom I was talking about.

But he never did anything. Perhaps because the piece, like my life, wasn't about him; he just made a cameo. It was about me.

By the time I moved to New York City my Teflon shield was almost finished. It was like the Death Star in Star Wars—nearly complete and constructed enough to function well and be close to invulnerable. I was able to repel incidents and negative opinions and microaggressions that might have sucked away my mental energy, that might have committed spirit-murder. Nothing could dent my self-confidence, nothing would stop me from achieving my dream of becoming a writer.

My first summer in New York, trying to get in the door as a magazine writer felt like trying to get deaf people to notice you in a pitch-black room. But I was socially aggressive and slowly made a few contacts that eventually mushroomed into more. There were already many great Black music writers in New York but most of them wanted to write for hip-hop-centric magazines. I chased bylines in older publications that were not focused on hiphop because I saw myself as building a career. Plus, I loved and understood hiphop culture and wanted to write about it in a more complex and accurate way than the vast majority of the white music writers in town were doing. When I pitched editors they respected my vision of hiphop and I think some felt that having a twenty-something Black man interview rappers and write about hiphop could have advantages over using thirty-something white guys who didn't seem to have the same tight grasp of the culture that I had. So I got to interview and write about Run-D.M.C., A Tribe Called Quest, De La Soul, the Jungle Brothers, Chubb Rock, Arrested Development, Digable Planets, The Coup, Tupac, Biggie, Snoop, and others.

I spent years freelancing for many magazines, taking all the assignments I could possibly get, often so overburdened with stories that I spent days on end sitting at the computer, writing from the time I woke up until the time I fell back into bed. The dream of a freelancer is to get a contract from a magazine so you don't have to worry about where your next assignment is coming from. The magazine agrees to give you a certain amount of stories for a good fee and you can focus on writing rather than scrambling to get assignments. Plus repeated exposure in one magazine helps build an audience: Readers see your name and hear your voice over and over and come to have a relationship with you and your work. But contracts are hard to get. It's like getting married to the magazine—you become part of the family. The magazine's editors have to believe in you, your voice, and your ability to be versatile enough to do enough stories to fulfill the contract.

One day, at a magazine where I was doing a lot of work, I was talking to an editor, campaigning for a contract, trying to get him to see that I deserved one. He leaned back and breathed in deep, then calmly made one of the more shocking comments I've heard in my professional life: "I know you can write about Run-D.M.C.," he said. "But can you write about Eric Clapton?" It wasn't a question, it was rhetorical. He was saying, "Your value to us as a Black writer is unquestioned but your value as a writer isn't there. On Black stuff you're valuable but outside of that you're either not able or not wanted."

I immediately felt this to be one of the more racist things anyone had ever said to me. It was assumed I was unable to write about a musician because he's white. This was the curse of affirmative action: We need you to talk about Black subjects but we won't use you in the larger conversation about non-Black subjects. This was the glass ceiling. I was perceived to be good enough to write about rappers but the artists who were unlike me and central to American culture in his mind were beyond my ability—or at least out of my purview. Even though I had written about Black music intelligently my skin remained a cloak of inferiority. To him. But if his words had taken physical form—as condescending, dismissive bullets fired at my mind from point blank range—they would've hit my bulletproof shield and bounced off and fallen to the floor, dented by the collision. Not for one second did I believe that I couldn't do an excellent story on Clapton or any other white superstar. I still to this day don't understand why someone would think I'd be unable to research and understand Clapton and spend a day talking and hanging with him, just like any white writer. Clapton in particular was a horrible example because he comes from Black music. He's a direct descendent of the blues and a devotee of Jimi Hendrix. It'd be valuable to have a Black writer talk to him.

That said, I also knew I couldn't have convinced him of that in that room. So I had to play it cool. You know that old story about the young bull who wants to run down the hill and screw a cow and the old bull who says no, let's walk down and screw them all? In my situation, the young bull would scream, "That's racist!" and never work with that magazine ever again. The old bull would lie back and calmly say, "I could write about Clapton, he's very interesting to me." Maybe he wouldn't convince that person in that room but he'd keep himself in the game. And eventually the old bull would get to write about Clapton or someone similar.

Some might say, "Well, I don't want to work for a racist," but you can't shut yourself off from working with every white person who's microaggressive toward you and you can't run every time you find a glass ceiling. Avoiding racism in the workplace is like avoiding the weather. If you want to work in any field that's not dominated by Blacks—i.e., anything outside of sports and entertainment (in front of the mic)—then you're going to encounter some sort of microaggression or bias or glass ceiling at some point. I just doubled my determination and looked for a white artist I could write about to prove my versatility. The reason why I was able to stand my emotional ground and not be swayed when an important, veteran editor basically told me, a barely experienced writer, that I wasn't good enough for the so-called big time—for serious white music—was because of my Teflon shield. Not for a second did I let his microaggression, his prejudice, his small mind define me or shrink my confidence.

I never did get to write about Clapton. But that's beside the point. I did not allow that moment to rattle my confidence in myself and two years later I got the contract.

A few weeks after the Clapton conversation I got a call out of the blue from *Details* magazine. It was early in my career and I had no relationship with them, and at that point magazines were not calling to pitch opportunities to me so I was surprised and thrilled. The editor said they were doing an issue on drugs and wanted me to write about a drug dealer. I remember standing in my kitchen on a cordless phone in the home office uniform, pajamas at noon, excited to be starting a new relationship with a good magazine. I put down my cereal and thought, Who knows how far this could go? Writing about a drug dealer is something different for me and if I do a good job maybe I can get more assignments from them. I told the editor I'd search for and find a drug dealer to write about and get back to him.

But after I hung up I thought, I wonder why they called me out of everyone in— and before I finished thinking that sentence I understood what had happened. They called me so they could have a Black writer talking about a drug dealer, thus insulating themselves from insinuations of racism. I wanted the assignment but didn't want to be a pawn in their game. I happened to know a white drug dealer who had a very sexy story: During the spring and summer he dealt expensive, designer drugs at hot New York clubs like the Paladium. He also worked as a cook in some of the city's trendy restaurants. At the end of each summer he'd embark on a five- or six-month-long trip, avoiding New York's cold to spend time exploring and reading in Tahiti or Rio or Vietnam or the Himalayas or South Africa or wherever. He'd been following this routine for years so by the time I met him he was quite the worldly renaissance man. He'd seen the globe, and had read everything you said you'd one day get around to reading, and had tasted everything you could imagine. Because of his dealing, he'd gotten in and out of all sorts of prickly situations, so he had a rugged street sense and a cosmopolitan air. He'd seen many sides of life, could tell amazing stories all night, and had a very interesting perspective on the world. He was an awesome magazine story subject. This was not your normal "stand on the corner and grind it out till death or jail comes" sort of drug dealer, not a Black kid with BORN TO LOSE stamped on his forehead. No, this was way more interesting: a guy who was dealing as a way to live life on his terms.

When I called the editor back I started to tell him about my man and he got excited. He said, "He sounds great!" I went on and on describing his dual existence, his erudite persona, his world travels, his way of using

101

dealing to snatch control of his life. The editor was virtually frothing at the mouth as I told him more and more. His tenth question about my subject was "Is he Black?" I said no. His whole tone changed. I could feel the air being sucked out of the conversation. There was an awkward silence and then he said, "Oh." Pause. "We were looking for someone more"—pause—"uptown." A moment later he caught himself, asked a few more questions, promised to call me back, and hung up. We never spoke again. And again I got the message that "You are valuable only as a Black writer discussing Black subjects, and when you stray from that—and try to be a writer—you're useless." But I refused to believe that.

I wanted to write about Black subjects because I loved them, I understood them, and I felt that when white writers covered them they often got them wrong and these were stories that were important to get right. So much about my generation was being shaped by people's opinions of hiphop and its culture, and those opinions were molded by media portrayals of it. Stories by white writers about hiphop that positioned MCs as aliens from another universe contributed to people looking at all Blacks as an other. I wanted to write about hiphop from the perspective of loving the culture and approaching MCs as smart, complex humans—a revolutionary concept. But I also wanted, sometimes, to write about interesting white people. I didn't want to be ghettoized and stuck with Black subjects alone. I wanted freedom. But the magazine world was saying it didn't want me to be post-Black—a writer who refused to be constrained by Blackness. Much of the world may not be ready for the post-Black liberty and complexity that so many of us feel within us, but we must fight for the right to assert it whether or not they are.

Despite efforts to push me into a box I have persevered. I did strong work, nurtured my relationships, let myself fall in love with interesting white artists, and thought about how I could expand my purview. Eventually I was given the latitude to write about Tori Amos, No Doubt, Radiohead, Dale Earnhardt Jr., Jennifer Capriati, and Coldplay. (When I showed up to interview Coldplay their tour manager greeted me warmly and then did a little resume check. He asked what other rock stars I'd written about and what rock I listened to. I didn't let him see my eyes rolling.)

In all these moments I relied on my shield to repel opinions that might have damaged my self-esteem. I listened only to inner voices on the subject of my import as a writer. I grew arrogant about my writing ability long before I had a right to be but if I hadn't been I might've succumbed to the idea that my voice was of limited value. It requires great inner resources to maintain a sense of personal importance in the face of multiple messages saying you are not. But that spiritual infrastructure can be constructed like muscles can be sculpted. You need exposure to people with strong shields and to carefully nurture the self-worth that you already have. Build a sense that you deserve self-esteem and have a right to self-confidence. You also must consciously understand and have experience with the ways in which your infrastructure will be attacked.

My shield came under heavy, sustained fire when, after having a long feature story I'd worked very hard on rejected by the *New Yorker*, I went to Columbia University's graduate MFA school for creative writing. I wanted to make sure I knew everything possible about writing so I might avoid disappointments like the *New Yorker* debacle again. Within a few months I had learned a lot but disliked that none of the work we were reading and deconstructing was by Black writers. The few other Black writers in school noticed this, too, and we all wondered if we were subtly being molded into a style that would not be palatable for Black readers. It's nearly impossible to put your finger on what's Black about Black writing, but intense study of white writers as taught by white teachers while surrounded almost completely by white writers would surely push your writing style in a certain direction. How were we going to form a style that vibed with the reading we prized and that resonated with the people we wanted reading us? So we formed a Black writers workshop in which we met to discuss the work we did for our classes. The workshop was relatively star-studded: future novelists Victor LaValle, Mat Johnson, and Nelly Rosario participated. We all just wanted to hear Black voices comb through our stuff to help our burgeoning writing styles grow properly.

That year I took the major nonfiction survey class taught by the head of the department, Richard Locke. Each session he read through a different text, deconstructing each line, showing us on a literary cellular level why great writers like George Orwell, Primo Levi, Joan Didion, and others had made each choice they'd made and how their work fit together. If there could be a biology of writing, his lectures were it. He taught an incredible class and his way of thinking about why writers place each word where they do impacts my process to this day. But there was not one Black writer on his syllabus. I longed to hear him go through the nonfiction of Baldwin, DuBois, Ellison, or Morrison and unlock something I had not previously seen in my readings. But his class did not go there and this I knew sent a subtle but audible message to the Black and white students—if the work of the giants of Black writing was not good enough for the toweringly important intro to creative nonfiction class taught by the head of the department, then our work was also not that important. This amplified the message I was already ignoring about the general unimportance of Black writing sent by a program that gave us no Black writers to read. This institutional microaggression cast the shadow of irrelevance on us as developing writers. Nothing could be done to change Professor Locke's curriculum mid-semester but I was determined to say something about it to him.

We all knew that on the last day of class the teachers stopped talking and gave students time to speak out and talk about what they'd liked and disliked about the class. Weeks before the final day I convinced the few people from our Black writers group who were in the class to do a sort of protest statement: All of us would stand at the same time and I would say that we did not understand the exclusion of Black writers from the class, that it made us feel as though our aesthetic was unimportant, and that we hoped that in the future the syllabus would grow broader. For weeks I thought about and edited what I was going to say so that at the moment I spoke I was insightful, concise, and persuasive. I wanted to win Professor Locke over to the idea that the exclusion was hurting the self-image of Black writers rather than making him feel like I was calling him racist in front of lots of students, because that would turn him defensive and shut down the discussion I wanted.

On the last day, at the end of our formal class, as soon as he turned the floor over to the students, I raised my hand but someone else was called on first. I looked around at my Black classmates, letting them know I knew I'd be called on next and we were going to do this. But one got up and went to the bathroom. Another saw me look at him and looked away. They were abandoning me at the moment of combat! Whatever. I had my shield and I was going to speak my truth because I knew I was right and I knew if I didn't say anything I would spend the rest of the week—maybe the rest of the year—crucifying myself for not believing enough in my cause and in historic Black writers to stand up and say what I felt. So when he called on me I stood. No one stood with me. Whatever. I calmed myself and got my Randall Dunn on. I said I thought he should rethink the curriculum a bit to include some Black writers because it was a glaring omission to go through a century of writing and not once deal with a Black writer. I explained that this exclusion made the Black writers in the program feel their work was unimportant. When I finished speaking I kept standing and had a flash daydream where another student stood up and then another and another until the whole room was standing with me to politely but firmly say hey, we need to include Black voices—all voices—in the conversation that is this important class.

My millisecond daydream was broken when Alexandra Styron, daughter of William, who was seated near me, said, "I agree with Touré." But no one else said a word. I was a bit heartbroken by that but kept my face stony so no one would know. As I sat down the professor stroked his chin as if to say this was something he had never once thought of. He said I should give him a list. He needed me to give him a list of great Black nonfiction writers? The curriculum, the silence of the room, and the chin-stroking all sent a message about the unimportance of Black writing. I had to crouch behind my shield as one hundred arrows of indifference flew at me, and remind myself that I knew my work, my voice was important, and the only judge who mattered was me.


A few years later I was in a pricey little Italian restaurant in Soho eating dinner with four Black men who are successful and well-off with mammoth self-esteem. These were brothers with gigantic Teflon shields. (They're friends and in some ways big brothers, and I often find myself listening to them talk and marveling at their massive shields and wondering how to make mine as big and strong as theirs. Because you can never stop fortifying your shield.) We were the only Blacks in the place but we didn't spend a second thinking about that until midway through our dinner. A tall, drunk white guy seated across the room who, for some reason, was wearing a giant afro wig, stood up and started semi-stumbling toward us. It wasn't an all-out stumble, but each time he picked up a foot, he didn't seem to be clear on exactly where it would land. But still, somehow, I knew he was coming our way. He walked in a bit of a serpentine path across the room to our table, draped his hands on the shoulders of two of my friends the way a maître d' would, and said in a deadpan voice, "They let Black people in here?"

He was trying to be funny but he was tawdry, pathetic, and racist. We were frozen by his ignorance and his arrogance. He stopped speaking and there was just a long, awkward silence. Everyone at the table assumed he must be a friend of someone else in the group because no one would dare say such a thing to a stranger. For three or four painful seconds we sat in stunned silence looking at each other—if it were a movie the sound would've dropped out and you would've seen eyes darting from man to man as we checked in with each other, waiting for someone to show recognition and say, "Yeah, uh, sorry, that's my friend Donald, excuse him, he had a lobotomy last week." But no one's face broke. We just kept looking at each other like, "Who does this stupid white man belong to?" But none of us knew him. And once all of us had looked at all of the others and everyone realized he wasn't being co-signed by anyone else, we did something really cool: We ignored him. He suddenly went invisible to us. He kept on talking but we didn't hear him. If he'd offended us we would've gotten angry but he didn't, he just embarrassed himself. There was no need for any response. He was dirt to be wiped off our collective shoulder. We knew we were the only Black people in there and we didn't care—that fact meant nothing in and of itself and him calling attention to it didn't affect us at all. His microaggression bounced off our shields and fell to the ground. I waved at his table and someone hustled over and led him away as he tried to apologize. Then we went right back to whatever it was we had been talking about. They say living well is the best revenge and we were already living well so we knew we'd already won.

But a few years later, in 2007, I found myself in a different universe where repelling racism was much harder. That summer I went to rural Indiana for a week to shoot an episode of the same TV show for which I'd jumped out of a plane. This time I was going to be in a demolition derby. I was frightened about getting in an old car and letting a bunch of rednecks crash into it until either I or the car couldn't take any more. Would they hit me extra hard, juiced up on racist hate? Yeah, they probably would according to my mentor for the week—Larry Staats, a short, tough, bald derby champ with thick glasses who looked like a nano-sized Wilfred Brimley or a tough-as-nails Mr. Magoo.

I knew I wasn't really wanted in town as soon as I got there. My first day someone told me, "Ten years ago you wouldn't have been able to spend ten minutes in this town." I said, what would've happened? They said, "Someone woulda got some guys together and come down here and made you leave." I quickly got the message that many still held that sentiment. When I thought about calming my shot nerves at a bar and asked which one I should hit I was told that of the nine bars in town, if I walked into eight of them I'd be greeted rudely and forced to leave by the patrons before I could taste a drink. I just went back to my hotel where I could drink in peace, an oasis away from the automatic hate surrounding me. This was an area where many people had parents or grandparents in the Klan. Or were in the Klan themselves. Confederate flags were all over the place. Feeling hate vibes raining down on me day after day, and the anxiety of looking over my shoulder and wondering what smiles were real and which ones were fake took a psychic toll on me. And I was planning on getting into a demolition derby with these people? Was I out of my mind? Would I look back at all this one day, trapped in a wheelchair because I was paralyzed, and think, "You stuck your head in the lion's mouth for a TV show?" On the day of the derby as my mentor drove me to the site of the race I wondered if I was willingly going to my own lynching. When we got there I walked away from my all-white film crew to clear my head and a group of young men went up to them and said, "Are y'all with the nigger? 'Cause he's not welcome around here."

I felt alone in a sea of racists, engulfed by enemies just waiting for their moment to get me. They couldn't dent my self-esteem but they could make me feel anxiously unwelcome and they could definitely damage my body. I felt myself retreating inward, unwilling to trust anyone, even those who seemed friendly. It seemed safer to assume the worst in everyone around me. But I was in serious emotional turmoil—feeling vulnerable and intensely afraid of the derby that would start in less than an hour. Anyone would be scared about their first demolition derby but I also had a second constellation of anxieties that no white host would've had to deal with. How much pain was I in for and how much more of a target would racism make me? My mentor kept telling me to keep my head on a swivel because the last thing you wanted was to get hit by someone you didn't see coming, especially if it was a full track shot—that is, someone targeting you from across the track, stomping the gas pedal to the floor, getting a head of steam, and crashing into you at top speed. Those were the hardest hits imaginable and if you didn't see them coming they'd rattle you to your core.

I needed someone's support to get through that muck of hatred as well as the fear I felt about my first demolition derby. I had a strong infrastructure but the strongest man in the world couldn't have powered through all those heavy emotions alone. My mentor wouldn't have let anyone beat me up but he was a man of few words and fewer hugs. He taught me the finer points of derbying but he wasn't able to soothe my soul before the terror of derbying with racists. I had a film crew with me but this was an adventure-reality show, and they wanted to film me being fearful and anxious. They weren't going to help me feel strong. Plus, that was the first episode so none of us knew the others very well. They were British, and admitted to having a dim understanding of American race and racism so they weren't picking up any of the signals that were bombarding me. I knew I was cracking up when they were interviewing me before the race and the producer asked me, "So, are you scared?" and I took the water bottle in my hand and threw water in her face and stomped off. I was scared and alone and needed someone to help me calm myself enough to overcome the fear of derbying, which was compounded because I felt surrounded by intense hate. I was inching toward a nervous breakdown.

Then someone came: my mentor's stepdaughter Samantha, a woman my age who was an experienced derbyer, a granddaughter of a local Klan leader, and, more important in this moment, a devoted Christian. She knew I was nervous because she had eyes and because she remembered her first race. Sam held my hand as she and her husband, also a derbyer, and their two sons formed a prayer circle with me in the center of the field where all the derbyers were preparing. She was someone known in that community and by holding my hand in prayer so publicly she communicated to everyone that I was not alone out there, I was not an other to be treated weirdly. She prayed for my safety during the race and told me I'd be all right. As long as I kept my head on a swivel. And Sam helped me find some of the peace I needed to do my thing in that race. I could not have been open to accepting her sacrament if I had not put aside my defensive mistrust of all the whites around me in that little town and let her comfort me.

Seconds before the race, as I sat in the revving car, I was freed enough to be excited. I didn't know what was about to happen but I was able to greet the uncertainty with joy. My adrenaline was soaring. The announcer called out each driver's name as if at a NASCAR race and when he boomed my name several people in the stands in front of my car gave me two thumbs down. But by then I didn't care.

The horn blew and we started moving around the track, hitting each other. I kept my head on a swivel, twisting every which way, trying to keep an eye on everyone at all times. At first the track was so congested the crashes were low-impact, like two people pulling out of a parking spot and bumping into each other. The first time I hit someone I instinctively yelled out, "Sorry!" I was the only rookie and everyone else had at least three or four old rivals in the race, so they went about attacking each other as I cruised around making light bumps and trying to avoid full-track shots. The expected racial animosity never arose. I think the lurking presence of my mentor—a local derbying legend—helped convince people not to attack me, as if I had a virtual bodyguard. But getting smashed into is part of the game and when someone finally bashed into the back of my car, sending me spinning, it was a rush like no other. The top of my helmet hit the ceiling and I felt my bones rattle and my brain smush against the edge of my skull, and I got a flash headache and I felt enough energy to lift a car. I was baptized and totally fear-free. That's what it's like to get hit? I can deal with that! Let's do this, boys! I targeted someone far away, stepped on the gas, and zoomed toward them. I aimed at their back wheel, fought my instinct to hit the brake, and gritted my teeth. I made contact and heard a loud *blam* that earned some cheers from the crowd and sent his car reeling. It was exhilarating.

I got hit some more but kept on going and before I knew it there weren't many cars left. I thought, "I can't believe how long I've lasted." Then I saw my mentor Larry's archrival, Jason, a much younger guy who used to be his friend and mentee but now barely spoke to him because he wanted the crown for himself. Jason smashed into Larry and sent him spinning. I said, nah, you can't do that to my homie! I took off and smashed into Jason, giving him what I thought was a tough hit. I saw his head turn toward me and he quickly backed up and curved into position to face me. I thought, "Bring it on!" Then he rammed into me way harder than I was ready for and left me woozy and shaken like I'd taken a solid punch to the head. Next thing I knew I was stuck on a log that marked the barriers, putting me out of the race. But the first person I saw was Samantha, jumping up and down and holding up five fingers. I'd finished in fifth place—Larry won, Jason was second—and more important for me I'd pushed past the racism and anxiety to get my job done.

A little while after that came one of the most racial "Twilight Zone"-y moments I've ever had in the post-Black era. One summery Saturday night a friend took me to a house party on Martha's Vineyard. Back then I knew I was heading toward having children so I spent a lot of time talking to people who seemed like good parents about how to raise kids. At the party I spent an hour talking to the hostess, a short brunette with blue eyes from Texas who was the wife of a congressman. She was a big proponent of spanking. I had never met a white person who was so enthusiastically pro-spanking. She had three young kids who were very respectful and well-mannered and she told me it was all thanks to spanking. Then I met a Black man with great, well-behaved kids and he said he didn't believe in spanking at all. He said he never spanked and never will because the home should not be a place of violence and kids should not fear their parents in that way. He made a lot of sense. Before meeting him I'd felt it was a Black parent's cultural duty to spank, as if that was a part of Blackness and I was short-changing my kids if I didn't. I didn't want to be a "Brady Bunch," "Leave It to Beaver," laissez-faire sort of parent. It's good to spank—spare the rod, spoil the child, as Blacks say. My parents spanked me plenty when I was little and my experience left me feeling that it was a valuable child-rearing tool. But suddenly I thought maybe I didn't have to follow the rule I'd heard since I was a kid. Perhaps there was a better way.

As I was leaving the party I said goodbye to the hostess and added, in what I intended as a compliment, "This has been an amazing night. I met a Black man who doesn't believe in spanking and a white woman who does. Blew my mind."

She furrowed her brow and shot back, "Who's white?"

Confused, I blurted out, "You're not white?"

She was infuriated. "What in the world made you think I was white?"

I had thought she was the downest white woman I'd ever met. She'd set my Black radar off in a way no white person ever had—just little things she said and attitudes she evinced and something in her spirit left me thinking that this was a white person who was better at over-standing Black mores and philosophies than any white person I'd ever encountered. So on some deep level I'd sensed she was a sister but the evidence from my eyes was so clear I ignored the feeling, as if assuming my radar was on the fritz. But I was confused: She looked so convincingly white that surely she could not be surprised about my mistake. I couldn't have been the first person in this forty-something woman's life to come to that incorrect conclusion. So I was shocked that she was shocked.

I said, "I can't believe this has never happened to you before."

She said, "I can't believe you thought I was white!"

And there we were in the middle of her party in a verbal standoff, with the whole room watching.

Her blond, blue-eyed sister ran up in a frenzy and yelled, "Did ya think I was white, too?"

I said, "Yeah!" (I'd meet her during the party and she didn't set off my Blackdar at all, so that convinced me to stop listening to my Blackdar about the hostess.)

At that point, given the audience, our investment in our positions, and our shared pig-headedness, no one was willing to give an inch so we stood there barking at each other until my friend squeezed through the crowd and dragged me away.

(Postscript: I hear the hostess later told the story to other Black people, telling them about the guy who came to her party and called her white and how shockingly unbelievable that was for her, and those Black people walked away and said behind her back, "I never knew she was Black." But I digress.)

I walked out of that party with a broadened sense of how complex race is in America today. What Blackness and whiteness mean have shifted and grown and become more amorphous, as if we're living in "Chappelle's Show."

The summer after my son Hendrix was born I was the only Black adult among the seven people at a tiny roof-deck house party in Brooklyn. The host was holding my ten-month-old on his lap when his wife brought out watermelon slices. For her a refreshing fruit. For me a passport to antebellum images of happy darkies. As soon as I see the red insides of a watermelon I feel ancient racist images slither into the room like a cold, sinewy, sinister breeze. When I was young my parents schooled me against eating watermelon in front of white people lest I confirm ancient stereotypes. I will eat fried chicken with impunity in front of anyone but because the anti-watermelon mind virus latched on to me early I have no taste for it. But my baby boy was, at that stage, an aggressive and adventurous eater who would try pretty much anything.

My friend took a watermelon slice from his wife and wondered aloud whether the baby would like some. As he said this he lazily held the slice just inches away from my boy's face. I knew what was going to happen. Before my friend could actually offer it to Hendrix, the baby lurched forward, mouth wide open, and chomped into the watermelon Pac-Man–style. He was so quick and aggressive it was a miracle he didn't bite off a smidge of my friend's finger, too. Everyone went into hysterics, everyone but me. I thought, "Great, they're laughing at the little Black baby's seemingly instinctual impulse to eat watermelon." My son is no pickaninny! But then I listened closer to the way they were laughing— the soft-edged, sentimental way you laugh when kids do funny things. A previous me would've been offended at a laugh that leapt from a stereotype seemingly coming to life, a microaggressive laugh, but I was able to step back for a moment and see that's not really what this was about. It was about the baby's cute lunge and his enthusiasm about food. I told my inner Sharpton to sit down. I was strong enough to see this laugh was offered with respect and love.

# Chapter 5

# The Most Racist Thing That Ever Happened . . .

There's a Chris Rock joke that is emblematic of modern racism. It's from his 2008 standup routine "Kill the Messenger," and it's about Alpine, New Jersey, the posh town where he lives in a multi-million-dollar home. His neighbors include Mary J. Blige, Patrick Ewing, and Eddie Murphy. Rock says Blige, Ewing, Murphy, and he are (or were) among the best in the world at their professions, legends in their line of work. They're also the only four Black homeowners in town. Then he says his next-door neighbor is a white dentist. "He ain't the best dentist in the world," Rock says. "He ain't going to the dental hall of fame. He's just a yank-your-tooth-out dentist." Rock spells out the point with a devastating punchline: "The Black man gotta fly to get to somethin the white man can walk to."

He's saying that in modern America Blacks can ascend to the upper class, it's possible, but they have to fight so much more to get there because white supremacy remains a tall barrier to entry. The fact that a few slip through the infinitesimal cracks is a way of advancing the idea that white supremacy does not exist, an attempt to mask it's awesome power, because the matrix doesn't want you to know its there. How can someone argue that Alpine, New Jersey, is racist when four Black families live there, welcomed by the community and unharassed by police? Of course this is a fake argument—these extraordinary Blacks would be welcome anywhere and Alpine itself is not racist because it doesn't need to be. There are institutional systems in place that keep the number of Blacks in Alpine and Beverly Hills and other exclusive communities very low, but not so low that Jesse Jackson can come and raise a ruckus. It's like releasing a tiny bit of air so the bottle doesn't explode.

Modern racism is a much more subtle, nuanced, slippery beast than its father or grandfather were. It has ways of making itself seem to not exist, which can drive you crazy trying to prove its existence sometimes. It's a powerful force shaping the post-Black experience because it combines the sense of you-don't-belong-you're-a-second-class-citizen that historic racism had with the subterfuge of a spy and creates, for some, a devil's bargain. You may ascend higher on the ladders of power than previous generations of Blacks could've imagined but when you smack into that glass ceiling and don't get as high as you feel you should go, it'll still drive you crazy and show you that your ability is not fully respected. Blackness is expanding and broadening as Black opportunities are improving but we all still must deal with the crucible called racism, and it has a pernicious impact on the modern Black persona.

Modern racism is, as the great Indian writer Arundhati Roy posits in one of the most mind-blowing analogies for it that I have ever encountered, like the president pardoning one turkey each year before Thanksgiving. In a 2004 speech at the World Social Forum in Mumbai, India, Roy broke it down. "Every year, in a show of ceremonial magnanimity, the president spares one particular bird. And eats another one. After receiving the presidential pardon, the Chosen One is sent to Frying Pan Park in Virginia to live out its natural life. The rest of the fifty million turkeys raised for Thanksgiving are slaughtered and eaten. ConAgra Foods, the company that has won the presidential turkey contract, says it trains the lucky birds to be sociable, to interact with dignitaries, schoolchildren, and the press. That's how new racism in the corporate era works. A few carefully bred turkeys—the local elites of various countries, a community of wealthy immigrants, investment bankers, the occasional Colin Powell, or Condoleezza Rice, some singers, some writers like myself—are given absolution and a pass to Frying Pan Park. The remaining millions lose their jobs, are evicted from their homes, have their water and electricity connections cut, and die of AIDS. Basically, they're for the pot. But the fortunate fowls in Frying Pan Park are doing fine. Some of them even work for the IMF and the World Trade Organization, so who can accuse those organizations of being anti-turkey? Some serve as board members on the Turkey Choosing Committee—so who can say that turkeys are against Thanksgiving? They participate in it! Who can say the poor are anti–corporate globalization? There's a stampede to get into Frying Pan Park! So what if most perish on the way?"

The post-Black era is a response to the rise in the number of Blacks who live in or are fighting to get into Frying Pan Park, or Alpine, New Jersey, but post-Blackness is no wonder drug that can cure or even significantly alter American white supremacy. The post-Black era suggests to me that what it means to be Black is broadening to infinity but it does not mean that racism is over, that white supremacy is laying down its almost impenetrable shield. Racism remains a daily fact of life for Blacks and a key component in shaping who we become as people even in the post-Black era. Indeed, where racism in our parents' and grandparents' generations was plainly visible, modern racism often seems to function like evaporating smoke: plainly visible but impossible to grab on to. As the number of Blacks in Frying Pan Park swells, it adds to the empirical data that attempts to argue that racism no longer exists, even though you know it does. The cognitive dissonance of that double consciousness can make you feel crazy.

You're in Target. Is the security guard following you? You're not sure. You think he is but you can't be certain. Maybe he is, maybe he's not—maybe he's actually following another Black person you can't see. But he's probably following you. Or is he? They were following you in the last store and you couldn't see it but you could feel it. Maybe the guard is Black, so if you tried to explain it to a white friend they might not understand it as racist, but the guard's boss isn't Black. Or maybe he is. Maybe they're watching all the Blacks in the store more closely. Maybe the guard himself feels badly about that directive but has to follow it because they're watching him, too. Maybe what you're feeling are his ashamed vibes as if he's sending you a silent signal of apology for following you. Or maybe . . . now you're looking for the Tylenol for migraines when you all you needed was toothpaste. And that's one of the basest examples of racism. That says nothing of the constellation of anxieties that could flash through you when the stakes are high—when you're applying for a job or competing for a promotion, or applying to a school, buying a house, or asking for a loan. When you're wondering if the white person who appears less qualified got the promotion because they were actually better than you or because they were better at networking upper management, or someone wrongly assumed you're not as good because you're Black or . . . "There's this sort of existential angst that Black people experience every day," Columbia professor Dr. Marc Lamont Hill said. "You're walking around the store, you just want some socks but in the process you're worried about the security guard and whether he's following you, and you either get angry or make sense of it somehow. But you have had to undergo so many psychological processes just between you and them socks that it's taxing on the spirit and on the intellect. We squander so much time dealing with those issues that we sort of miss out on opportunities to do other good stuff like expanding, growing, developing, and so forth."

Columbia professor Patricia Williams told me, "There's nothing that Black people would like more than to be happy in the world and to have the freedom to go through the world without being constantly self-conscious." But that's nearly impossible. Maybe the storekeeper's kind of scowling because he's tired and having a bad day and it has nothing to do with you. Or maybe he doesn't want his clothes to be seen out in the world on your Black body. You just can't know. "That's the necessary nuttiness of racism," Professor Williams said. "And a kind of defensiveness is just a consequence of what we have to negotiate. And I don't think that that's victimhood." She compared the necessary nuttiness of racism—the maddening, funhouse-mirror untouchability of modern racism—to one day in law school when someone sent her a bouquet of flowers on Valentine's Day and didn't sign it. "I went through the entire rest of the day smiling at people because it could've been this person, it could've been that person. I loved everybody. Well, prejudice can do the same thing in a negative degree." When a moment of racism occurs, especially a subtle one, you can find yourself walking around distrustful of everyone white, wondering who else feels that way.

This is often what the face of modern racism is: invisible or hard to discern, lurking in shadows or hidden. Institutional inequities and glass ceilings and even racial profiling can be hard to see at times and can be easily dismissed by dissenters. Modern racism is often an amorphous beast. Dr. John Jackson of the University of Pennsylvania said, "This idea that there's this sort of clichéd vision of someone who is racist from the time they brush their teeth in the morning and only thinks about ending the life of every Black person isn't the only way to talk about what racism looks like. The category of 'you are racist' or 'you're not' isn't useful. I think what's more useful is to get people to think about the ways in which we perpetuate the kinds of racial differentiations and inequalities on purpose or inadvertently that thus reproduce differences that are real and powerful and that we see every day. Unless you're going to tell me that there's some biological, hardwired reason why people of color at academic institutions are always the people serving you food or cleaning your bathroom and not necessarily in your classrooms teaching classes, then I think you're going to have to be honest with yourself about all the ways in which there's a privilege that accrues to people. One of the things that we need to do is to recognize that race is more subliminal, race is more subjective, and race is more subtle in the contemporary moment. And I think we need to find a way to really articulate that subtlety. There are very few smoking guns, thank God, anymore."

Jackson continued, "I think everything we've understood about race up until 1970 and the kind of racial environment we're living in now are diametrically opposed to one another and if we try to think about our current racial landscape using that old terminology, using the organizing principles of civil rights and the stuff that came before, we won't get it right and we'll make a bad situation worse. Part of what we're used to doing is finding black-hat bad guys when we thought about racism. This was the Klan, this is the white line separating the fronts and the backs of buses, this is bodies hanging from trees. And although that's terrifying, although that is horrible, though that's an entire society organized around the marginalization of Black people, existentially I would argue there's something about knowing your enemy that at least allowed you to figure out how to orient yourself in the universe. And a part of what we're dealing with now is a scenario where you recognize that the public discourse has been sanitized of all those earlier forms of racial animus and hatred but at the same time, just because people talk a good game and the letter of the law is such that people are purportedly equal, you're still recognizing the reproduction of social difference. And there's no way to easily reconcile those things except to recognize that what you see is never what you get in the contemporary moment.

"In some ways I would say we long for the kind of black-hatted bad guys of yore because we knew who our enemies were. In the contemporary moment not only do we realize racism is still alive and well, but now we recognize that we can't always see it. Even though that's very unnerving and unmoored. But there are tons of moments where folks are realizing that they have to interpret something that they don't even have the kind of conceptual baggage to unpack and make sense of. What does it mean to say, as in Dave Chappelle's case, that you're feeling like someone's laughing at you feel in some ways violated and how do you articulate that to someone, especially someone who doesn't identify as Black and says you just sound crazy, you sound like you're being paranoid? We don't have to buy into this rhetoric of shut up, prove it, or dismiss it, it's only racism if you can prove it beyond a shadow of a doubt. If the only racism is the 'bodies hanging from trees' variety or you got to apologize for making the accusation because the accusation itself is equal to the crime of racism—well, I want to say that dance concedes too much. You can't always try to set up this zero-sum game, either/or scenario, where it's racism or it's not, where you're the good or bad guy."

I asked my 105 interviewees, What is the most racist thing that has ever happened to you? The response I received most often was indicative of modern racism: The answer is unknowable. "I imagine it'd be a thing I don't even know ever happened," Aaron McGruder said. "It would be that opportunity that never manifested and I'll never know that it was even possible." A decision is made in a back room or a high-level office, perhaps by someone you'll never see, about whether or not you get a job or a home loan or admission to a school. Or perhaps you'll never be allowed to know that a home in a certain area or a job is available. This is how modern institutional racism functions and it can weigh on and shape a Black person differently than the more overt, simplistic racism of the past did.

People who told me that the most racist thing that ever happened to them is unknowable gave me that answer quickly—it's in the front of their minds that secret incidences of racism are happening behind their back. They're walking around constantly and consciously aware of racism as a ghost in the machine, following them, impacting them, even though they can't see it or know what it's taken away. There's a sense of malevolent ghosts darting around you, screwing with you, often out of sight but never out of mind. The poet and Yale professor Dr. Elizabeth Alexander, who read an original poem at Obama's inauguration, said, "The most racist thing that ever happened to me would likely be a continual underestimation of my intellectual ability and capacity, and the real insidious aspect of that kind of racism is that we don't know half the time when people are underestimating us. We don't know half the time when we're being cut out of something because someone is unable to see us at full capacity. And so I presume that that happens, and has happened, a lot." She presumes this racist miscalculation of her brilliance happens quite often even though it never makes itself plain. How tragic. I can see Alexander walking down the street, the inverse of Patricia Williams the day she got anonymous flowers, correctly assuming anyone she's passing by or talking to could be looking at her as a cut far below the genius she is. Alexander says she fights it by evaluating herself outside of the judgment of others. But how can this daily, even hourly, battle to constantly reconvince yourself of your ability not become an exhausting mental drain? "What's scary about prejudice is that it's not a measurable force," Malcolm Gladwell said. "We just know that it's all around and it matters sometimes a lot and sometimes it doesn't matter as much but we don't really know how much."

Many people said they could definitely put a finger on the most racist moment of their lives. These stories also, usually, came out quickly. People tend not to have to search their memory banks for these stories no matter how long ago they occurred: They keep them easily accessible and close to the front of their memory, like baggage sitting by the door. Some of these stories were classic examples of blatant old-school racism: whites saying or doing things meant to keep Blacks in a lesser place, as if policing the line between first- and second-class citizen by reminding one of the de jure and/or de facto strictures—or the inherent and inescapable inferiority of the Black mind and unimportance of the Black body—while also attempting to break the spirit. "There's just a kind of perpetual reminder," Kara Walker said, "that in this culture a Black body is not safe and my humanity is not real, somehow."

I expected that examples of new-school racism would be wholly different but the stories I heard were similar to old-school racism, only they played out on new fields. Instead of being called nigger on the street you're called nigger at a major university. One big difference I noticed in many of the modern racism stories is that there is less of an expectation that people will be racist, so encountering racism is a shock even when it's delivered with less of a crushing blow. When Paul Mooney felt the tangible tentacles of oppression in the deep South in the 1940s he was hurt but unsurprised. When those tentacles smack you in the 1990s on an ivy-tinged campus in New England it's a blow you didn't see coming. Poet and University of Vermont professor Major Jackson went on a romantic date with a white woman in Portland in the 90s that ended with them sprinting from six-foot skinheads carrying blades and screaming, "White power! Nigger lover! Chocolate-eating whore!" He hadn't seen that coming. Their love connection, displayed in public restaurants, seemed itself evidence of progress. Then, in a heartbeat, he went from being Sidney Poitier to Usain Bolt. "Being Black is incredibly random," said writer Harry Allen. "We know that at any given time something that completely shakes up anything in which we were engaged can happen. Racism is like a monster in a movie that can come from anywhere. It can come out of the toilet, out of the bed at night, it can come from

122

any doggone place. And you can't outrun it. You run as fast as you can and it's right there. It walks and it's right behind you."

We get surprised by the monster because even though we're hyper-aware of racism, you can't make professional, or personal, progress nowadays assuming every white person you interact with is guilty until proven innocent. If you move through the world expecting racism at every turn you'll lose—carrying around a shield like that would spend tremendous spiritual energy and would more often cut you off from positive interactions than protect you from destructive ones. "If you expect everyone to be racist you're not going to get any business done," said Nelson George. "You can't build a career in any major way coming into every meeting with white people expecting racism. You have to go in assuming the best. Now, if they show you their ass somehow then you have to decide whether this is racism or it's because they're assholes." That said, we're also sometimes shocked when we are treated with humanity by white people. Mumia Abu-Jamal wrote, "Once, when I was walking down Market Street in Philly, a middle-aged white woman walked out of Reading Terminal, walked right up to me, and asked me to walk her somewhere. I was shocked by this, for neither of us knew each other, and she was old enough to be my mother. Here I was, dressed like a 'militant,' with a full beard, a big, tall, young Black guy." This is the double consciousness at play—he knows he's a peaceful guy and also knows that to some others he looks frightening, so when someone doesn't treat him as threatening he's surprised. "I walked her where she wanted to go, her clutching my arm. When we got there, I couldn't resist asking her, well—why did she walk over to me? She explained that she was Jewish and with my bearded face it reminded her of her husband, and as I had a nice face she knew she was safe. It blew me away."

It's tempting to remain vigilant and on the lookout because major racism moments are never peripheral moments in people's lives, they are transformative. Many times these moments lead people to do the work they later become known for or be the person they later become known as. Reverend Al Sharpton told me, "I remember once in the sixties we went down South. We were driving in a Cadillac. I was maybe seven or eight years old. And my father had been an amateur boxer so I felt no-body could beat my father. We stopped in North Carolina and they told him he couldn't eat in that restaurant. And that was the first time I saw my father emasculated. And I never forgot. He got back in the car and pulled off and didn't stand up to them and I didn't understand why. And that bothered me. And he explained to me what racism was. He said in parts of the country Blacks are barred from basic things like hotels. And I'm seven, eight years old. I didn't understand. But I remembered and I think that's what sparked my activism."

As inspiration, racism can spiral in many different ways. The artist Fred Wilson said his family was ostracized when, in the 1960s, they moved to Westchester, a suburb north of New York City. As their home was being built someone put up a sign that said NIGGERS GO BACK TO AFRICA. Wilson ended up making no friends in town or at school and spent a lot of his childhood by himself. "We had a big backyard so my fantasy life flourished because I was alone all the time, which is why I am the artist that I am today." Gary Simmons was an experienced artist in the midst of an exhibition in Paris when someone said to him, "What does it mean to be Black? Because we don't have racism here." But he could see French racism quite plainly and his anger about their inability or refusal to see it was epiphanic. "That was a kind of a turning point in my work," Simmons said, "because I think prior to that I was in a little American microcosm in the art world, thinking that my work goes out into the world and it's understood in a certain way. That trip redefined for me how the work was getting read and it became clear to me that I needed to open up the dialogue to not just one isolated experience—my own—and make it something broader that everybody else can access. People were looking at the work and being able to separate themselves from it and saying, "Well, that's a Black experience, that doesn't happen here, we don't have that, that's y'all's thing," and I was like, "No, that's not true. This happens everywhere." So the work shifted at that point from some of those forties and fifties race cartoons into things that had more of a class underpinning and I started to use other sources for the language that I was trying to make. That was an important moment."

These episodes are epiphanal because they can be spirit-killers, leaving permanent psychological damage and lasting scars that never fully heal. In many cases even though the stories are decades old the wounds remain fresh. "Just thinking about it now," Simmons said of an assault that was thirty years old, "it gets my blood boiling."

And they are never isolated incidents within a life—people never said, "This is the only moment of racism I've had." They picked the biggest, most painful, most impactful moment but always there are many other stories that they could tell. "The most racist experience you have," said Ben Jealous, president of the NAACP, "is the one that's worst, and the one that's worst is usually the one that transforms the way you look at the world."

These moments of suddenly discovering the pain and lack of status and power that attends being Black is what comedian Paul Mooney refers to as "a nigger wake-up call." Skip Gates calls them "the scene of instruction" and he says they exist in classic Black autobiographies from slavery to recent days: a moment where someone discovers they're Black and what that means—the societal limitations and the emotional assault that comes along with Blackness. It's where the Black American is taught the negative side of what it means to be Black. "For W.E.B. Dubois it was a little girl who wouldn't take his Valentine card," Gates said. "For James Weldon Johnson in *Autobiography of an Ex-Colored Man* it was when the teacher said, "Would all the white scholars stand up," and he stands up and she goes "No, you can sit down." It's always a moment of trauma. There's always something lacking, a deprivation that makes you realize what being Black means. So discursively Blackness is an absence, a scar, even if you become the most celebrated person."

New York Governor David Paterson had a classic scene of instruction when he helped integrate a segregated school as a nine-year-old entering the fourth grade. "I don't think I knew what race was," he said. "And then all of a sudden I found out in a couple of weeks what race was and I think it was a little disturbing because for the first time I felt that there were limits on me. And it was clear that some of the teachers kind of looked down on us." This sense of being taught the absence of importance, of relevance, of status, of power, of humanity runs throughout the Black experience. The painter Barkley Hendricks said: "There's that area of thinking that you're really not painting people until you're painting white people."

In the late 1940s Paul Mooney was about six or seven and living in either Mississippi or Louisiana—he can't recall which. He drank out of a white drinking fountain—he surely knew it was a violation of convention but even as a child he was flouting norms and defying whites to their faces. But someone tried to put him back in his place: A thirteen-year-old white girl beat him up and called him nigger. But if you know about Paul Mooney you can imagine it wasn't easy to put him in his place even then. "My grandmother beat her ass," Mooney said.

At this point in the story I was scared for his grandmother. What happened to her? Did she get beaten or lynched or run out of town? "No," he said. "Nothing happened." How could that be? How could she get away with beating a white child?

"My grandmother took care of white kids and she whooped ass," Mooney said. "That's what she was known for. When they wanted their kids to get their ass whooped they'd get my grandmother. They would tell their kids, we goin to get Mama Ealy to beat your ass. They used her to scare their kids. Oh you not going to do that homework? Then Mama Ealy gonna come whoop that ass. So they couldn't lynch her or beat her because the white folks protected her." She was a woman with a special place in the community, a valuable role—the designated spanker and sometime bogeywoman whose presence allowed white parents to keep their hands clean and avoid the messy work of meting out corporal punishment. That special position allowed her to get away with this rogue, unsanctioned beating of a white girl attempting to enforce order. And in that way she was able to protect Paul and help him become the person he's become. Mooney said his grandmother was a big influence on him and I'm sure a woman who was able to get away with beating white children—and perhaps quietly enjoying it—was able to teach young Paul how to be the Brer Rabbit he's become. "There was a parakeet that lived next to us that said nigger," Mooney said. "One day she told me, it won't be saying nigger no more. I said, 'Why grandma?' She said, 'I poisoned it.'"

In the fall of 1960, in Greenville, South Carolina, an eighteen-year-old Jesse Jackson tried to use the public library. He was home from college and needed a certain book for a speech he had to give. "I went to the colored library," he told me. "Librarian said, 'I don't have that book but my friend at the Central Library does. I'll write you a note and I'll call her. She's my friend.' I ran about two and a half miles. I was so anxious to go because I had to read the book, write the speech, and memorize it. When I got there I went in the back of the library and two police-men were standing there talking with her. No doubt she told 'em I was coming.

"So I give her the note. Said, 'May I get the books?' She said, 'I'll have 'em in about six days.' I said, 'I need 'em so bad.' I knew not to ask to sit down. I said, 'Can I go down in the stacks to get them?' She said, 'Six days.' Policeman said, 'You heard what she said.' I went out the back of the library and I saw the sign said PUBLIC LIBRARY. I cried." Jackson said what made him cry was thinking of the man he called his father—his stepfather, Charles Henry Jackson. He'd fought in World War II but was barred from certain places on the military base that even Nazi POWs could enter. That sort of bizarre restriction could make your head explode—these evil, captured, enemy soldiers had rights that val-iant American soldiers who'd risked their lives did not? How could one understand or accept that? "Couldn't get it out of my mind."

The following summer when Jackson returned home he and several college classmates went to jail for trying to integrate the public library. "It was kinda my baptism in officially fighting back. I'd grown up to resent the limitations, resent the walls; that was the first time I'd taken definitive action." It was the beginning of the activist the world would come to know and revere.

"I came home from jail that day," Jackson said, "and my dad was sitting there watching television, his feet in the tub. I was in there getting some ice cream. I heard him get up. 'How you doin', Dad?' 'All right. Lookie here, watchin' television here, seen y'all down there goin' to jail or something. If you gonna do that kinda stuff, them fools might bomb this house or something. If you gonna do that stuff, you do it up at school. Do that kinda stuff up yonder.' Dad was gently, in the name of love, askin' me to cease or get out the house. Daddy tightened up with fear 'cause you'd get killed doing that stuff. He didn't want me to get killed. 'Cause he knew when Willie Earl got lynched in our town. He was in jail . . . they took him out the jail at night, left his head in the garbage can."

Jackson had been spurred to fight back by the memory of deep and perplexing injustice done to his father and yet when he did fight back his father asked him not to. And that hurt him anew. "The contradiction," he said, his voice breaking as a single plump tear rolled down his face, "was our sense of dignity came from him." Jackson's sense of refusing to give in was cemented, he said, one Sunday long before his ill-fated library trip, when he followed his father as he cleaned up a bank and two office buildings. The man he was working for came in with two friends. "Big ol' guy," Jackson recalled. "Said, 'Hey, Charlie, come here.' In that tone. A belittling tone. I heard that. His friends laughing. 'Charlie, I said come here.' Heart on the floor. 'You don't come here, I'ma kick you.' I was petrified. Dad took his keys off and said, 'Mr. Temple, you take these keys. I can't stop you from kicking me. But you won't get the leg back. Let's call it even.' Walked out the bank." Jackson paused. "So I got my dignity from him. That was my politic right there." Deep in the Jim Crow South, amidst backdoor entrances and policemen always ready to maintain Negro second-class citizenship and white men who pulled men out of prison in the thick of the night to lynch and decapitate them, Jackson saw his father debased and physically endangered and refusing to accept it. And when Jackson encountered racism that broke his heart and saw a life ahead of him that would insist he have fewer rights than a Nazi prisoner of war he said no, at the risk of death, I refuse, and in the name of justice, I refuse. Because my father taught me better, even if he didn't realize it. At his scene of instruction, Jackson began to blossom into greatness.

In 1964, in West Virginia a fourteen-year-old Henry Louis Gates Jr. broke his hip and went to a doctor who x-rayed his knee, which was also in pain. The doctor saw nothing wrong with his knee and deemed his pain psychosomatic. "He said that I had a nervous breakdown because I was an overachiever," Gates said. "He said colored people weren't supposed to do as well as I had done. I had been stressed out and there was nothing wrong with my knee. White guy thought I was imagining things. And that's why I walk with a cane and I've had a dozen operations since I was fourteen." Gates remains bitter about the whole thing. "I hope that motherfucker's burning in hell."

It seems like the doctor thought too little of Gates's body and his intellectual potential to take him seriously enough to do his job thoroughly—instead landing on a bizarre explanation for his searing pain. This is an example of disrespecting both a Black mind and a Black body and Gates has suffered the consequences his entire life. One of his legs is an inch and a half shorter than the other and has required medical attention on numerous occasions. He was scarred by it literally and figuratively and remains as angry as if it were a fresh wound, but he refused to internalize any sense of inferiority or demoralization. "I was just like, this asshole's stupid!" he spat. "I can talk about somebody calling me nigger but that is nothing compared to this!"

Duke Professor Wahneema Lubiano, who was introduced to me by a brilliant college professor as "one of the smartest people in America," did internalize a racist comment and it shifted the course of her life. It's as if she and Gates got the same flu bug but where he was for some reason able to fight it off, Lubiano was felled by it.

In the early seventies, in Pennsylvania, in high school, she took the

National Merit Scholar's test and placed as a semifinalist. But when she went to the guidance counselor, he suggested she go to secretarial school. "And I believed it," she said. "I went home crying but I believed it. I internalized it that quickly. So maybe I shouldn't go to college." When she told her mother of her decision her mom was apoplectic. "I knew she was going to explode and go up to the school. And I said, 'No, it's okay, Mom. I haven't gotten A's in every single thing, maybe he's right.' And she said, 'Wahneema, you took those exams. You are one of the few. Why are you gonna let this cracker tell you that you're not going to college?' And I didn't really have the language to tell her that in that moment he had wiped out everything that she had and my father had ever said to me. 'Cause in that moment he was the world, they were just my personal cheerleaders." This is why Elizabeth Alexander fights to be the ultimate judge of herself—because if you allow white people to gauge the value of your mind you will most likely be undervalued.

Lubiano ended up going to the University of Pittsburgh but she left after freshman year. "I dropped out, thinking, 'You're too stupid to do this,'" she said. "The damage had been done." She didn't return to college for ten years. When she went back she went to Howard University and it changed her life. "I was surrounded by really smart Black people who were pretty casual about it," she said. "It's not like you walked into a class and sat down and said, 'This is a miracle there are so many smart Black people here.' No, you normalized it, it was routine. And in that way it was really nurturing because being smart was routine." Howard imbued her with a sense that being Black and intellectual was regular stuff. For someone with tremendous mental capability and a self-esteem so fragile that it could be broken by a slight comment from a white man she respected, Howard was a life-saver. "By the time I finished with Howard I could go to grad school at Stanford because I was ready."

In the mid-seventies, in Detroit, when Michael Eric Dyson was around age sixteen, his girlfriend's father, a federal judge, arranged for him to take an IQ test. The test revealed him to be a genius, and the judge

decided to help Dyson get into an elite private boarding school in the
suburbs of Bloomfield Hills, Michigan. But he was one of only a few
Black kids in the school and had no support system. As a kid from the
ghetto who'd grown up in what he called "the womb of segregation," he
found it difficult to fit in and feel comfortable. And other kids were bla-
tantly racist. "I came home to my dorm room one day and affixed to the
door was a caricature of Kunta Kinte from *Roots* and underneath it said,
'Nigger go home.'" [The irony of that message—"Nigger go home"—is
not lost on people who are descendants of the only people brought to
America by force. We didn't ask to come so how dare you tell us to
go home! NC State history professor Blair Kelly said, "The majority of
African-Americans in this country today had ancestors here before the
nation's founding, so if you want us to go back it's going to be kinda difficult."] Then, in the middle of the quad of Dyson's school someone put
a bottle labeled 'Sickle Cell Anemia. To kill off all the undesirables.' The
self-confidence Dyson had gained from earning the respect of a federal
judge, testing at genius level, and being admitted to an elite selective
school was quickly eroding. This is old-school racism in a new location,
little different than what Jackson and Mooney experienced—whites enforcing boundaries, telling him he did not belong. But it sparked great
dissonance in him because he knew that he belonged intellectually—he
had tested and proved he was a genius.

"It was horrible," Dyson said. "It made you feel that no matter
how smart you are, no matter how much smarter than your white col-
leagues you are said to be—not all of them were claimed to be at genius
level—no matter what you do, no matter what you say, no matter how
smart you are, no matter how early you get up, no matter how good you
are, no matter how well you write, no matter how articulate you are,
it doesn't make a difference." As the old joke says: What's a Black man
with a PhD? A nigger. "We knew then the terror of white supremacy
and the refusal of white brothers and sisters to love and embrace us,"
Dyson said. "And it gave me a kind of vertigo, a Hitchcockian vertigo:
The verdant fields began to spin for me. They're attacking me, they're
assaulting me, they're directing racism toward me. My culture is being

subject to all kinds of vicious and incriminating prejudice and I don't have a community to sustain me. I mean, I got the other fellas out there but it's very small. I was unmoored. I'd lost a sense of connection: One year I'm in the ghetto and then all of the sudden the next year I'm going to school with wealthy white kids." After a year and a half Dyson was expelled from the school. Soon after he became a father. He was still in his teens. He went to night school to finish high school and didn't start college until he was twenty-one.

Many people told stories involving the police, who still seem to often function as a tool used to enforce racial dominance and remind Blacks of their lack of status in America. Ben Jealous was a young man in Washington, D.C., sitting on a porch with some friends in front of an apartment he was renting when the cops pulled up. As they got out, one of Jealous's friends stood up. A cop said to him, "Where do you think you're going?" He said, "I'm not going anywhere." The cop said, "That's good. You wouldn't want to have me make up something." It was like he was saying, 'Nigger, don't run cause I'll just shoot you and create a reason later.' "That made me feel most hopeless," Jealous said.

The visual artist Deborah Grant was pulled over by the police for a reason that was unclear to her, and had the back window of her Toyota smashed as she sat in the car. "It was a humiliating moment and it changed my entire existence and how I felt. It made me angry and it made me very bitter for a very long time. And it's one of the reasons I became an artist. Because your work can be out there and can consciously do something that changes people's perceptions."

Some also spoke about the Ku Klux Klan. Gary Simmons was seven or eight when his mother took him and his sister on a Greyhound bus to Disney World. "We drove through a really small town outside of Savannah, Georgia," Simmons said. "It was night. There was a billboard that said YOU'RE PASSING THROUGH THE LAND OF THE KU KLUX KLAN and it had a Klansman on it. And I was fucking terrified, dude. I mean, like, terrified." When the bus stopped he was afraid to get off and when his mom got off he thought she would never come back. They made it to Disney World but his entire trip was ruined. "I was so freaked out I just couldn't deal. To me that was the defining moment of the South. I was like, 'Oh, I'm not, I'm never coming down here, I don't even want any part of this. I don't want to be here at this Disney World shit.' It struck a fear in me for years, man." Simmons said the memory burned in his mind and inspired him years later when he became an artist. "That's one of the moments that I looked back on when I first started making work," he said. "That's why I would do some of that stuff with the Klan imagery. That's one of the moments that I look back on as a source because it involved so many things. It was anger, fear of being in an unknown place, and being defenseless, at the mercy of other people. That's just one of those situations that you'll never forget."

Not all Klan stories are tragic. Abiodun Oyewole of the Last Poets, a proto-hiphop spoken word group from the early 1970s, famously robbed the Klan in North Carolina, thus living a dream for some Black Americans. It all started on Fayetteville Street in Raleigh as he watched a Klan parade in 1970. "I was amazed," Oyewole said. "And while we're looking at these white men walk down the block with hoods on, a rock comes out of the crowd and hits a white guy in the head and when red blood hits something white it looks vicious." Oyewole found out the rock-thrower was white. He was someone the Klan had tried to recruit, which the rock thrower found offensive. He tried to enlist Oyewole in burning down their headquarters and told him where it was located.

Oyewole was unwilling to trust the man but still wanted to attack the Klan's headquarters. But when he mentioned it to fellow revolutionaries in his group the Yoruba Society they laughed at him because they didn't have guns. "Somebody said what you going to do? Get a bulletproof dashiki? You gonna knock 'em out with your afro?" But Oyewole was undeterrable: he and some friends stole weapons from two gun shops in Raleigh. The plot thickened when two of his partners lost their guns and their freedom. "Two of the boys dropped a duffel bag of guns," he said, "cause they heard a sound. They ran and left the guns. When they went back to retrieve them they got picked up by the police."

Now he needed money to bail the men out. And he still wanted to stick it to the Klan. He knew a way to do both. "I said, man, I know where we could probably kill two birds with one stone, to get the money to get the boys out and we can embarrass the damn Klan." So he and two men set out toward Klan headquarters with their guns. "It was like a motor lodge. It's a building where the would gather and they had a filling station, a general store and a lodge. And the lodge is where they had their meetings."

Oyewole and his men walked in the front door around one p.m.: a daylight caper. "Our whole thing was the bolder the better." As soon as they got inside he went into tough guy mode—Oyewole has a revolutionary spirit but he's a poet. The Last Poets debut album had already been recorded then. But, he said, it takes nothing for any Black man to make any white person afraid and he played on that. "I'm not a robber," he said. "I'm not any of that but I was trying to play the role. If the dudes had said boo I might have dropped the gun. But the gun I had was scary. I was showing a .357 magnum which is a pretty big gun. I pointed that big boy at the guy and I think he peed on himself. I looked at him I said you know what this is. It must have been a line I heard on TV or something."

There were only two Klansmen there, the Watkins brothers, but one of them was the local Grand Dragon. The Grand Dragon went to the cash register and opened it. Oyewole said, "I want the real money I don't want this pocket change. He could see I knew what was going on and he was scared. You know, you put a gun in a Black man's hands against a white southerner and they feel like this is my day, this is the last day of my life!"

They went to the safe. Oyewole got about $6,000 and they ran. But as they escaped they were fired at. A Pepsi-Cola delivery man who happened to be starting a drop-off as they were robbing the place had pulled his gun. They got scared and ran faster, then stopped. "I said, we got guns. Why we running?" He turned and fired and then, afraid he'd killed the Pepsi man, they ran more, then hid in the woods for about six hours. During that time they buried the money. In time they came to a house where a Black woman lived with several kids and asked her to help them. She refused and as they were leaving they saw a boy run out the back door. One of Oyewole's men aimed his gun but Oyewole stopped him. He said, "We're not killing our kids," even though he knew the boy was going to run and tell the cops, which he did. The cops caught them but didn't get the money so they were able to bail out their comrades. Oyewole did three years and nine months during which the first Last Poets album came out. "I can't get none of the rewards or the glory and people are walking around me quoting my stuff." He wrote thousands of poems, songs, essays, and stories and two books, setting himself up for the rest of his Last Poets career. "It was a great, great, great recess period for a crazy revolutionary." It was a necessary and invaluable period in his life that he was able to enjoy partly because he had slain the Klan. "When I went to jail I was the king."


The artist Rashid Johnson told me a story that's emblematic of modern microaggressions, those passive-aggressive but painful flicked jabs. One of those little moments where you find yourself reminded how little is expected of a Black mind. At the wedding of one of his art dealers Johnson fell into a conversation with a prominent collector. "She asked me to put this [his becoming an artist] into context," he said. "So just, the idea of like, imagining pedigree in some degree." I read that as she was resume-checking him. How did you, young Black man, become an artist? But perhaps he felt from her an even lower vibe: He used the word "pedigree" to explain what she was asking for. "Pedigree" may be used to describe the ancestry of a person but it's primarily for the ancestry of animals, especially dogs.

"My mom is a PhD," Johnson told the collector. "My father is an attorney. My brother went to Harvard. I went to Northwestern and took classes at University of Chicago and I have a master's degree from the Art Institute. She said, 'Are your parents happy that you're an artist?' And my parents are. My mother was a poet before she was an academic and my father was a sculptor for a period and they're happy that they made

WHO'S AFRAID OF POST-BLACKNESS

an artist instead of an attorney or an accountant or a businessman. So I said, 'I think they're happy they made an artist.' And she said, 'Instead of a drug dealer.' And it just relocated me, you know. It just made me feel . . . wow. It was a nigger wake-up-call scenario." When Johnson's guard was down in the midst of an intimate conversation with someone he presumed respected him, he found out she thought he was fortunate to not have become a street hustler thug, as if every Black man has that as an option.

The story I heard from Professor Derek Conrad Murray is the one that for me best captured one of the central collisions of modern racism—the belief that you can possibly move on up and all but escape racism can arise but will always crash and burn. Some think that because of the times and their class ascension and presenting themselves to society in a certain way they will avoid certain indignities, but eventually find out that racism remains inescapable. A Black man with a PhD from Harvard Law in a suit from Savile Row is still a nigger. Murray and his family were brought back to Earth by a spectacularly messy, public nigger wake-up call that damaged the family deeply, creating fissures that last to this day. The incident is over two decades old but the family will still not discuss it among themselves. "It was too painful of an experience," Murray said. "I try to address it with my family to try to heal but it's still damaging the psyche of my family. I brought it up to my mother two days ago and she said, 'Uh-huh. Why you bringing that up for?'" Murray thinks about it once or twice a week.

Murray was fourteen in the early 1980s when his father, a hospital administrator at the University of Washington Medical Center, moved the family to Lake Forest Park, an exclusive community outside of Seattle. The Murrays were the only Black family in the area. They were a very religious family who prayed every day, sent the kids to Catholic schools, and went to church every Sunday. The move to Lake Forest Park meant they needed to find a new church. They landed at a large suburban church where they were the only Black family. They'd attended service there a few times when one Sunday, during a moment of prayer it got very quiet. A white man on the other side of the church stood up and stared in their direction but the church was so large it wasn't clear at first whom he was looking at. Then he pointed at the Murrays and yelled, "You niggers don't belong here! You niggers should get out of here! You don't belong here!"

Murray's father leapt from his seat and started running at the man, full speed. The man took off running and raced out of the church. Murray's father followed him, as did many of the men in the church and, naturally, Murray and his older brother. They watched their father chase the man down the block, catch him, jump on him, drag him to the ground, and begin choking him as if to stop more venomous breaths from coming through the man's throat. You stabbed me and my family with your throat and now I'm going to crush it! Murray saw his father in a place of rage he'd never before seen as he choked the man while several men tried to pull him away. Finally, the men extracted Murray's father from the man's throat. He calmed himself down, and the Murrays got in their car and drove home.

A few hours later one of the church leaders visited the Murrays in their home and apologized profusely and begged for forgiveness. He explained that the man who'd called them niggers was the son of another church leader. He was a schizophrenic who had been in and out of institutions all of his life and if the story became widely known he would be institutionalized again, probably forever. So Murray's father agreed to let it go. But the family never really did.

"It changed everyone in my family," Murray said. "My family was very religious up until that moment. After that moment no one in my family ever had any relationship to religion ever again. My parents never went to church, they never prayed, none of my siblings ever did. I became an atheist. It effectively destroyed our relationship to religion. I haven't gone to church since that moment. Whenever I think about religion I think about that moment. People say, 'You gotta get past that,' and I know they're right but it's still in me. To be sitting in church and feeling like this is a place of acceptance and safety and have this horrific racist incident happen to us was so damaging to my family."

The sudden, shocking loss of peace and grace and dignity in a place they thought was safe extended beyond the church and into Lake Forest Park, and also into what Murray's parents thought upper-middle-classness had bought them. "That moment tapped in to a lot of the aspirations of my parents," Murray said. "They moved us there because they thought we would be better off in that environment and not subject to the pathologies of the Black community, and I think our presence there was very much wrapped up in those kinds of attitudes. I think a lot of the Black bourgeoisie had those attitudes in that period in time. And that moment kind of vulgarized the distorted Black middle-class aspirations of assimilation that my parents had. It impacted the way we perceived our parents and their understanding of what our lives should be and how we should go out in the world. It caused us to think a lot about our parents' values and what they thought about what it means to be an upwardly mobile Black person.

"Our presence in that church was supposed to be the embodiment of some kind of success as Black people, some kind of transcendence, and that moment dismantled all of those notions. They thought they could avoid racism and ran into it. That superseded the reality that this man was not well. That didn't matter. My parents back then were really concerned with the way whites perceived us and we were raised to be the embodiment of everything respectable and appropriate. Acceptable Blackness. We dressed very preppy and conservative and were extremely well mannered and in many respects it was about impressing whites and illustrating that we were not like common Black people. I think what had been programmed into me by my parents was achievement in America meant assimilation into whiteness. So there we were, this beautiful, well-mannered, middle-class Black family amongst all these whites and to be called niggers in that environment—it didn't matter how we dressed, it didn't matter what job my dad had or how big our house was. We were just niggers.

"After that there was a certain criticality that I started to have toward the way I'd been raised. I started to see another vision of what it meant to be Black. And that relates to post-Blackness because to me, if that's so, then I'm gonna do whatever I want and be who I wanna be. I'm not gonna try to pencil myself in to some notion of appropriateness to whites because you're not gonna achieve that acceptance. You just have to live your life, be free, be happy, and do what you want to do."

All these stories show white attempts to break the Black spirit but they also show Black resiliency. Though deep wounds are created and lasting anger and bitterness may ensue and people often change, in no story I heard was anyone permanently broken by racism. People either brush themselves off and press ahead or coil inward, rethink parts of themselves, and then explode in a new direction with steely purpose. Murray absorbed a painful body blow, went down on one knee, heard the ref count to eight, but he got up and learned from the moment and grew. Though his family is still grieving and unable to talk about what happened, he became a better person because of it. He lost his religion but he gained a sharper sense of himself and saw through the off-base, idealist, assimilationist notions his parents had fed him. That is the moment when he changed course in life and began becoming the man he is today. Black people are damaged by these moments of racism, we are shaped by them, but we are not victims. We revitalize ourselves like the phoenix—rebuilding our spirits and coming back stronger. And still I rise.

Racism to us seems like a complex, multi-faceted obstacle to surmount—Goliath to our David. Having any chance to defeat it requires all the mental and spiritual skills acquired by people who always had to be like the wily, witty trickster Brer Rabbit just to get by. The quintessentially Black emotional approach to racism is evinced by the mother of Spelman professor Dr. Jelani Cobb. "My mother believes that white people everywhere are always conspiring against her," Cobb says. "But my mother doesn't see racism as an excuse not to achieve. She sees herself as constantly outsmarting the racist forces that are trying to keep her back, which makes the most simple aspect of life, like going to the supermarket, become an adventure. And I think it relates to how Black people can both see racism as ever present and not see themselves as victims. My mother tells all of these stories where white people are conspiring against her but she always manages to outsmart them at the last minute. Every single one of her stories includes this one line: 'Now, what them crackers didn't know I knew . . . ' There's always something that she knows that enables her to outsmart them or some kind of knowledge that keeps her from falling victim to the white conspiracy. And that's cool."

There are other strategies Black people can employ to help them deal with racism. Claude Steele suggests four. In an environment where there aren't many Black people, where you're, say, the only one or one of a very few, find existence-proof role models: Blacks who went before you and succeeded, thus lessening the pressure of being out on a limb. "That affects your moment-to-moment interpretation of your experience," Steele said. "If he made it, or if some number of people made it, you think, Okay the stereotype's out there but it's not gonna kill me. Others have made it. So now I'm not as easily upset by the cues in the environment that might suggest otherwise.' It makes things less threatening." Steele also suggests we remember that ability is changeable—we can always get better at something—rather than seeing it as static, God-given, and preset. If improvement is available to everyone then excellence is possible for everyone willing to work hard enough: a democratic vision of potential. "America's saturated with the ideology that ability is genetically allocated and there's a fixed amount that is assessable," Steele said. "But ability yields to deliberate, organized practice. The brain is the most expansive organ we have; it really does change. You learn something and your brain changes." When ability is considered pre-determined then usually Black minds are perceived to have less of it and white minds are assumed to have more.

Steele says that being aware of stereotype threat is helpful in allowing us to get through times where we're being stereotyped and dealing with microaggressions, and are thus better able to deflect the passive-aggressive attacks coming our way or the anxiety we're feeling. "There's research that shows if you teach people about it they'll get through these moments better." Stereotype threat has a large impact when those attributes you hold dearest to your self and public image seem challenged by outsiders' prejudices that are based on stereotypes. If you value being thought of as smart and want to be known as smart, when you encounter people who seem to think you are not because you are Black, you are under threat. What do you do? The more you know about stereotype threat the more you can combat those emotions and stay on an even keel.

Perhaps the most important strategy is Elizabeth Alexander's concept of relying on yourself to be the main judge of you. When you allow your self-image to be determined by whites you will probably be sold short. "In academia you're always around people who think ability is genetically rooted," Steele said. "That people either have it or don't and there's no use in you entertaining someone who doesn't have it. I had to disbelieve what these people believe. I knew that they'd never see me as someone who had genius. 'Cause genius is white, maybe Jewish, maybe got a European accent. It would never be a Negro. That's impossible. So I always had to have a private theory about what my capacities were."

Some of these strategies you may not need or you may find you're already practicing naturally, without realizing it. We are resilient people because we have had to be. Still, in many of us, beneath our layers of resilience, there's a deep spiritual ache and exhaustion. "We are a people in pain," said Terrie Williams, the author of *Black Pain: It Just Looks Like We're Not Hurting.* "We are all dealing with the pain and wounds and scars of our parents and our ancestors." She said people pass their pain and their pain avoidance strategies down to their kids and grandkids. We are people with unspeakable horrors in our collective memory, who feel searing vicarious pain when those horrors are referenced either in media or in incidents that remind us of the violence America so often inflicts on our bodies. And we must fend off the multi-tentacled onslaught of constant oppression and attempts at spirit-murder in our own lives and also deal with our own difficult memories. All that leads to us carrying a ton of pain and expending a lot of spiritual energy. We may be phoenixes, but rebuilding yourself uses up a lot of your power.

"Racism is damaging us," Williams said. "We are literally walking around, looking like we're not hurting, looking like we're sane and just dying inside. Just because you have become accustomed to it, just because it's second nature that you're not going to get a cab when you step out on the street, doesn't mean that it doesn't have a profound impact on your psyche. And every time you gotta go into that mode, even though you consider it like second nature, it takes something out of you. It sits inside of you." Williams pointed to the hundred-plus studies that document the long-term physical impact of racism. In the 1800s abolitionist physicians argued that Blacks had poorer health than whites not because they were innately inferior but because of the accumulated impact of white privilege. It cannot be coincidental that today Blacks are more likely to die from heart disease, diabetes, stroke, and hypertension than any other racial group. Some of the problem is related to class and culture but some of it is not—affluent Blacks suffer more health problems on average than poor whites. Studies indicate that racism has at least five major ways of impacting health. The first three are almost exclusive to the working class: exposure to inadequate medical care; commodities specifically marketed to or easily available in Black communities (like junk food, substandard food, malt liquor, drugs; one may also include here unhealthy cultural norms like an affinity for fried foods); and toxic substances and hazardous conditions (like asbestos or other sorts of harmful chemicals used in housing projects or on blue-collar job sites). But two more factors span the classes—these are where the potential health advantages of not being working class are squandered. One is the impact of socially inflicted trauma (both mental and physical, stemming from racism experienced either directly or vicariously). By "vicarious" I mean racism need not happen to you for you to experience it as painful and stressful. Blacks understand the act of putting one Black person in their place, or inflicting violence on one Black body, is an attack on us all and these are often felt with an intensity similar to the intensity felt as a result of racist incidents that happen to you. Someone may ask me, "What racist incidents have happened to you?" Well, putting aside the litany of events cataloged previously, I experience the shootings of Oscar Grant, Aiyanna Jones, Sean

Bell, Amadou Diallo, and many others as things that could've happened to me or a family member and as painful reminders of the vulnerability of the Black body, even though I'd never heard of those people before they were killed. Even if I felt nothing racist had ever happened to me, being aware of America's constant racist incidents brings me in touch with racism because the vicarious experience of it is painful enough. One of the central moments of racism in my young life was Randall Dunn discussing an incident of racism in his life: Nothing happened to me specifically but I knew that if people felt that way about him they would surely feel it about me, too, and thus, emotionally, the incident happened to me as well.

Many of those I interviewed spoke about the intense pain of watching the aftermath of Hurricane Katrina—Black Americans stranded and begging for help and basic human necessities—and they emotionalized it as if this horrific deprivation was occurring to their blood relatives. "I was, like, walking around my apartment screaming about they are killing Black children! They are killing our children!" said Karen Finney, a Democratic political consultant. "And I remember feeling so angry and I felt like only my Black friends really understood how deep that was and how real that was and how we weren't just imagining what was really going on there." It is this vicarious experience of racism and the resultant stress that endangers the health of every Black American regardless of class. That and the fifth way that racism can impact Black health: John Henryism.

John Henry was a steel-driving railroad worker in the South in the 1800s whose story has become legend. He was known as the strongest and best of all railroad workers. When the steel-driving machine arrived to replace Henry and the other steel-drivers he battled the machine, carrying with him his pride and the honor of humankind. For a man to compete with a machine of that sort he would have to work at the edge of his capabilities, perhaps beyond them. Henry surely pushed his heart and lungs well past their potential because he won the battle against the steel-driving machine and then he collapsed, dead of a stroke or a heart attack. The intense effort of battling the machine taxed him beyond what his body was able to do and even though he won, he paid the ultimate price.

In modern psychology John Henryism is the idea that exposure to social discrimination can lead some Blacks to put in extraordinary effort in pursuit of success and a repudiation of racism, resulting in a steep physiological cost. Blacks who have extrahuman reasons why they need to win—to prove that they have been wrongly judged and the stereotype against Blacks is wrong and that the expectation of failure is undeserved—may find themselves working incredibly hard and straining the edge of their physical, mental, and human capabilities as John Henry did. They drive themselves to be twice as good, as my mother instructed me to be, working in the spirit of "I'll show them." They may overcome and achieve but they will pay with their bodies: with higher rates of blood pressure, hypertension, heart disease, or other physical breakdowns brought on by the extra effort of being at war with racism.

Oppression's impact on health goes deeper than those five factors—the body is also impacted by your response to it. Some tend to internalize racism, some bury it by using drugs or alcohol or other emotional masking agents, some engage in reflective coping, and some resist either as individuals or by organizing and mobilizing against their oppressors. The more external the response, the healthier the response to racism, but Black cultural norms strongly encourage us to hold in our pain. We don't have ways to expunge the bullets in our soul. "We end up taking it out on ourselves because we have been taught not to voice it," Terrie Williams said. "It's the learned silence that we picked up when we were enslaved. Horrific things we would experience and not speak about, and so you learned to hold it in. That's what we had to do in order to survive and it's something that we have passed on from generation to generation: that you suck it up and do whatever it is that you gotta do to stay sane." I know the Black stoicism she's talking about. The way we hold our head high in the face of emotional racialized pain, the way we bottle it up and find a way to keep on keepin' on. "I just know too many Black folk who are impatient about other Black folk who complain about racism," said Dr. Cobb. The dumb comment a white co-worker made is good for a laugh when you repeat it to Black friends but when the promotions you deserve continuously go to white people who are less qualified than you, that's not so easy to share. "That silence worked for us back then," Williams said. "It's what we had to do in order to live, but now it is literally destroying our community."

# Chapter 6

# The Blacker the Berry the Sweeter the Juice,

# But Nobody Wants Diabetes

Paul Mooney tells a joke that always makes me laugh, about a little white boy who's in the kitchen with his mother as she's making a chocolate cake. When she turns around he dunks his face in the batter and spreads it all around. When she turns back he says, "Look, Mommy! I'm Black!" She grabs a broomstick and beats his ass. Then she says, "Go in the living room and show your father what you've done!" He struts into the living room, certain his father will understand. Excitedly he says, "Look, Daddy! I'm Black!" Dad rips off his belt and beats the kid till his butt is bright red. Then Dad says, "Now go on the porch and show your grandfather what you've done!" Kid drags himself outside, knowing what's to come. Lifelessly he says, "Grandpa. I'm Black." Grandpa leaps up, grabs a switch off the nearest tree, and beats the last remaining tears out of the boy. Then he says, "Now get back in the kitchen with your mama!" He trudges into the kitchen. His mom says, "I hope you've learned your lesson!" Kid says, "I sure have. I been Black five minutes and I already hate white people!"

Black people are clear, I think, about why we dislike white people and a moment in our shoes can reveal why. We are angry and in pain because of the oppression and assaults we've suffered over centuries. That anger and pain inspires both the intense joy that draws the world's eyes to us and the infamous lash-outs that make white people afraid of us. Racism leaves lasting psychological and physical damage but, like true family members, Blacks know how to devastate each other.

Black people are conscious of how difficult it is to be Black and how we must go two hundred yards to score a touchdown instead of one hundred, and yet at the same time we're deeply in love with being Black. We complain about racism but we don't wish to change races. "In the costumes of life it's the best costume," Mooney said. "It's been a movie to me. It's been laughter, it's been a musical, it's been a horror movie, it's been a violent movie, it's been a very entertaining movie. It's been . . . amazing. If I had it all to do over again I wouldn't do it any other way." We love Blackness even as the harsh realities of Blackness weigh heavily on our shoulders. "When we were young women," Sharon Pratt the former mayor of D.C. said, "we would all laugh at how if you were a white woman you just had this sort of giddy smile, you could just be so happy. Whereas if you were an African-American woman you probably started the day with a little bit more of an attitude, anticipating problems, anticipating rejection, anticipating barriers that robbed you of that giddiness that is easier to express and to experience if you're not African-American."

Psychologists say there's an infinitesimally small number of Blacks who actually want to be white and most of them have a serious sort of psychopathology. Blackness dumps a heavy weight on your back but we know the benefits of being in this family are worth it. "Being Black is one of the great blessings in my life," Cornel West said. "Because to be Black means that you are tied to a tradition of a people who have produced levels of excellence and elegance and dignity from Ellington to King, from Sarah Vaughan to Toni Morrison to my mother. So any time I hear the word 'Black' I think first and foremost of elegant style and dignity. Black people have no monopoly on these things, it's just we have our own forms of 'em."

As a writer I'm inspired by the stylish excellence of the peerless Black artists who preceded me—not just Ellison and Baldwin and Morrison and Greg Tate, but also Nas and Miles and Monk and Sonia Sanchez.

We are a people who know it don't mean a thing if it ain't got that swing: style matters. That ethos runs through every aspect of Blackness from music to dance to cooking to clothes to language. As a Black writer I've got to confront the reality that a well-built sentence full of substance may permeate the mind, but style is also required to impress minds that have already been penetrated by Baldwin's sheets of sound and the poetics of the Black pulpit and the everyday linguistic gymnastics of so many non-famous Black folk.

As a person I'm buoyed by the courage and determination of our legendary freedom fighters—people who fought through levels of adversity I'll never have to battle. "I come from a people who faced insurmountable odds and overcame 'em," Reverend Sharpton said. "We took the worst crap in the history of the world and made it anyway. It's a great feeling: we are not victims, we're victors." I know there are land mines in the ground I'm trying to cross to reach my professional goals, and I draw strength from knowing there were many more land mines in the Earth crossed by Blacks who came generations before me. That knowledge gives me inspiration to keep pressing forward. My battle to be a host at a cable TV station is nothing compared to the battles fought by Max Robinson to become the first Black network news anchor or by Jackie Robinson to play in the major leagues or by the army's earliest Black fighter pilots to show their brilliance and mettle. If they had the grit and strength of character to succeed against crushing odds then how could I ever feel down when I hit roadblocks? Those Blacks opened doors for me so how can I not honor their victories with my own resolve and steely determination?

Alas, we are not excellent and dignified ubiquitously. Every time I hear of a grisly crime I pray the perpetrator isn't Black because too often they are. Every time I see someone cooning on TV—ahem, Flavor Flav—I cringe to my soul. Yet there's no criminal and no buffoon who could make me think less of Black people. Most Blacks would agree: We are bombarded by images of Black criminality and degradation as if there is a planned effort to make the nation think little of us, yet still we know we are beautiful and dignified.

"There's a lot of evidence," Claude Steele said, "that Black people are pretty good at not internalizing these negative images of Black people as much as white people do. From a young age in America you know you're shrouded in some identity that is problematic but you don't know why it's problematic. There's a conditioning, a pairing of race with this negative image of the race. That doesn't mean for a minute that you believe it's true or that you internalize it." We know the dregs of our society are not representative of us.

I remember the night the D.C. Snipers were caught after three weeks of mysteriously killing ten and injuring six people in the D.C. area. They terrorized a nation by murdering people at random at a Home Depot, a mall, a school, a Mobil station, and then vanishing, poof, seemingly undetectable. A Black police chief was the face of ineptitude, standing before a bank of microphones and cameras after shootings, looking befuddled and at the mercy of an invisible villain. The nation watched in horror as bodies piled up over weeks. Everyone assumed the perpetrator was a white man because the vast majority of serial killers are. I was watching CNN the night it all ended and when the anchor announced they'd been caught I exhaled with relief. But who'd done it? CNN had no photos of the killers to show us when the anchor said he was just then being told that one or both of the killers was from . . . Jamaica. My heart sank. I thought: "There are white people who are from Jamaica," hoping against the odds that this heinous, insane crime spree had not been committed by Black people. I watched CNN for hours to see pictures of the suspects, like waiting to see if my team had really lost the big game. And then confirmation came. CNN showed us pictures. One of the most horrific crimes of my lifetime had been perpetrated by Black men. I was crestfallen. But there was not a moment when I thought a speck less of Black people. That never occurred to me. We can separate our disappointment with those who mortify us from our love for the family that has made us so proud so many times, because real love is not rocked by moments of bad behavior. As my mother often said when I was growing up, "I may not always like you, but I'll always love you." We may not always like what we see from our brothers and sisters but we will always love Black people.

150

So our double-consciousness is elastic enough to be able to hold op-posing concepts in the mind at once: to know that Blacks are brilliant, beautiful, and dignified even though we are sometimes ugly, embarrass-ing, and immoral and often scorned and hated. I suspect the difficulty of being Black is part of what makes us proud to be Black: We know we're tough because of what we have to deal with just to get through a day. That aspect of Blackness is essential to what Blackness is. But with each generation it's slowly lessening. "Race used to manifest itself as this con-sistent oppressive burden in everyday life," Dr. Charles Mills of North-western said. "Think of Richard Wright in the thirties and forties, or Ellison when *Invisible Man* comes out in the fifties. That sense of things is not the case anymore." The gradual decrease in how difficult—how warlike—Blackness is on a day-to-day basis has left some wondering what it means to be Black now. "I remember in college," said Professor Dorian Warren of Columbia, "discussing the Black Panthers and being mad and wishing I could have been there in the late sixties or early sev-enties. So I started acting that out in campus politics, saying, I'm gonna be as radical as those guys. It was like we missed out on something, on the movement a lot of us were searching for. You hear the stories, you see the footage, you see *Eyes on the Prize* and it's romantic and it's uplifting and you're like, wow, I want to be there. I want to make a contribu-tion. I think we're searching for what our unique role is as part of this centuries-old struggle for racial equality. And yet I don't think any other generation of Black people have had as much access and opportunity in the white world. So I don't think any generation of Black people has ever had that dilemma in the same way." The way racism functions has shifted such that there are more Black people having more success than ever and the sorts of issues we're fighting against are not as sexy as the issues that previous generations battled. "We're in such a different time period," Dr. Mills said. "The period of sixties, seventies militants has passed. Part of the thing is, what exactly would one do? What are you protesting? You can protest de facto segregation but it's not as catchy as segregation by law. The structures of exclusion are still there but they're not thought of in such a clear-cut way so mobilizing a population is harder." We still feel the revolutionary impulses that make us love Malcolm X, Huey P. Newton, Assata Shakur, Angela Davis, Thurgood Marshall, Marcus Garvey, Frederick Douglass, and Harriet Tubman, but where do we put those impulses in a world where Blacks get into Ivy League colleges and are Fortune 500 CEOs, federal judges, and secretaries of state? How do we say, "fight the power" with the same gusto when the commander in chief is a brother? And when you stifle the revolutionary impulse does it change what it means to be Black?

The post-Black era has seen a fluidly mutating sense of what it means to be Black and a variety of different Black experiences and opinions about what it means to be Black. There are ideas floating around about what it means to be Black but it's as hard to nail down a fixed definition as it is to grab a wet water balloon. Whenever you think you've got one, it seems to squirt away. Professor Blair Kelley likes to give her students a Blackness test. She gives examples of people, some famous, some not, and asks the students to say who's definitively Black or not and why. First, Kelley points out someone with brown skin and two Black parents. Students say they're Black because of parentage and culture. Then she makes things more complicated. "I'll say a Black person who's brown-skinned but who says that they're actually Native American," Kelley says. "The students are like, 'Ha! That's stupid,' and then they tell me that self-identity is not really important here, it's what you look like that matters. Then we get to the person who could pass for white but has a Black parent. They're mixed race, they have straight blond hair and light eyes and most people who see them think they're white. Are they Black or white? And they're like, well, it's not just who you look like. When we talk about Tiger Woods, Mariah Carey, Vin Diesel, and Jennifer Beals they get all tied up in knots and they can't answer the questions and they can't make a rule that they can follow. By the end of the exercise the board is covered with all these different, contradictory notions of who a Black person is or what race means and then they get it—race is socially constructed and there is no fixed notion of race and it's this messy thing. It's not neat. Blackness and whiteness don't actually have real meanings. They're socially constructed and we're always shifting what they mean.

I think people want hard answers and like truisms but we have to teach people that it is messy and that it's okay to be messy." The mind grasps for clarity and certainty on all matters; it dislikes confusion, ineffability, and mystification. On the thorny and crucial issue of race it demands lucidity but race refuses to give it up.

In an attempt to codify Blackness, many Black minds create a hierarchy of authenticity. Roland Martin from CNN broke down the authenticity pecking order that exists. "The platinum-level authentic Negro," Martin said, "is you grew up in public housing, crime, drugs, poverty. The gold level is you grew up in a middle-class Black neighborhood and you went to public schools and maybe to a Black college so you got a pretty good Black experience. Silver is you lived in a neighborhood that was really diverse where you had a mix of educated African-Americans and whites and you may have gone to a Black church but it wasn't a Black Baptist church, it probably was Episcopalian or something on those lines. You might be in Jack and Jill, a whole different kind of Black thing. And then there's bronze. You grew up in the suburbs and you didn't really see many of us. You went to a prep school and an all-white college and your experience of Blackness is really third person, something you heard and read about versus what you know and experienced."

Those levels are based on proximity to the ghetto experience, as if that were the sun around which Blackness revolves. The further the planet you live on is from the ghetto the less authentically Black you are. I reject the idea that the 'hood is the center of Blackness and that Blackness is somehow lost the further you go up the class ladder, like milk moving toward spoiling as it sits longer and longer outside the fridge. To suggest that underclass Blackness is authentic and middle-class is not is self-destructive thinking. It suggests that Blackness requires us to stay poor in order for it to survive and it dies as more of us become economically successful. Get real. I've been to too many wildly negrified BBQs in well-tended backyards in Oak Bluffs, the Hamptons, D.C., and Beverly Hills to believe down-home Blackness and class can't co-exist. I also reject the concept of Black life experiences as rankable rather than sitting on a continuum where all experiences are equally valuable, equally

WHO'S AFRAID OF POST-BLACKNESS

Black. How is a Black person who grows up around white people not Black when they are reminded of their Blackness constantly? Why is Blackness necessarily synonymous with the underclass? Why's Blackness burnished by life in the projects but somehow damaged by life in the suburbs? Why's Blackness validated by a trip to prison and challenged by a stint at Yale? Do you really think Blackness is not portable? Do you think Blackness is like a chemical that's so fragile that it requires extreme exposure to itself in order to survive and extended exposure to whiteness will somehow destroy it? Does it lead to communal upward mobility and mass economic empowerment when we tell each other that you can be Black or you can be successful but doing both will be impossible? Why must I choose between romanticizing the ghetto and creating a Black personality that could lead to an office at a corporation with a ticker on the NYSE? I've seen too many brothers and sisters in suits strutting stylishly through the halls of Merrill Lynch and NBC and Harvard, refined enough to be respected by the whites in charge but still Black enough to be down—brothers and sisters fluent in several dialects of American English and smart enough to code-switch on a dime. No, I cannot fall for the lie that Blackness is so perishable that extended interaction with whites will somehow ruin it.

Roland Martin also rejects the hierarchical way of looking at the community that he broke down. "Hell, yeah, we gotta stop doing that," he said. "What is real and authentic Blackness is solely based on your experience. How you grew up, how you were raised, what you saw, what you went through. That is your authentic experience as a Black person and you cannot define what I saw, what I witnessed, what I went through as not representative. That's you. That's what you went through."

Still, the debates over authenticity remain as passionate and pernicious as ever. "It's like couples have things they can say to each other that they know will really cut into the other," Henry Louis Gates, Jr., said. "Well the most painful thing for a Black person is 'You're not Black enough.'" "You're not Black" and "you're acting white" are essentially two sides of the same coin, both meaning your understanding of what it means to be Black is wrong. You're not wielding Blackness correctly.

You're not living right. Perhaps even you're ashamed of Blackness and trying to pretend you're white. Or we both know it's hard to be Black but I'm not trying to sneak out of the race so why are you? Why are you trying to act like whitey? Whasamatter? Don't you love being Black? The accusation can cut to the core of a person. It can hurt so deeply it can change lives.

As a tween in New Jersey, Professor Blair Kelley was, she admits, a bit corny. She listened to James Taylor and played violin and piano and, according to her, had a somewhat white-sounding tone to her voice. She also listened to Diana Ross and the Supremes but not to Black music of the day. Then one day the authenticity police shined a light on her. "Someone told my father that I acted like a white girl," she said. "He was really disappointed that that's what people thought of me. He was hurt and he didn't want to tell me, but he was hurt." He didn't say anything to her but her mother did and that led to exploration. "I could have not worried about that. I could have said, 'Who cares? I'm not a white girl.' But it became a question for me. Ever since then it's been a question for me: who are Black people and what do Black people do and what do they consume and who were they in the past?" This is a woman who grew up to become a Black history professor. "It didn't necessarily change me, I wasn't interested in not speaking well or quitting the violin, but I did fall in love with hiphop that next year." That gave her a bridge into contemporary Black culture. "Loving hiphop gave me something to identify with and a sense that I could go be with my cousins in Philly in an all-Black environment and know how to blend in. I always wanted to not feel cut off from what was an urban Black experience, so I chose that. That was a conscious engagement."

Barry Michael Cooper was a ninth grader in Harlem when the authenticity police came for him. "I remember getting off of the bus," he said, "and a guy was asking me something and he said, 'You sound just like a fucking white boy when you talk.' I said, 'What?' He was a scramblin' kid, a drug kid, so I couldn't tell him I'm reading Richard Wright's *Black Boy*. I couldn't tell him that I just read *Invisible Man*. I can't tell him none of that because I don't want to stand out like a sore thumb.

And from that moment on I said I can't sound like that. I can't do that cause I stick out like a sore thumb. And I fell into the shadows. Maybe a year or two later I started getting high. I was getting cheeba'ed up [smoking weed]. I started sniffing coke, all of that. I said, 'Man, they're not gonna put me on front street. I gotta fit in.'"

When the artist Rashid Johnson was in graduate school a white fellow student told him, "You know, man, your work just doesn't scare me so I just don't think it's really about identity and race because I'm not scared. You didn't hurt me or offend me." So the expectation of being frightened or unhinged by Blackness was so deeply ingrained in that white man that when he didn't get that response from Johnson's work he concluded the work was dishonest. He wasn't painting Black enough. "I was so fucking flabbergasted by that," Johnson said. "It just blew me away that my goal, if I was ever to discuss race in my work, was that I had to scare white folks."

The accusation of not being Black enough is impactful and damaging and can spark an epiphany, sending people plunging into themselves to question who they are and what they value and often lead them to change. It is painful to be called not Black or acting white and is not always easy to repel. It surely changed my life to be called not Black, as it changed Kelley and Cooper and many others. That's why psychologist Dr. Angela Neal-Barnett of Kent State has spent years studying the "acting white" accusation.

Focus groups told Dr. Neal-Barnett that examples of behavior that led to the accusation include speaking standard English, dressing in clothes from The Gap or Abercrombie & Fitch or other preppy brands, wearing shorts in the winter, listening to white music, or one of the most crucial, sitting at lunch tables with non-Blacks. You see there an assault on symbols of abandoning the group mentality: If you don't talk like us, don't dress like us, don't listen to the music we worship, or fail to sit with us during free moments then you are taking steps away from the herd and for that you will be harshly censured. It's bad enough that attempting to cultivate an independent personality will be attacked but somehow the idea is also spread that mental development is not Black. A nightmare meme. But Dr. Neal-Barnett said students reported: "People around me say because I'm in honors courses, I don't act my race," and "I get talked about because I go to class every day" and "Kids look at me differently because I want to go to college," and "My peers say I study too much and that I am always in the library," and "My peers criticize me because I try to use big words," and "Kids look at me differently because I want to make something of myself." Black kids are telling each other it's antithetical to Blackness to try to develop your mind. And on top of that, they're socially penalizing those who do.

Several researchers have shown the "acting white" accusation can lead to academic underachievement because many Black students will choose not being ostracized, and not having to hear they're acting white, instead of doing the work it takes to excel in the classroom. A 2006 study by Roland Fryer and Paul Torelli, both at Harvard's economics department, found that if you rank students by GPA, Blacks with GPAs above 3.5 become less popular as you go up the GPA scale while white students gain in popularity as their grades increase. Fryer and Torelli found a Black student who gets a 4.0 has, on average, 1.5 fewer Black friends than a white student with a 4.0 has white friends. So white students at the top of the grade pyramid are popular and respected while Black students up there are not and are lashed with perhaps the most painful Black pejorative there is—thus doubly punishing Black students for being academically successful. So many Black students are faced with the choice of either getting good grades or being accepted by their Black peers—they cannot have both. And the better grades they get the more shunned they'll be. That's an alarming communal dysfunction. It's a horrible choice to give to a teenager because for them popularity is of paramount importance. And what does it say about us that we're spreading an anti-intellectual, self-sabotaging message that being Black means doing those things that'll ensure lesser grades, while doing things necessary to be successful in school is to be white? Since when is brilliance antithetical to Blackness? Slaves who risked their lives to learn how to read are surely turning over in their graves about this.

Some kids who are accused of acting white don't change their personalities or their approach to academics, but some adolescents become so distressed that they make significant changes in an effort to be more like other Black kids. This is beyond frightening. Our children are making it more difficult for each other to improve themselves and aligning Blackness with intellectual mediocrity. Why? What's the psychological underpinning of the "acting white" accusation?

Dr. Neal-Barnett said slaves who were seen as acting white could command more on the auction block. So the acting white accusation started as a way of saying: Don't be what white people want you to be. Being of greater value to them was of no value to us. But now when the fruits of America are much more available to us, and mastering the King's English and developing your mind can bring tremendous economic benefits, the "acting white" accusation seems to be part of the crabs-in-a-barrel phenomenon. "The 'acting white' accusation is to put people in their place," Dr. Neal-Barnett said. "To make them remember. To make them come back over to the Black side. I was half expecting to find it was about throwing people out of the Black race but in people's minds it is not. I haven't found anyone who wants to throw people out of the Black race. It's trying to bring them back in." Bring them back in or bring them back down?

In a community that feels under siege it can seem crucial to keep all your soldiers together and not let people stray and so markers of staying with the herd become very important. "When you're walking down the street," Dr. Neal-Barnett said, "and you see another Black person you know how they give you the nod?" I do. I was very young when my father taught me that we should in some way acknowledge all the Black men we pass on the street and encounter in rooms—a nod, a wave, a smile, a hello, a whass happenin', something. To this day I still do the nod and most Black men I pass on the street do, too. Those few Black men who do not nod, who walk past without giving any sort of recognition, I judge to be a little strange. In college the nod was a crucial part of community membership and if you failed to wave at another Black person you passed you would be eviscerated at the Black table in the cafeteria. Not acknowledging them in some way was a major social felony. And if you had been walking with white students when you failed to wave—suggesting you were perhaps embarrassed about your Black friends while talking to whites—well, then, there'd be hell to pay. The nod is crucial. "That nod," Dr. Neal-Barnett said, "is saying, 'We're all in this together, you're part of my kinship, you're part of my network, we're all Black people together.' And so when people are perceived as not recognizing what is called in the literature the 'fictive kinship,' it makes them suspect."

Dr. Neal-Barnett said some kids who are hit with the "acting white" assertion are sent into a sort of personality tailspin, change who they are, and fall into what she called the Acting White Trap. In this adolescents will explore overt expressions of Blackness that may or may not reflect their true beliefs, but they do it because they feel forced to pile on the Black tropes in order to fit in. But other kids are able to let the assertion roll off their backs and do not allow it to change them. What's the difference between them? The answer may lie in how they were raised to think about race and what their parents' approach to race was. Dr. Beverly Tatum, the president of Spelman, is a psychologist who spent twenty years studying racial identity development among Blacks who grew up in predominantly white communities. She is the author of several books about race including *Why Are All the Black Kids Sitting Together in the Cafeteria?* She found most Black parents raising children in overwhelmingly white environments fall into one of three strategies for teaching their kids about race and racial identity: "race-conscious," "race-avoidant," or "race-neutral." Race-conscious families talk about race a lot and are active in building a social network for their kids to interact with other Blacks—church, sports, Jack and Jill, or visits with members of the extended family, which, for Blacks, often means going down South. Race-avoidant families are silent about race, they just don't talk about it, leaving kids on their own to figure it all out. Race-neutral families feel it's important to have a Black social network but don't know how to create one, and may give their kids more information about race and Black identity than a race-avoidant family would but a fraction of the knowledge that kids in a race-conscious family will get. It seems that some people think race will dissipate if you don't discuss it but it's more like the weather, constantly impacting your life no matter what you do, even though sometimes you're able to stop consciously noticing it for brief stretches of time. "I sometimes use the analogy of sex education," Dr. Tatum said. "If you don't talk about it, they're still gonna get information but it may not be the information you want them to have."

These strategies had a direct and predictable impact that manifested when the kids became adults. "All of them described racial incidents of one kind or another occurring at the college level," Dr. Tatum said. "But the ones who had grown up in a race-conscious way could recognize other people's nonsense and call it that. As opposed to those who had grown up in race-avoidant families, who were more likely to internalize in a kind of depressed or sad way when they encountered other people's nonsense." The nonsense includes not just racism or negativity from whites but the "acting white" accusation from Blacks. People who grow up in race-conscious homes seem to have a better sense of self and of race that allows them to not be devastated by the assertion, while those who grow up on the other end of the spectrum are more vulnerable to having their sense of self crushed.

I grew up in an otherwise all-white neighborhood but in a race-conscious home. We talked openly about race and racism. My parents weaved what it meant to be Black into our daily lives, pointed out Black stars we be could proud of, and weren't quiet when they noticed racism. I can recall walking out of more than one restaurant because my mother was offended that we'd been seated in a location she considered demeaning. I can also recall her beaming whenever Ed Bradley and Philip Michael Thomas came on TV. And if we went to a movie where the first person to die was Black, Mom was quick to say, "Why'd they have to kill off the Blacks?" We had Ernie Barnes prints on the walls and Romare Bearden monographs on the coffee table. My parents had cookouts where I talked to Black architects, lawyers, and artists. We were encouraged to read Toni Morrison and Ralph Ellison and watched "The Cosby Show" as a family. Our home away from home was a Black tennis club in the 'hood. All this gave me a strong sense of what it meant to be a Black person and a vision of Blackness that included the 'hood mores but also saw Blackness as much more than that. As a teenager and an emerging adult I had a slew of messages coming at me—I had spent all my life in an overwhelmingly white school and neighborhood—and was as confused as anyone my age about who I was. When I was assaulted with the "acting white" accusation—when he said, "You ain't Black!"—it sparked an epiphany and sent me inside, questioning who I was, but I was ultimately able to look in the mirror and like what I saw. I knew that I was indeed Black and could repel his attack because I had already spent years being conscious of what it meant to be Black. I had grown up spending so much time in white environments that I did not radiate all the tropes of coolness that signified Blackness to my attacker but I had a clear sense that Blackness was more than just what the 'hood said it was. So after he rocked my world I was able to re-center myself and re-focus myself on what I thought about race. "I think as people get more secure in who they are," Dr. Tatum said, "and their definition of quote 'Blackness' expands, you see a much more self-confident, internalized definition that is not so dependent on external views." The more at ease you are about Blackness the more you can define it for yourself.

Dr. Neal-Barnett says skin color has no impact on the "acting white" accusation but we know it has a massive impact on Black lives. The way we are perceived by both whites and Blacks is partly shaped by skin color and the stereotypical perceptions assigned to our hues. Michael Eric Dyson and his brother, Everett, share a mother but not a father. They grew up together in the same home. Michael is light skinned, Everett is dark skinned. That's not the only factor that determined how their lives would turn out, but it is a major one. "I saw the different treatment accorded to him," Dyson said. "I saw how people assumed certain things about him: a behemoth, a brute, a person who was incapable of intelligence. I saw the treatment he got and I saw the relative favor that I received as a result of being light skinned. The assumption of intelligence, then, reinforced their willingness to work with me and to make sure that my gifts were realized and supported, whereas other people were cast aside. I saw that very early. Not only from white people but from Black people especially. Especially. Valorizing me, celebrating me, I know damn well the way I looked got me into certain circles, gained me acceptance." Dyson constantly got the extra helping hand adults give to a promising child and the gifts of "light-skin-ness" accumulated, helping to shape him into one of the premier scholars of his generation. Meanwhile, his brother got entirely different expectations from society and ended up far away from where Dyson did. "I've gotten tremendous privilege from being light skinned," Dyson said. "My brother is in prison. Been there for twenty-one years. I'm not blaming his being in prison on being a dark-skinned man, I'm saying that the trajectory of his life was certainly curtailed and shaped by his dark skin and the relative treatment he got, the failure to identify his talents early on."

Race is far more than the color of your skin but color still matters. America remains colorstruck—Black America definitely remains colorstruck—because the aesthetics of white supremacy are so deeply embedded in so many of us. Dr. Alvin Poussaint of Harvard said, "I think that darker-skinned Black people are more likely to be victims of a lot of color prejudice and even rejection within the Black community and even sometimes rejections within the Black family. I have seen some Black families where there was a lighter-skinned child who was rejected because parents would feel the light-skinned kid was going to have an easier time in society and the darker-skinned kid would have a harder time so they'd show favoritism toward the darker-skinned kid." So they're being almost pitied in their own home. That same overcompensation happened to Professor Farah Griffin of Columbia. "I grew up as a dark-skinned child in the context of my family and I think my family overdid it because they expected that I would have challenges, so my family always talked about how beautiful I was and that I was this little queen. Then I remember when I first started getting friends and peers. Kids will tease you about everything, but the thing that I got teased about was being dark-skinned and it was painful. I remember thinking that Black and ugly was one word. My father would say to me, 'Oh that's just because our people have been blinded to their own beauty and one day, when the revolution comes, everybody's going to see how beautiful you are and they're going to throw roses at your feet.' So I had this sense of self that was like, 'Man, I was born at the wrong time.'

"I remember," Professor Griffin continued, "someone saying that one of Clarence Thomas's issues was that he was hazed about being dark and that was some of the issue that he had with Black people and I remember thinking, 'Well, then I have reason to hate Black people.' And I really did think, 'Why don't I?'" Her family had to spend extra time and energy telling her that dark skin could also be beautiful, as if she were an aesthetic special education student who needed extra classes to build her self-esteem in preparation for a world filled with Black people who would spit on her. But such is the lot for many dark-skinned Blacks. "The harshest racism that I've ever experienced in my life," said the poet Saul Williams, "has come from the hands of other Black people."

Growing up, Williams dealt with a lot of pain from constant jabs about being dark skinned. "I'm not talking about white kids," he said. "I'm talking about Black kids calling me frying-pan black and telling me, 'You better date a really light girl or your kids are gonna be invisible.' I knew every dark-skinned joke by the time I was fourteen." He said his mother gave him ammunition in the form of retorts like "The blacker the berry, the sweeter the juice." He would also tell kids, "So you're over here bragging about the fact that your great-grandparents were raped by their slave masters?" But these retorts did not always work out well. "One day a good friend of mine and I were playing the dozens and he teased me about being dark. I just laughed it off and said, 'Ah, man, the blacker the berry the sweeter the juice,' and he comes back and says, right on time, 'Yeah, but nobody wants diabetes.'"

Williams's self-esteem took a beating. "I didn't feel beautiful," he said. "I remained extremely insecure about myself." This impacted almost every aspect of his life. "I got so paranoid about it that I would walk into a room and see people whispering and automatically assume that they were whispering about me. It made me feel like my life and experience would be a little better if I were a little lighter." So Williams decided to do something about it.

As a teenager, for years he used part of his allowance to buy a bleach-

163

ing cream from Ambi and applied it every day before school. "It looked like Michael Jackson was doing it at the time so it was something I didn't even question in myself at the time," he said. "I was completely oblivious to what I was doing. It just became a quick part of my morning ritual." These are not self-hatreds brought on by white people but by Blacks. You could say Blacks are actually acting like ventriloquist's dummies, repeating the deeply baked-in attitudes of white supremacy, but I don't know if that makes things any better.

I asked all of my dark-skinned interviewees if they could name any advantage to being dark. They all either said no or struggled to come up with something. Photographer Dwayne Rodgers said, "You get fetishized." Major Jackson said, "There's a particular kind of virility and masculinity that we attach to the brother who's appearance feels closer to Africa. I would even go so far as to say that there's an authenticity that we somehow project upon people who are darker." Farah Griffin said that as an adult she "became exoticized in a white world and my color was celebrated in weird ways." She also said, "Certain groups of Black women are willing to give me a hearing because I am dark skinned, because they don't think that I have been given privilege because of skin color. So there's a certain way that it authenticates me with some Black people, so in that way I guess that, you know, that's been an advantage." Saul Williams said, "There's a certain amount of privilege that comes with being dark and articulate, if you want to be real." What's the privilege? "You get to witness the shock on people's faces when you open your mouth."

Williams said that in recent years he has felt a move away from the perception of dark skinned as ugly and he cited the perceived sexiness of Michael Jordan, Wesley Snipes, Big Daddy Kane, and the actor Djimon Hounsou as normalizing the idea that dark is attractive, making him feel better about his color. He said, "I went from being 'kind of cute to be so dark' to being beautiful and, to some Black people, exotic." Again, that word "exotic." It seems like a backhanded compliment.

When I asked light-skinned people if there was an advantage in being lighter they had one of two responses. They either hemmed and hawed in a way that admitted they knew it was socially inappropriate to discuss the advantages of light skin, similar to the way it is to talk about being born into money, or they began listing the many advantages. "I am a light-skinned, pretty Black girl, so my experience is everybody loved me," said Professor Melissa Harris-Perry. She said the assumptions about light-skin-ness went beyond intelligence and into an expectation of being attractive, well behaved, and from a good family. "Mariah Carey talks about how hard it was to be gorgeous and light skinned," Professor Harris-Perry said, "and I'm like, 'Really? Life was hard? You gotta be fucking kidding me.' I mean, my experience was that I basically benefited from light-skinned privilege within Black communities that said that I was essentially valuable because I was yella and I benefited from light-skinned privilege within white communities that said, 'Thank God you are well spoken, well educated, and light skinned because now you can be our Black friend and not scare us.' I gotta say, I lived in a cocoon of naiveté and privilege for the most part. Not economic privilege, but really of social privilege.

"I can even," Harris-Perry continued, "ramp up or down my light-skinned privilege depending on whether I'm wearing a perm or braids. Or whether I'm wearing my hair long or short or coloring it or not. There's all kinds of weird things you can do, like the whiter you can make yourself the more likely, for example, they'll put you on television. The privileges of light-skin-ness are real and tangible and they're tangible within the community, maybe even more so within the community than outside of it."

We have swallowed the lessons of white supremacy whole. The psychological weapons that have been used against us are inside us and coming out of our own mouths. We don't ostensibly hate Blackness but we aid white supremacy by valuing light skin over dark—lionizing a visual likeness to whiteness—and also by punishing those who think of building themselves and their minds into forces that could help us succeed in America. I cringe to think what could've happened if teenage Barry Obama had let some Black classmates tug him down and away from the path that would lead to Harvard Law School and the Oval Office. Several people said Obama's unusually high senses of esteem and efficacy could perhaps stem from having grown up in a white household where it was conveyed to him that the sky's the limit. We've got to give all our children the same freedom to develop their minds and chase their dreams that Obama had.

There is too much self-hatred baked into too many of the messages we send each other. We are witlessly operating the machinery perpetuating our own oppression. It's as if we've been in prison so long we're guarding ourselves and telling each other it's wrong to leave.

If words were people, nigga would be a celebrity. A hugely famous and infamous man. English doesn't view words as gendered, but many languages do and nigga's definitely masculine given his aggression, his cockiness, his obsession with obscenity, his love of shocking others. Nigga would have presence and radiance and a big reputation preceding him. He knows how powerful and frightening he is so he has a badass walk like Shaft and when he enters a room or a sentence he easily dominates it. Nigga would be like Michael Corleone in *The Godfather* saga: a criminal who says he's trying to go straight but is having a hard time separating himself from his history. He says he's trying to change, to spread love instead of hate, but no one will let him forget his nefarious past and secretly, he doesn't want them to forget because his wicked past is what supersizes him.

Nigga has been a seminal word for the hiphop generation, which has used nigga in the way Richard Pryor showed us. Paul Mooney, who worked and partied with Pryor, said the two of them loved to say nigga because it stripped the word of power while simultaneously giving them power. "It was like having a bomb and we were diffusing it," Mooney said of himself and Pryor. "A very dangerous bomb. But we said, 'We're going to take this bomb, they tried to blow us up with this bomb, and we're going to fix these motherfuckers. We'll be using this bomb. We'll be in your face with this motherfucker. We're going to make you eat this motherfucking bomb. It's not going to control us, we're going to control it.'"

You may understand why nigga has felt so right for so many in the hiphop generation when you remember that the hiphop generation is also called by many the crack generation, putting an ominous but accurate bow on it. In the eighties, the defining force in many Black lives was the impact of crack, whether it was families ripped apart, or people lost for decades in the prison system, or the crack millionaires who set the standard for materialistic desires and violent tendencies. Questlove believes crack is a big reason why hiphop developed into the shape that it took. "It's blasphemy to say this," he says, "but crack is responsible for the hiphop movement. It's a direct result. Hiphop is created thanks to the conditions that crack set: easy money but a lot of work, the violence involved, the stories it produced—crack helped birth hiphop. It injected startup money. Crack brought a lot of money to the inner-city youth who didn't go to college. Which enabled them to become businessmen. Half the narratives of hiphop would've been erased, the street cred, the danger, so hiphop would've been more of a jazz thing with virtuoso rhyming and it could've easily faded away." With such a rugged, violent, psychotic, chaotic, and apocalyptic backdrop to our lives it's no wonder we chose to take ownership of a self-appellation that's synonymous with monster.

For over fifteen years I relished using nigga whenever it fit—to my parents' dismay. I can't remember the first time I used the word but I know I was in my early twenties when it was in almost every hiphop song and it seemed every Black man around me was using it. Some think Black people say nigga blithely and uncritically, just following the thing their peers are doing, and for many that's true. Talib Kweli, the acclaimed Brooklyn MC, said, "When I first used nigga, I used it to fit in. I grew up being taught it was a bad word with negative connotations—I grew up with all the knowledge I needed. But to me, it was hard to juxtapose that with the fact that the dudes on the street were using it in such an endearing way. A teacher or parent or someone on TV could tell you 'till they're blue in the face that it's wrong to use the word nigga, but if the ones using that word are the ones who got your back, all that other stuff doesn't mean anything."

But I never used nigga nonchalantly. It's deep with history, weight, and controversy, and I could feel all that when I said it. Each time I used it I was thumbing my nose at a taboo and as a Black man that felt right—being a Black man sometimes feels like being a walking taboo so I have a certain sympathy for nigga, as if we have a lot in common. It's an outlaw word, an electric word—you can almost feel the charge when you say nigga at the right moment, as if the word were giving you and your listeners a tangible shock. When I said it I felt rebellious and badass and connected to the Black men of my generation. I felt like I was giving a linguistic middle finger to a system that doesn't love me. I felt like I was holding Massa's wretched flag and waving it around—we captured your flag. It's our word now, as if nigga were a parcel of linguistic real estate that we'd invaded.

Everyone in my generation does not use nigga as a political tool, but it is one because we've used it so publicly—rhymed in songs and shouted on subway platforms. In forcing nigga out of closed circles and into public spaces we've carved it into a political tool. There's a certain gallows humor in our embrace of the biggest anti-Black epithet—we're having a laugh about our status. We're acknowledging that we know the country sees us as monsters and even though we think that's ridiculous, we see there's power in owning monster status. Dwayne Rodgers said, "I think it's about an embracing of a shared underdog status. But an underdog status that's been ascribed major cool points in the world. We're underfoot but we're the coolest motherfuckers out at the same time." At a deep level I think Black men enjoy our power to scare white America and find it fun to use. "Some kids think playing the role of the monster is a profitable game," says Reggie Hudlin. "So they say, 'I'm not gonna fight the stereotype, I'm gonna exploit it.'" We're also rejecting a fear of the white gaze. It seems my generation very much wants to be on the subway—a public space where races and classes are squeezed together— shouting nigga because that seems to prove we're unconcerned with the white gaze. Writer and filmmaker dream hampton has spent years living in Martha's Vineyard with few Blacks around and finds saying nigga to be very liberating out there in that white world. "There are times when

I'm in the Vineyard," she said, "and I'm totally rebelling against their politeness and their manners. It's not just to shock, it's a tool of resistance to their bullshit."

We also tell ourselves we're reclaiming nigga, but are we? No matter what our overuse is doing to nigga, nothing could ever blunt its power when someone white or Black spits nigger with venom. "It still carries force," Dwayne Rodgers said. "If you're being knocked on the skull and someone's calling you nigger simultaneously, then you have a clear indication as to why you're being knocked on the skull." As much as I love the feeling that using nigga is subversive, I wonder if we're truly subverting anything or if we're just playing with a loaded gun.

Some people think hiphop or Richard Pryor gave birth to the modern, affirmative, subversive usage of nigga, but Blacks used nigga as a closed-circle, in-group word as far back as the fifties and sixties. Nelson George says, "I was a little kid in the sixties and I heard it in barbershops, everywhere. Nigga was always used. People wouldn't say, 'You my nigga,' but they'd say, 'Nigga, please.' That was definitely around. And 'Nigga, what?' Those kind of phraseologies. Nigga was a very typical word used among Black men in social situations. I heard it all the time." Stanley Crouch was a teenager in Watts in the sixties and says the word was widely used then but the crucial difference is that it was used much more carefully. Crouch says, "I came up in a period when nigga wasn't public property and it wasn't something you used around people who weren't Black. Culture wasn't as ethnically porous in earlier periods as it is today. There were things Black people just wouldn't say to or around white people. That just wasn't done." The lack of care that my generation takes with the word, our using it publicly and in mixed company, is in large part what rankles the older generation. "My issue isn't the use of the word," Harry Allen said. "My issue is not using it scientifically. If Blacks used it to draw attention to both the white supremacist system and our victim status, I would completely approve of that use. But we use it playfully, which either blunts its force or misdirects attention to its counter-racist meaning. To me the issue is less that we use it than that we use it in this playful kind of way. I don't have a problem with people

169

working with benzene, I just don't want people playing with benzene." Benzene is a highly flammable liquid that can kill.

Many from that older generation continue to use nigga as a closed-circle word even while schooling the younger generation on morality. Stanley Crouch surprised me by admitting that even though he's often lecturing the younger generation on its moral failing in its overuse of nigga, he occasionally uses nigga in conversation. Perhaps more surprisingly, several people said they've heard the ultimate Black moral authority, the Reverend Jesse Jackson, using nigga. Someone who asked to remain anonymous told me, "Jesse uses it all the time. I was at a Congressional Black Caucus event in the mid-eighties when Jesse ran for president, during the whole thing with Hymietown. Jesse turns to me and says, 'We gotta get them niggas in New York motivated.' I was like, 'Holy shit, did he just say the n-word to me like that?' I know other people who've been in the Reverend's company and it flows off his lips pretty easily." I saw that when I interviewed him. After the tape recorder went off, he said nigga in two or three sentences—in the classic colloquial way, i.e., with affection, not as a condemnation. When I asked him why he did that he initially said he hadn't said it. I think it had flowed out so easily he hadn't noticed he'd said it. I gently pressed him on it and he said, "It's like we know fried chicken is wrong but we eat it a little anyway. Look, it's unacceptable. It's wrong. Even those who rationalize it as affectionate or endearment, it must be resisted. But addictions are deep. Sometimes unlearning bad habits that were taught well is difficult."

Dr. King also said it. "Martin used it," Cornel West said. "The day he died, he saw Andrew [Young] and said, 'There's my nigga.' It's part of the Black preacher's culture. That's where Jesse gets it from. Now, Martin was a sterling figure as a citizen, the greatest lover and freedom fighter—cat's willing to die for us any minute. If you love negroes as much as he did, I guess he can call us anything he want because the love is still there, you know."

The key difference between the way the older generation employs the word and the way mine does, according to many in that older group, is that we do it publicly and wantonly and with a flair that suggests nigga is part of how we're marketing modern Blackness, saying, 'Hey, y'all, we still got that badass, seditious edge.' Reverend Jackson said, "We never tried to commercialize it like it was armor."

Nigga turned a corner and went from in-group word to mainstream thanks to Dick Gregory, whose 1964 autobiography was titled *nigger*; and comedian Redd Foxx; and poet LeRoi Jones (who later changed his name to Amiri Baraka); and the Black Panthers; and Pryor. "*That Nigger's Crazy* [Pryor's seminal 1974 album] was a revolution," says Larry Wilmore, an Emmy-winning TV producer and writer who plays the Black Correspondent on "The Daily Show with Jon Stewart." "People used to say stuff like nigga but Richard Pryor took it to a whole new level. He made it so it was okay for us to laugh at it in public." Pryor and the others said nigga in public spaces and in mixed company, which showed off the word's shock value. My generation, hungry to give the middle finger to the white gaze, jumped on Pryor's example and used nigga in public spaces with enthusiasm—from albums to street corners. We were pushing past the limits of political correctness, reveling in the power to shock that comes from using the taboo pejorative in public, enjoying the subversive thrill of feeling we'd captured the enemy's machete and could now flaunt it, and waving race and racism in people's faces like a Jewish person walking through the streets yelling, "Auschwitz! Auschwitz!" Nigga says, "I don't care what you think, I don't care if I'm making you uncomfortable, I don't care about you. And we're not just attacking the white gaze, we're turning our back on America."

Black people have long had those and far more nihilistic feelings toward America. We resent the hypocrisy of America, promising liberty and justice to all, and not delivering for us. We're bitter about our history—from slavery and Dred Scott to modern atrocities like the murders of Sean Bell and Amadou Diallo and the insanity of post-Katrina New Orleans—as well as the tragedies in our lives. The times we were racially profiled or unjustly attacked by cops. The jobs we didn't get or the promotions we lost to people less qualified than we were. The loans we didn't get to nudge our lives upward that someone with lesser qualifications snagged. "White people have done some really fucked-up shit," said Santigold, "it's had a permanent imprint on our psyche. It's permanent damage. So the reaction to that is being like, 'Fuck them.'" We know in our heart the country hasn't been good to us in many ways and on many levels. We know that if America were razed and the whole thing rebuilt from scratch, we couldn't end up with a position any lower than what we've had. So screw it all. It's a word that seeks to remind everyone of our divisions—it's anti-communal and anti-progress. Where brother and sister were attempts to build connections and community and reassert the familial nature of Black Americans, nigga is interested in none of that. "Nigga is a word Black males use," Harry Allen said, "as a way of affirming mutual low status under the system of white supremacy."

The night Obama was elected I did some soul-searching because the election told me I didn't know my country as well as I thought I did. Knowing that millions of Americans would trust a Black man to lead this country forced me to reevaluate America. Rashid Johnson said, "I was very proud of Barack. But I wasn't proud for Black people—I was kind of proud for white people." For so long I've felt unloved by the country that views Black men as fascinating and frightening but I remember walking home the night of the election feeling numb, on a surreal high, hearing people yell out in joy from several blocks away—"Bah-rock Oooo-bama!" The ancient, seemingly impossible dream of a Black president had finally come true and I felt as though I was walking through an entirely new country, one that I hadn't previously known existed. If this was a new country then I had to be a new man. I had to change in response to the country I was now living in. And I thought, Does nigga fit the Zeitgeist of the country anymore? How can I continue giving the linguistic middle-finger to the country and approach America as if it hates us when America picked a progressive brother who fist-bumps his wife to be president?

The night of the election, as the streets were filled with people partying like it was New Year's, my heart pounded at the dawn of an unthinkable moment and I tried to drink in every second of this new reality. That night my son, then eleven months old, woke up around one a.m., as if he could feel the ground shaking beneath us all. I peeled myself away from the television and held him in his dark room, thinking of how this loving gesture from America would change his future. How he would not grow up feeling as though America has a presidential glass ceiling. And it wasn't just Obama. Other Black successes in politics, business, finance, and a slew of fields that have nothing to do with entertainment or sports proved that more Black people than ever are reaching higher levels of achievement and status—the ceiling is not only getting higher, it's also getting wider, so the potential for success is greater than ever. That's the America my boy will grow up in. And there, holding my boy while the world partied, I said, "I need to stop calling myself and my brothers nigga. It no longer fits. It's no longer accurate. I want language that seeks communion, that stretches toward progress, that honors the maturity of a nation that would have a Black man as its leader." Greg Tate sees Obama inspiring many Blacks to reconsider everything. "His presidency is the most radical experiment in Blackness of our time. We don't know how it's gonna play out but he's definitely a game-changer. We haven't seen anyone so define how Black people are gonna think about themselves since King. You really got to be in almost like some deep Buddhist state of mind to be able to wrap your head around the totality of Barack Obama's Blackness and what it implies for us."

Now I see nigga as an old toxic friend I need to distance myself from. He's an enabler and he's not leading me down a good path. I need to stop getting high with him on the cheap narcotic he's always got plenty of: rebelliousness. I need to leave nigga alone and spend more time with a word that's about empowerment, love, freedom, and the American way: post-Black.

Postscript: While researching the history of nigger/nigga I stumbled onto the history of the word motherfucker. There's confusion on the word's etymology but the word seems to come from Black American English, popularized by Black World War II soldiers and originating in slavery. I found citations of it in Texas court records from 1889. Motherfucker, many say, is the word slaves used to refer to masters who impregnated slave women. "Motherfucker" was used in lieu of father. They linguistically reduced master from the import imbued by "father" to a literal, scientific description of an action.

I recall distinctly the first time I consciously thought about motherfucker: I was in the seventh grade walking through school and I felt that meaning. I thought, "I bet that's what slaves thought about masters." I just knew it. It was as if the word were a bottle with a message inside it tossed from a deserted island and found centuries later.

I pushed the meaning I felt into a drawer in my mind and used the word anyway, because it seemed badass. I mean, Richard Pryor loved it so it must be cool. But then I found research seconding what I had felt, and I became unbearably conscious of the fact that the history of slavery was baked into the word and suddenly I could hear inside the word the sounds of unwanted incidents happening in the crevices of plantations. And I had to stop using that word, too.

# Chapter 7

# How to Build More Baracks

I am told that Robert Reffkin, age thirty, wants to be the mayor of New York City. "He's plotting to run for mayor of New York in 2017," said Columbia political science professor Dorian Warren. "He's climbing, he's picking 2017, that's on his mind every day." Reffkin, of course, denies this. Smart politicians never show their hand early.

Reffkin grew up in Berkeley, California, raised by his mom. He joined A Better Chance, which led him to Columbia University and then Columbia Business School. He's now a Wall Street millionaire with lots of moneyed friends and is the founder of the Bronx Success Academy charter school and New York Needs You, a career mentorship program for first-generation college students. He's raised a million dollars for A Better Chance and other youth education programs by running fifty marathons, one in each state in America. "He has the same drive that I think a young Barack Obama did," says Warren, who's friends with Reffkin. "This guy, he's so careful and strategic about every single thing he does in his life."

There are surely many others like Reffkin in America—young Blacks with an eye on political office. How will they need to campaign and to carry themselves in order to make their dream come true? Years away from an election it's unknowable what issues will matter most to voters, but identity and character are crucial in every election and in the post-Black era there's a playbook developing for how Black candidates can

175

get elected to major offices. Where some Black politicians of previous eras seemed to run by presenting themselves as part of redressing racial wrongs of the past, modern Black politicians tread lighter. They wield Blackness far differently. They don't discuss race or racial history, or don't discuss it until forced to, and above all try not to use race in ways that will make white voters feel guilty about the past—they want their Blackness to help voters feel hopeful about the future.

During Obama's presidential campaign you could see a self-congratulatory glee in many of his white supporters: they were proud of themselves for being so far beyond racism that they could support a Black man for president and proud of their nation for being open-minded about having a Black man lead. Campaigning for Obama threw some whites into unsettling conversations with other whites who unveiled racist attitudes while Obama supporters got to be on the right side of things. This was a far different vibe than when Reverend Jackson ran for president in 1984 and 1988, when tropes in his self-presentation reminded whites of the guilt they felt about the past. He seemed to be the president whom Blacks were owed for our suffering. Obama was the president whom America, in its multiracial glory, had created. He was someone you could vote for as a sign of a better racial future, indeed someone who some whites saw as a harbinger of the end of racism or at least the first light at the end of the tunnel. Blacks knew he was neither, but racial pride and the thrill of breaking the highest glass ceiling helped lead us to vote for him almost unanimously. So Obama and his campaign staff were successful at shaping his race as one of the reasons for whites and Blacks to vote for him by employing hope for the future rather than guilt about the past. Governor Paterson told me, "I think the pain argument or the guilt argument has worn off and now you're going to have to show that you're the best person. And by the way, I don't know that pain and guilt got too many people elected in the first place." Even Reverend Sharpton, who is a polarizing, Rorschach test sort of candidate, stresses the importance of campaigning as a candidate for everyone. "If you have an inclusive style then it's easier to sell that message," Sharpton told me. "If you don't have an inclusive style then you may not be able to sell that message. If you're trying to gain the favor of everybody you've gotta appeal to everybody. You can't expand the base with a limited message." Sharpton said his counsel to a young Black political aspirant would be: "Don't wear race as a badge but don't put it in your pocket, either. Stand up for what is right for everybody. But at the same time remember you're not running to represent the Black community, you're running to represent everybody." Before the election of President Obama we saw Massachusetts governor Deval Patrick, Tennessee congressman Harold Ford Jr., Alabama congressman Artur Davis, Newark mayor Cory Booker, and others portray themselves not as Black politicians but politicians who happen to be Black but can and will represent—and should be voted for by—everyone. "I never thought of myself as a Black candidate," Ford told me. "I thought of my experiences as a Black as being additive in huge ways, but not as a defining thing." But what exactly are these politicians doing to transmit that in front of the white voters who will ultimately determine whether or not they are elected?

The real campaign begins many years before the official race starts by creating a network of moneyed friends who can help build a war chest and the high-powered relationships necessary to get someone into office. These are almost always started at elite colleges and graduate programs. It's not necessary to go to an ivy league school to get elected to a major office, but being Black is never an electoral advantage so having the sort of powerful network behind you that can only be built at the big name-brand schools is an extraordinary counterbalance, asset, and resource. It's no coincidence that Obama, Patrick, and Davis all went to Harvard Law School and Booker to Yale Law School. Reffkin's educational resume, double Columbia, definitely puts him in the ballgame. (Harold Ford went to an ivy for undergrad, the University of Pennsylvania, and to a prestigious law school, the University of Michigan Law, but he was the son of a longtime congressman so was born into a network that others must go to school to acquire.)

Part of what happens for Blacks at these elite schools is learning to become extremely comfortable with white people and with being one of very few Blacks in the room. The more a Black person can learn to put the whites around them at ease, and also to feel comfortable doing so, the more powerful they can become. And, perhaps more important, the more love a Black person can find for whites—in specific and in general—the further up the ladder he or she can climb. Politicians can seem like a selfish, cold-hearted, egotistical bunch, but in order to get elected to major office you must convince people that you really care about them and will take care of them and will fight for them and on some level that you love them. We're obviously not talking about some sense of preferring whites to Blacks but rather ascribing to them the same sense of humanity, respect, and trustworthiness that Blacks extend to those we think of as brothers and sisters. Some Black politicians are better positioned than others to find real love for whites in their heart. "I think Barack and Cory Booker and Harold Ford actually do love white people, like in a very specific and personal way," said Professor Harris-Perry. "Part of the evil that is racial difference and racial division in this country is that so many of us live in and grew up in worlds where the racial other was truly the other, someone we just didn't know in any kind of intimate way. And even though you may not hold strong stereotypes or negative opinions, you also don't hold any particularly strong emotional affective attachment. Many Black people I know would be perfectly happy if they literally never saw another white person. They don't lynch them but they really could not care less. But part of what happens for people like Booker and Ford and Patrick is that because of the intimacy of their familial or romantic or school relationships, there's a recognition of the humanity of white people that makes them more attached to them. So it's genuine and it works, or is convincing, because it is in fact true. It's not strategic: They actually see their family there."

Black people who can make the leap to loving and trusting white people as confidantes, friends, neighbors, and a general populace, and to feeling comfortable being loved by them, have far more ability to climb the ladders of power than those who cannot bring themselves to feel that way and retain a distrust or disdain for them. In my life, despite going to an almost all-white school and living in an almost all-white neighborhood throughout my childhood, there was a long period in high school when I struggled with white approval. I wondered: "If they like me and respect me am I doing something wrong? Am I wielding Blackness wrong?" It was almost like I thought of Blackness as a sort of sword—was I using it as a kitchen knife when it was supposed to be a machete? Years later a friend said, "If you're not making the white people around you uncomfortable then you're not doing your job as a Black man in America properly." I felt that sentiment in my bones long before I heard it articulated. But my survival at school was predicated on the approval of white teachers, administrators, and students whom I knew and respected. So this sense of uncertainty about how to wield Blackness in the midst of whiteness, and a teenager's confused motives, led me to say and do little things to subvert their approval and undermine my relationships. I would bring up race to try to make people uncomfortable and demand they confront it and show them that I was hyperaware of it. These things happened almost subconsciously and I sometimes found myself walking away, wondering why I'd said or did what I had. I felt uneasy about being able to relate to white people because some voice deep in my mind told me maybe I shouldn't emotionally trust white people and shouldn't be okay with being liked by them because maybe that suggested something was wrong with me. This after growing up around a lot of white people! I imagine some Blacks who don't grow up with as much close experience with whites as I did might find it a bit more work to master the emotional skills needed to be so deeply comfortable with whites—comfortable on a subconscious level—that you can move together with them through the long, hard war of chasing electoral office. But in another aspect of comfort with Caucasians I never wavered: In my entire childhood it never once occurred to me that whites as a group were one iota smarter than Blacks as a group or that I had anything to fear in competing with them mentally. I was always intellectually confident among them and never felt a need to prove my intelligence to whites. The myth of white mental superiority, and some of the sting of stereotype threat, never reached my consciousness because I had such intense familiarity with them. That sort of deep self-certainty is crucial when entering any arena where Blacks must engage mental combat with whites. "Frankly a lot of it does have to do with how comfortable you are dealing with white people," said Mark Whitaker, executive vice president and managing editor for CNN Worldwide. "We still live in a white-dominated society. It's changing, it's becoming more diverse, but most people with influence and power in America are white and I think in professional life and political life comfort level is just a very big factor. And the onus is still on Black folks to make white people feel comfortable rather than the other way around and I think it is just easier if you've grown up around white people to feel more at ease around them and therefore put them at ease. And some of the success of this generation of politicians has to do with the fact that they're just comfortable around white people. They're not intimidated, they're not uncomfortable, they can be at ease and I think that puts white people at ease."

The potential elected official must make sure he or she is comfortable with making white people comfortable and must also perform the personality traits that put white people at ease. If you want to be an MC you can construct a persona that's like yelling, "Boo!" at quaking white people but you can't do that and have success in politics—or in almost any field beside sports and entertainment. If you want to have a seat at one of the tables of power in politics or business or so many other fields then discomforting white people is going to be counterproductive to your mission.

Wielding Blackness in a non-threatening way can mean many things. A Black person who whites know will never rob them can take something even more valuable by throwing in their faces the pain of oppression or the embarrassment of white supremacy. Obama, while campaigning for president, never did that. "The manner in which he addressed the issue of race during the campaign was absolutely brilliant," Sharon Pratt said, "and one reason he was so good is he could soar above the pain. You watch his manners, his energy—he doesn't have those scars. He didn't have to worry about the police. He didn't have to worry about whether he could use that water fountain. He didn't have to stay on a road and try to figure out where you go to a restroom. He had none of that and he was reared by a very loving white family from Kansas so he doesn't bring that to the party, whereas that edge is there with Michelle. She is in her forties so she has a little bit more of a reality about that era. It gives her an advantage in terms of speaking to our concerns and to our yearnings and our experience but I don't think she could have addressed the issue of race as effectively as Barack did because there is no edge. There was clearly no bias, no cruelty, no 'got you,' no nothing. He just said, 'Folks, these are the facts. This is where we are, this is who we've been,' and it was so masterful because he is so centered and he can sail and navigate above the sky."

UCLA social psychology professor Dr. Phil Goff has conducted several studies on the impact of how Black candidates talk and what the most successful rhetorical strategies are. "The Obama-era candidate," said Goff, "takes great pains to make sure that their language is designed to never make whites feel racist. It's never an indictment, it's always about allowing people to be off the hook. That may be the most central part of it all: the message that we're all in this together and you're not supposed to feel badly for being white." Goff has studied stereotype threat in whites and found that they are often afraid of being thought of as racist. If you want white people to vote for you, you must not activate those fears. Goff has noticed in the speeches of Obama, Patrick, Davis, and Booker a crucial rhetorical strategy for easing tricky discussions about race and taking some of the thorns out of the cactus: the intergroup analogy. "We spent a long time doing a search in terms of what makes white people feel comfortable and uncomfortable having interracial conversations," Goff said. "If we make analogies between different things, you know, this group is like that group, that makes people feel comfortable because if everybody is like everybody else than nobody has dominance over everybody else. In Obama's speech on race he said, 'I can no more disown my Black preacher than I could my white grandmother.' And the analogy was that they're both family, but it was explicitly saying this radical Black male is equivalent to this white female. And when you do something like that the audience hears, 'Oh, okay, it's not their racial differences, it's about the fact that they say controversial or difficult things from time to time.'" Blacks know there is not an analogous relationship between the Black man who says mean things about white people and the white woman who need do nothing to benefit from white privilege, who's accessing her white supremacy card constantly and quietly, but if you want to get into elective office make that distinction in private and use intergroup analogies when talking to voters. And talk as little as you can about how hard it is to be Black. "You do not put Black suffering front and center," says political science professor Farah Griffin. "You just don't do it. You may acknowledge the dark and difficult past that we're coming through but Black suffering cannot be at the core of your message. You cannot appear to be overly concerned with it."

The Black candidate must also allay subliminal associations to those Black men by whom whites feel physically threatened. Obama realized as a teenager that people were comfortable with him if, as he famously wrote in *Dreams from My Father*, he "smiled and made no sudden moves." In the campaign one of his mantras was "No Drama Obama." As president, during certain crises people publicly longed for him to seem angry, and thus emotionally engaged, while he insisted on presenting a cool exterior that sometimes seemed emotionally detached from the turbulence of the situation. All this is part of conveying the non-threatening Blackness that's necessary to be seen as a credible Black leader of whites. Where a white man banging his shoe on a desk while yelling would seem like a no-nonsense tough guy, a Black man doing the same thing would be perceived as frightening, and even if he were the president banging his own wingtip on his own desk in the Oval Office, you can bet someone would think about calling security.

On a personal level, the Black candidate must be beyond reproach—the private life blunders that many officials have gotten away with would never be tolerated in a Black candidate or officeholder. Unless you're like Marion Barry or Charles Rangel with an overwhelmingly Black electorate, the rules are more stringent for Blacks. "During the 2008 campaign Sarah Palin was allowed to have a granddaughter born out of wedlock," said Malcolm Gladwell. "Do you think Obama was? Are you kidding me? You know that kind of thing is not available to a Black man running. He has to be straighter and squarer than anyone else in the race. Remember that famous photo of Obama wearing the mommy jeans? That's calculated. It's very important for him not to be a kind of hipster and for him to be square because if you're going to be the token Black person you're safer if you're square. You're not safe if you're kind of hip and sexually threatening. I mean, there's all these kinds of subtle and not so subtle ways in which Black politicians have got to play a very specific, narrow part or they're out."

It helps if you can evoke a certain innocence with your face. A 2009 study by social scientists at Northwestern University's Kellogg Graduate School of Management quantified the power of a non-threatening Black face by studying what it means to be Black and have a baby face at Fortune 500 corporations. The study was called "The Teddy Bear Effect: Does Babyfaceness Benefit Black CEOs?" Many earlier studies had shown babyfaceness as a handicap for white men striving for leadership because it made them seem less competent. But the disarming nature of a baby face helped talented Black executives circumvent an association with being threatening Black men. The study found the more babyfaced the Black CEO, the more prestigious the company they led, reflected by both Fortune 500 ranking and annual corporate revenue. The study also found that white executives shown pictures of Black executives guessed that the more babyfaced the Black CEO, the more he earns. "To function effectively as an African-American male in the U.S. it helps to have a disarming mechanism," said the study's author, professor Robert Livingston. "Apart from impeccable credentials, demonstrated competence, and tireless diligence, successful Black leaders possess disarming mechanisms—physical, psychological, or behavioral traits that attenuate perceptions of threat by the dominant group. Babyfaceness is but one example. Political conservatism, style of speech or dress, smiling behavior, or even a Harvard education might also serve a similar disarming function." Just because we're in a post-Black era doesn't mean all the rules of white supremacy have changed.

It makes me sick to think of needing to constantly mollify whites and remind them they needn't fear me but such are the rules of the game of acquiring power in America. You're either going to master the game or lose it. And playing the game is so much more worthwhile now than when our grandfathers were our age. When the reward for smiling and placating whites was a demeaning low-level job with no chance of advancement, the game was hardly worth playing. But when the reward for pacifying whites is a shot at becoming the CEO or a vice president of the company—or rising high enough to gain enough experience to leave and become a powerful entrepreneur—then the game is absolutely worth playing.

Livingston concedes that Obama does not have a classic baby face but says his protruding ears and big, quick, easy smile are effective disarming traits. Another classic Caucasian-calming trait that Obama has—one that few want to discuss but is real—is light-colored skin. We know whites attach feelings of trust and expectations of intelligence to lighter-skinned Blacks. It's not a coincidence that over the past four decades almost all of the five Blacks who've been elected to one of the big three jobs, president, senator, and governor, are lighter-skinned—Obama, Massachusetts senator Edward Brooke, Illinois senator Carol Moseley Braun, Virginia governor Doug Wilder, and Massachusetts governor Deval Patrick.

"If Barack Obama were dark like Clarence Thomas he would not be the president of the United States," said Michael Eric Dyson. This is not merely about voters choosing one face over another but the end result of a lifetime of advantages. "Light-skinned privilege is operating at every point along a child and an adult's path," said Melissa Harris-Perry, "so it's not so much a willingness for voters to choose the light-skinned person over the brown-skinned person as it is that the brown-skinned person never even gets there because there's a whole set of choices and experiences, leading up to that moment."

The way you talk—the grammar, articulation, and diction you choose to employ as well as the specific tone that comes from your throat—is also a critical way of either disarming and comforting whites and subtly suggesting that you deserve to be a leader, or of scaring them and cancelling yourself from the game. "I don't think it's talking white," said Professor Patricia Williams. "I think it's a class marker. I think they speak that way in a certain class and there haven't been many of us who have had access to those class levels. To get into that level you have to do it really well without thinking, you have to master all of the subtler aspects of class marking. You don't say, 'between you and I,' but 'between you and me.' You don't say, 'axe,' you say, 'ask.' You know, the very subtle things that the real upper class hears and are hard to master unless you've gone through an educational system or work to make it part of your ordinary speech." Blacks often tease or deride those who speak English in its more textbook form as talking white but those who are said to do so will grow up to have greater access to higher levels of power than those who do not, just as the computer nerds we teased in high school became powerful and valued in the computer age.

Modern Black politicos must also be very careful to never appear like emissaries for the Black community. They must insist that they're enthusiastic about representing all their constituents. "When asked, 'What are you going to do about unemployment for Black people?'" said CNN political analyst Roland Martin, "the president says, 'I want every American to get a job.'" The expectation that the Black officeholder will give special attention to Black concerns is always lurking, so as a candidate they must prove they will not put Black people first—something that candidates from no other racial group must do. Indeed, to establish your bona fides as a serious Black candidate you must at some point be critical of Black people. You have to prove that you're so uncontrolled by the group that you're unafraid to publicly critique Blacks, that you're willing to get tough with Blacks—to show you're willing to say "Pull up your pants," as Obama did. "This never happens with any other group," notes Dr. Marc Lamont Hill. "Joe Lieberman doesn't have to say, 'Look, I'll get tough with Jews in the West Bank.' But Black candidates have to show that they don't have a sort of chauvinistic allegiance to Black people. The Black politician has to say, look, I'm more American than I am Black."

But at the same time voters want to feel that the candidate is comfortable in their own skin and at peace with being himself. So while you're proving that you're non-threatening, able to speak the King's English, able to love white people, not going to make them feel guilty about whiteness, and willing to rhetorically spank Black people once in a blue moon, you also must show you love Black people and being Black. You must proudly evince Black personality tropes. That can be done in many ways: worshipping in a Black church, preaching (not just "speaking") when you campaign in one, publicly playing basketball, occasionally quoting Jay-Z, having a Black wife and giving her fist bumps. Who you marry is extremely important: Since Edward Brooke in the seventies it has been exceedingly rare for a Black elected official to win major office (mayor, congressman, senator, governor, or president) with a white spouse. In 2000 Congressman Albert Wynn of Maryland won re-election after divorcing his Black wife and marrying a white woman. (In what must have seemed like a scene from a madcap political parody film, Wynn's ex-wife became the campaign manager for his little-known GOP opponent. In robocalls she told voters: "Albert Wynn does not respect Black women. He left me for a white woman." Wynn still won.) No one I interviewed thought Obama could have won election with a white wife. A Black man or woman campaigning for votes with a white spouse at their side presents an image that is too confusing and/or threatening to many whites and too off-putting to many Blacks.

Marrying Black communicates a comfort with Blackness that both Black and white voters want to see. So does a healthy and robust relationship with the Black community. Even if Blacks do not constitute a majority of the electorate they can be a powerful voting bloc when properly mobilized. And whites may not trust a Black candidate who's shunned by his own people. "The Black politician," said filmmaker Reggie Hudlin, "must have credibility and clout in the Black community. Whites know the power of the Black vote and influence, sometimes more than Black folks themselves, and if you cannot interpret, translate, and motivate the Black community you are seen as weak." So while you can't appear to be a representative focused on the Black community, you must be able to draw on their support as any ethnic candidate would. Governor Paterson said, "I don't think that you can have some sort of color blindness. If you're Italian and you're running for office, you are going to be working the Italian community, same as if you're Jewish or Irish or Chinese or Puerto Rican. I think that there's a necessary recognition that people who've lived in neighborhoods like yours and who've gone through some of the same experiences and have a sort of homogeneity about life, would be drawn to you. I think that some candidates who have distanced themselves so much have had trouble trying to get back home when they needed those votes. So I'd advise you to don't forget where you came from."

So while your political style must be doggedly inclusive—you can't let white voters think you'll put Black legislative concerns first—you still must make them think you're personally comfortable living within their expectations of a Black person. "I have certainly seen that there are ways in which you must show that you strongly identify with your Blackness so that there's no sense that you're hiding who you are," said Phil Goff, speaking of his studies of Black politicians. "You don't want to say, 'I'm not a Black person,' you want to say, 'I'm not that kind of Black person.' So Obama's decision to regularly play basketball was, I think, as much a personal decision as it was a political image decision. It says, 'I'm genuine, I'm Black, and I don't have to hide it.'"

This confusing constellation of demands seems like playing Twister on a tightrope, but once in office Black politicians find themselves with greater and more nuanced power than previous generations of Black politicians. Harold Ford Jr., whose father was a congressman for two decades, told me, "My dad's generation essentially gave this generation of politicians an expanded toolbox. When my dad was in office they pretty much had one tool: a hammer. Whatever the problem was they showed up with a hammer. It could have been a problem that required just a screwdriver—let's finesse this a little bit—but they showed up with a hammer. They meant no harm, it was the only tool they had. Now I got wrenches, screwdrivers, saws, tape measures, I mean, I got a more complete set."

But what about the Black voter? If you can win the Mollifying Whites Decathalon it will be because you've learned many different ways of making whites trust you while holding on to the love and admiration of your Black constituents. But, like Obama, you will not have gained power solely from the Black community and thus you will owe us less. For artists the freedoms of post-Blackness seem to expand what's possible and give them more power to create to the edge of their imaginations, but in politics it seems to constrict what Black politicians can do for the Black community. After campaigning by convincing white voters they wouldn't give Blacks any special favors, once in office they must keep that promise. Where John Edwards looked noble in making a battle against poverty the centerpiece of his doomed 2008 presidential campaign, a Black candidate could not take up that mantle despite millions of whites being in poverty. "You can't talk race policywise in the same way that Jesse does," said Dorian Warren. This is why Obama has not proven to be the racial savior that some thought he might be. It would seem like cronyism. And Black voters who gain the spiritual uplift and group esteem powerboost from having a Black president (or governor or senator or even mayor) lose out on specific political advancement. "I'm not so certain," Dyson said, "that this notion of a complicated Blackness translates politically as smoothly or easily without tremendous sacrifice and without tremendous, I think, surrender of legitimate territory that Black people have gained."

We need to somehow find a middle ground where Black politicians can get elected without having to all but turn their political back on the Black community. This is not a bargain that Jewish or female candidates need make and it's a very costly deal for Blacks to make. "We see breakthroughs," Reverend Jackson told me. "We see the morning coming, but if the price we pay for getting the crossover vote is to miss base needs, it's too expensive. You can't trade off the rights of the base to a privileged access to the majority. That's too expensive."

# Chapter 8

# We Are Quintessential Americans

America is a nation enthralled with the potential of personal reinvention. In America anyone can go from poor to rich, from outsider to powerful. You may not make that leap because of steep institutional boundaries or a paucity of ability or bad luck—and obviously most will not. But America is uniquely shaped by being a nation of people who know it's possible for anyone to hit the life lottery. We know Blacks must work twice as hard to get half a chance, but we do have a shot. We know the average Black person has less of a shot than the average white person but we do have more of a shot now than at any time in Black history. You can grow up poor in Mississippi and become a billionaire like Bob Johnson or Oprah. You can grow up in the South Bronx and become secretary of state, you can grow up in Hawaii and become president. Even a grandchild of slaves, a child of a farm worker and a maid, raised in a tiny Georgia town without paved roads, can become a Supreme Court justice. In America hope abounds.

As a collective, Black America has lived the American dream of personal reinvention and class ascension. We were dragged through a nightmare, brought here unwilling and in chains, people who were the living asterisk giving lie to the idea that this was the land where all men were created equal. But through four centuries we have gone from enslaved to president, from 3/5ths of a person to CEOs of and executives at Fortune 500s, from chattel to seminal. There's still tremendous work to be

189

done—the American dream is still a nightmare for millions and inaccessible to too many—but there's no question extraordinary progress has been made. We weren't even sure how much progress had been made until Obama's election—before the night he won the Iowa primary the vast majority of Black people did not believe he had a chance. "I'm wondering what did we get wrong?" said Jelani Cobb. "Because even those of us who study this for a living did not see Obama coming. So we didn't know that this was possible and as a community it forces us to take a step back and say, 'Okay, what else do we have wrong and where are we racially?' And I don't think people are necessarily ready to do that. I think that it was disturbing for some folk to actually realize that there was quantitatively less racism in America than we thought there was. None of us like data that contradicts our assumptions. We like the world to be the way, exact way that we imagine it."

After that presidential glass ceiling was broken many Black Americans reassessed America—and let themselves feel a spiritual release, perhaps even the homecoming we had thought would never come. "Obama is a fulfillment moment," Blair Kelley said. "I was crying like a baby the night of the election. I just kept saying, 'Is it real? Are we citizens now?'" It was as if suddenly many of us could finally feel valued by America. "When Barack won," said Sharon Pratt, "people said, 'I feel my country has embraced me.'" We felt, as Michelle Obama famously said during the campaign, pride in our country for the first time. We felt fully part of America for the first time.

While many Black people felt a homecoming in Obama's victory, none confused it with the end of racism. The onward march of racism has been symbolized by the acute racist backlash Obama has absorbed—from a congressman yelling out, "You lie!" during a nationally televised speech, breaking Parliamentary protocol and the rules of basic political and human decorum; to the overt hatred of Glenn Beck, who has charged Obama with hating white culture and kept his jobs; or the hostility of the Tea Party, who, in a barely disguised message, have vowed to "Take the country back!" All that has conveniently reminded us that while the reaction to Obama's candidacy showed us there's perhaps less racism than we thought, the reaction to his presidency has reminded us there is still a great fear of Black power in America. "Obama is a prince," Malcolm Gladwell said. "He is smarter than almost everyone around him, he's more capable, he's an alpha male. And that kind of figure in America in Black form is problematic because part of what they're reacting to is 'I'm not going to be instructed by a Black person.'" America has never offered the full freedom of America to Blacks, so Blacks have never had an easy emotional relationship with America. It's always been complicated. Even with a Black president it remains a relationship dripping with pain.

Many Blacks are reluctant Americans, more loyal to and in love with the chocolate city they live in or the Black nation within the nation. "It's hard to love America," Nelson George said. "The history is so, so, so overwhelming. Your grandparents have terrible stories and then every time there's an Abner Louima or any kind of shooting it becomes a high-tech lynching." A Black president helps matters but we're still too deeply scarred by the things America has done and continues to do to us, things we've experienced specifically and vicariously, still too hurt by attempts to exclude us from the American dream and the violence unleashed on the Black body, to be able to love America with abandon. "We have an affection for people around us, our families, and for non-sentient things like land, maybe the red clay of Georgia," Harry Allen said. "That's soil, that's matter, and that can move people and make them emotional and it is part of America. But there's anger and there's hurt as well. I would love nothing more than to love my country. It sounds like a really cool thing to do." But he can't.

Many Blacks do love America deeply but they seem to me to be glass-half-full types—their love is difficult and complicated and no less fraught than those who say they struggle to love the country. "My claim is that we actually really do love America," said Melissa Harris-Perry. "'Love' is actually a pretty good word for it because it's almost a romantic rather than completely patriotic love, and therefore we get our feelings hurt a lot just as you might expect in the context of a romantic love. I actually think we're really incredibly invested in our identity as Americans and see Americanness and Blackness as constitutive of each other. We really are invested in this idea of it as our place but are deeply hurt by the fact that it doesn't love us back. We're highly critical of it the way that you might be of a rejecting lover in a kind of dysfunctional relationship."

Our deeply fraught love gets expressed in many ways. I once walked behind a boy moving through Brooklyn in a T-shirt with the American flag hanging vertically. Several Black passersby told him rudely to take it off. Another example: "I'm a big baseball fan," said Rashid Johnson. "I'm the guy who doesn't want to sing the 'National Anthem' at the ballpark cause this country has such a perverse history." Johnson actively engages in America's love affair with baseball, which was once the nation's central sport, but eschews an overt signifier of Americanness thrown at him during the game. But baseball itself is classic Americana, perhaps as emblematic as the flag itself. So while embracing one Americana trope, he rejects another, a twoness symbolic of how many Blacks simultaneously love and hate America. As Chris Rock said, for Blacks, America is like an uncle who put you through college but molested you.

We know the past is not done with us. We know it's not even close to past. So deep down I feel, as I think many Blacks do, a sense of not being completely at home in America. Obama's election rocked the foundation of that sentiment and sent cracks running through it and made many of us wonder if it's a dead idea. But it's not dead yet. We have felt unwelcome for so long it's in the blood memory and it will take a while to shake it off. We still feel not fully welcome and even though we helped build the house, we're still not quite ready to take off our shoes. We've been officially shunned and hated by this country and constantly reminded of our worthlessness and whenever we've gotten the first inkling of a thought to maybe reach down to take off those shoes, we get slapped with another nigger wake-up-call, and snap back to stiffness.

How do you survive centuries of sitting stiffly in your house, never really getting comfortable? Sometimes we've soothed ourselves by laughing at America, by getting drunk on the strongest moonshine around— schadenfreude: pleasure derived from the misfortune of others. We reacted to O.J. Simpson's famous not-guilty verdict with a celebratory sneer at the country, taking joy in the government falling on its face. We didn't particularly love O.J., he was never a Black icon, but we loved seeing the system fight and lose, reveled at a seemingly guilty Black man winning, for once, as if that was, somehow payback for centuries of injustice. As if.

That same schadenfreude sneer at America was rampant after 9/11, when I heard many Black New Yorkers express a sadness for America and the innocent lives lost but, in the macro view, a sense of righteousness: The chickens had come home to roost. Some felt America had gotten what it deserved for its long-term foreign policy and did not grieve with quite the same intensity as the white people around us, because we had not gone into 9/11 with the same sense of America as a great nation. Many Blacks saw a self-righteous bully get knocked on his ass, a spoiled country getting the comeuppance it deserved. Obviously not every Black person felt that way and I'm not saying that those assessments are correct or that those feelings are right or fair—I'm saying those feelings were real and indicative of the emotional distance many of us feel from our country. We feel that because the cognitive dissonance of feeling unloved in the country that's supposed to love and treat all its citizens equally is an exhausting stressor, a knot in the soul. How can you feel at spiritual peace in a nation that brags to the world that it accepts the world's poor, huddled masses but doesn't accept you?

I think it's our awareness of being Americanized and our deeply conflicted emotions about that—our righteous unhappiness with America—and our intense desire for a tangible connection with an alternate national identity that led us to Afrocentrism. We have craved a relationship with Africa, we have needed to be from and connected to some other place because our relationship with this country is very problematic and we feel so unrooted here. But Africa, too, is an unrequiting lover because it is a long-distance lover—long-distance temporally. By that I mean we haven't lived there in a very long time. We may retain Africanisms that run deeper than our consciousness can grasp, but our relationship with Africa is wrapped in an overly romantic notion, like a love for someone we no longer know. Or like massaging a body part that's been amputated. "I understand the kind of African detour, if that's what it is," Malcolm Gladwell said. "It's understandable and important because you're dealing with a form of grieving. You're dealing with this trauma of slavery and you've got to close a door on it if you're going to move on. You do have to kind of touch base with that and think it through, but I agree with you, it ultimately doesn't solve your problems and ultimately you've got to move on from it."

How many Black Americans have never been to Africa? How many have no intention of ever going? How many of us can name most of the countries or are aware of what's really going on there politically or culturally or even in sports? Some of us retain a meme called "Africa" in our minds that has little to do with what Africa really is. How many of us can say they know Africa? Or even one country in it? Or even one tribe? How can Black people who've never been to Africa call themselves African-American and at the same time assert that the term is not applicable to, for example, the actress Charlize Theron, who lives in LA but grew up in Johannesburg.

Afrocentrism was necessary, powerful, and beautiful. It gave us a sense of rootedness and a connection with the people, the land, and the culture that birthed us. It helped infuse us with pride and a deeper understanding of what it meant to be us. It helped repair some of the bitterness we felt at being forcibly ripped from our homeland and convey an empowering sense of agency: We were returning ourselves, at least mentally, to the place where we came from. As a teenager in the eighties I read Molefi Asante and Maulana Karenga, owned a kente cloth bow-tie (a now embarrassing teenage fashion choice), and tried to think of myself as African. In college I majored in African and African-American Studies. But despite the spiritual imperative and political necessity of Afrocentrism it has diminished, perhaps because there was something not quite real about it. Our relationship to Africa is a construct like Kwanzaa—a holiday created in Philadelphia in 1966 that does not take place in Africa. It symbolizes Africanness in the Black American mind, which is rightly hungry for a cultural bridge back to Africa, but as a tool to reclaim true Africanness it is as honest as African statues built in a union factory in New Jersey. "I think for me the problem is that the Africa we are naming is imagined," said Melissa Harris-Perry. "So we end up with bastardizations like Kwanzaa and you're not actually tapping into a meaningful cultural or historical legacy. You're tapping into a romanticized vision of what this place is. If it were actually Africa that would be okay, but the imagined Africa is so silly."

I have been to Africa—Ghana, Senegal, Cote d'Ivoire, Morocco— and marveled at its beauty. It was epiphanous for me to feel a human connection I had never known. I ate, I danced, I talked, I people-watched, I played soccer, I saw the remnants of the beginnings of Black culture. I was deeply stirred and inspired. I walked through a door of no return— where slaves went onto ships, never to return home—and almost cried. I wanted to feel at home because I never truly can in America. I wanted to feel the way my white and Asian friends do in returning to their old countries. In some ways I did. But I also had severe moments of disconnect. Africans sometimes let you know you're not one of them.

It started at the airport in Accra, Ghana, where I was skillfully intercepted by a local hustler (there are always many of them waiting for tourists) who quickly smooth-talked his way into being my guide, which I realized after a day meant I had to pay for all his meals and drinks and buy him gifts. He continued to manipulate by promising that tomorrow he'd take me someplace special where tourists could not go. Whenever I had just about had enough of him he'd come up with some amazing experience that justified the expense and erased the frustration of having him attached at my hip throughout my stay in Accra. I don't blame him for his hustle, but his entreaties to intercontinental brotherhood were a smokescreen allowing him to treat me as an ATM. Before I finally shook him loose he let me know that he saw me as a rich American cousin who owed him for the good fortune of having been born in America. You can't imagine my struggle to hold my tongue.

That was a city guy's hustle. In villages they were more blunt. I was wandering through a village outside Accra with small one-room apartments made from packed clay—places where in many ways people lived the same way they did one hundred years ago. This was a place where they sacrificed a goat in my honor and I distributed bags of meat to every family in the village. As I walked along, carrying a bag, a small boy who may have been four or five years old ran up to me and said, "Toubab!" This means "foreigner" or "white man," which is pretty much the same thing in the African sense of race. To them a little white blood means you're white, rather than the American sense in which a little Black blood means you're Black. To the African child who called me white man I said calmly, "No, I'm not white. I'm Black like you." Three women standing several feet behind him burst out laughing as if it were the funniest thing they'd ever heard. In their laugh I could hear them saying, "You're not from here! You don't look like us, you don't talk like us, and you don't even understand what it means to us to be Black!"

Many Black people have had similar experiences. The painter Barkley Hendricks went into a store in Ghana to get water and a gaggle of children followed him in, just watching him. The storekeeper said, "They don't see white men that often." Hendricks said, "White?! Look at my skin color!" She said, "You got a Ghanaians' white color. They're artificial. You're a genuine white man." In Togo, children ran up to Hendricks saying, "Lovo! Lovo!" He asked what that meant. They said, "White man coming!" He said where? They said, "You."

This is not to say that I'm angry or hurt because many Africans mistake light-skinned Black Americans for the people we went to Africa to get away from. I overstand the cultural differences that lead to those misunderstandings. Black Americans and Africans are speaking different languages when it comes to race because of histories on different sides of slavery and the Atlantic. So, while we must love Africa and appreciate its significance in the Black American soul we must also embrace the reality that we are deeply and indelibly American. We are, like jazz, rock 'n roll, and hiphop, a child of Africa molded by distinctly American longings, joys, and pains as well as uniquely shaped by being in America. Our sense of still being strangers in a strange land is so ingrained that it feels like apostasy to say this but it's true: Black Americans are quintessential Americans. We are quintessential to America and American is who we are.

We are among the prime architects of this country. We built its infrastructure with our hands and our backs in slavery. We electrify its cultural stages and sporting fields. But most important, we have helped shape America's laws, forcing it to become as democratic as it claimed it was, demanding our rights and thus forging a more perfect Union, molding this country into the nation the founders set out to create. America would not be what it is without Black America because the multi-generational Black freedom struggle transformed the laws and the soul of America. We demanded the equal protection guarantees of the 14th Amendment include us, too, so we would have the right to vote, the right to attend any school, the right to buy a home, a product, or a meal almost anywhere, and the right to marry whomever we choose. We got all that and the Black Civil Rights movement became the template for civil rights movements fought by women, gays, and Latinos—meaning the Black struggle had an impact on all of America. Black America is like the woman who matures her guy into a better man than he ever thought he could be. We may be, in that analogy, a battered wife in an abusive marriage, but we are still married, by which I mean we are still absolutely, undoubtedly, and indelibly American. "We feel like strangers in a strange land," Mumia Abu-Jamal wrote to me, "because we are treated as strangers. In the white American collective psyche 'citizen' means 'white,' not 'nonwhite.' But I think African-Americans are more American than any people on this land."

Many people told me they sense in Black Americans an urge to reject America before it rejects us. I understand that. It makes perfect sense as a reaction to the past. Blacks have had insurrection in our blood because we've felt America's power and hypocrisies pressing down on our necks. But is that reject-America-before-it-rejects-us ethos the most pragmatic answer for our future? Is the pessimism inherent in that ethos valuable? A prominent Black psychiatrist told me a white executive told her one reason why some Blacks don't get further in major corporations has to do with a constellation of behaviors that stem from failing to identify with the corporation in the way that many white people can. "In order to succeed," Dr. Carlotta Miles said, "you've got to care not just about your job, you've got to care about the company. You've got to feel that you have a vested interest in the company, not that you're just visiting as an executive and collecting your salary. You gotta love the company. And Black people tend not to love it. They like their salaries and they like doing the job, but the job is a job and the company belongs to 'them.'"

That is analogous to our relationship to America. We like the economic possibilities of America, but we may not emotionally identify with America as completely as we could. We may subscribe to the "strangers in a strange land" philosophy enough that it holds us back from success. We may need to more fully embrace our Americanness in order to maximize the power we have as individuals and as a collective. We have every right to feel like strangers here but are we adding to the challenge of being Black by feeling that way? At what point are we dealing with a self-fulfilling prophecy?

I'm obviously not saying our problems in America are our fault. But at what point in a bad marriage with no possibility for divorce—which is what we have with America—do you need to say, "Okay, my partner needs to change but I also need to think about what can I do to make this relationship better for me." We have changed America in the past with less political, economic, and institutional power than we have today and we can change America even further now. Many of us refuse to vote because we don't feel like the system serves us, thus giving us politicians who don't—and needn't—speak to us because we don't vote. Then Obama arrives and we vote for him en masse and push him over the top. That's just one example of modern Black power. Can we flex our power in other ways? Too many Blacks are finding success in America to continue the revolutionary insurrectionism of the sixties. New tactics and mores are required. Can we continue to demand justice, righteousness, respect, and our share of the pie but do so while feeling not like we are owed by America, but that we are co-owners of America and key architects of the nation? "I'm a great patriot," said Kamala Harris, the attorney general of California. "But I'm the kind of patriot who believes in the promise of our country based on the foundation of our country. Who believes in the ideal of our country as outlined in that great manifesto from 1776. And I believe to fight for the ideals of our country is truly what patriotism is about."

We are American. And we are so American that rejecting this country means rejecting part of ourselves. A person who hates their family must also hate themselves, for they will surely manifest family traits. That's a migraine-inducing sort of double-consciousness. "I don't have hatred for white people," Paul Mooney said, "because then I would have to hate myself." Being an American who cannot fully love America means you cannot fully love yourself. "I gotta love these white brothers and sisters," Cornel West said. "Even though I've seen some real sick ones. Gotta learn how to embrace 'em. And inspire 'em to be better."

It may feel dangerous to love America but we must have faith. America's story is still unfolding, its character is still forming. It's a young nation, it's like a teenager among nations, and we must retain hope that it will continue to mature because giving up on it is giving up on part of ourselves. We must believe in the marriage because we can no more divorce ourselves from America than we can divorce America. And because it is the only pragmatic course: Why stay here just growling at America night and day like the world's angriest dog, when the American life lottery is available to you and the chance to acquire power may be within reach?

One day many years ago Barack Obama decided he was going to be president and he wasn't going to let being Black keep him from his dream. Clearly he began shaping himself and his resume into presidential material well before he ran for the Senate, so it was sometime in the early 2000s, or perhaps years before, that he began taking steps toward the presidency. At that point no one else in America thought a Black person could become president. Many thought it would happen someday but not then. Surely "not now" would extend forever. "Someday" would be like the horizon: permanently visible but well out of reach. But Obama had confidence in himself and he had faith in his country that he would not be denied the presidency because of racism. He must have wondered if being Black would be an insurmountable hurdle that would negate years of work—how could he not?—but he pressed on anyway. And he taught us something about America: that believing in yourself and in the country can lead to towering rewards. You will probably not become president someday—though someone reading this will find a golden ticket in their life and become the Larry Doby of Black presidents to Obama's Jackie Robinson. But even if that's not you, there are so many other prizes that you can win in the American life lottery. And for those who opt to hate America and refuse to play the game and reject it before it rejects you, there are no rewards. You'll get the coal-filled stocking you anticipated and never know if it was a self-fulfilling prophecy.

If Obama succeeded at a massive task that almost everyone thought was impossible, then what smaller mountains can we climb that are currently deemed insurmountable? Are there other areas where we are undercapitalizing on our potential and underutilizing the economic, educational, and political resources we have to attack our problems? Are there problems we think we can't solve that we can? Are we blaming white supremacy for things we don't realize that we can tackle? Where else are we limiting ourselves and our possibilities? What if the answer is everywhere?

Reggie Hudlin compared us to being trapped in that classic science-fiction construct where you're put into an alternate reality where your limitations are equal to what you think they are. If you accept the rules of the world you're in, then you'll fail or die; but if you refuse to believe you are limited then you can succeed. We are obviously not in a science fiction world but we are in a matrix and this is a math we can take advantage of: When we accept the constraints that white supremacy suggests we have then we are chained. When we insist that we can go through the wall—as Obama did—then we have a chance to create our own reality. And to acquire power. Obama is a harbinger of a self-determinable future. He is a Black person who decided not to believe that a Black presidency was impossible despite everyone in the country telling him it was so. The result was that he acquired massive power. Hudlin says: "Don't fight the power, be the power." You can stand outside the system protesting and throwing rocks or you can join the system and create change from inside it. That doesn't mean everyone should become a politician:

There are many ways to gain power. I think for too long we have prized the revolutionary sexiness of outside agitation over the workmanlike possibilities of insider capability. We need more insiders to acquire power and effect lasting change by infiltrating white American institutions the way our government once infiltrated Black Power groups. Obama did not fight the power, he became powerful. And so can you.

But America continues to hate you and how could you love something that keeps trying to kill your body and soul? How can you just will yourself over the three-hundred-sixty-foot wall that is white supremacy? Well, America has definitely done its best to try to kill us—physically and spiritually. It has dumped everything imaginable on us. In the movie about America made from America's point of view we are the monster that could not be killed. Imagine Black America as a peaceful but feared giant, moving through the street with 1,001 arrows sticking out of him, countless bulletholes on him, and fragments of exploded grenades all over him. We've been attacked so many times in so many ways, but we've never stopped, forever marching forward, not invulnerable but invincible. Their attempts to kill us have failed. We're still here. We may be in pain but we're still whole. And we're still rising. And I need not fear that which cannot kill me. So let's think like co-owners of the nation while continuing to demand equity and parity and access to those arenas Reverend Jackson says are the crucial battlefields for Black America now—education, capital, industry, technology, and deal flow. All that requires being part of America, penetrating its systems, gaining power, and competing for its spoils. We don't gain from rejecting America before it rejects us and from shunning voting and education. We progress by getting as much education as we can and launching ourselves into corporations and entrepreneurialism and politics and finance and real estate. We need more and more Blacks sitting at tables of real power. Let's be like Barack. Let's get what we want from America in spite of racism. Let's buy into the promise of America and get what we deserve. Let's come home. You can fight the power, but I want us to be the power.

# Outtakes

There were many great quotes, stories, and thoughts that just couldn't be shoe-horned into the text but still demanded inclusion somehow. So, a few Outtakes.

Asked what is Blackness, Kehinde Wiley said, "Blackness is a nomadic aesthetic." He means Blackness itself is fluid and changing—a shape-shifter. "It's a way of making music and art that's about survival in hostile territory. Getting on with falling in love and making babies and creating great food in a world that could give a shit whether or not you live or die. When I say nomadic aesthetic I mean the idea that you're constantly moving, you never have a sense of security or space. And there's a type of soulfulness that comes out of this. The ability to improvise is what gives us jazz, is what gives us this radical response to violence in the street that we call street poetry, which begat hiphop. And radical contingency as a state of affairs is the nature of Blackness."

Henry Louis Gates Jr. said, "I give this lecture where I read quotes from people arguing over what the race should be called. They're arguing and postulating about what the race should be called and why it would be liberatory if we changed to being called 'colored.' Or why everything with the name 'African' in it should be chiseled off the fucking map. Some people said Negro, some people said colored, one person said Africamericans, one person then says how about Afro-American? And you know when all this happened? Between the years 1831 and 1845. When I tell them that everybody in the class almost has a heart attack."

Vera Grant gave me one of my favorite quotes of the interview process. "All of those arguments about what Blackness is have been with us for decades, just kinda intertwined and unraveling, so for me it will be postmodern once it accepts the unraveling. Once you say, 'Ok, let the center be decentered. Let the margin be the center.' That's post-modern." "Decenter" means to displace something from a central position, to disconnect it from assumptions of priority or essence. So she's saying the only way we get to a progressive, accurate, and honest vision of Blackness is to let whatever is considered central be dispersed and become marginalized so that it becomes equal to that which is currently marginalized.

Asked for his definition of post-Blackness Dr. Mark Anthony Neal said, "For me it's the idea of having the freedom to explore the world through a particular Black aesthetic without the reference of always having to be Black. Kathleen Battle [the legendary opera singer] is a kind of good example of this. She's like lots of folks who want to have the freedom to explore their world without it always being a constant reference to their Blackness. I know part of what Glenn [Ligon] and Thelma [Golden] were responding to was this notion that Black art would only be recognized if it so visibly embraced a certain Black aesthetic and they found that limiting. I think there are a lot of folks who feel that way. Not just in terms of artists but folks who are in corporate America, folks who are in academe. I think there are all kinds of ways that folks are trying to find a certain kind of freedom within their identity. And they're thinking of post-Black not as 'not Black' or 'anti-Black' but articulating a much more expansive notion of Blackness."

"Being Black," says Paula Madison, "is no longer as black and white as it used to be. What I mean by that is whatever the historical definitions of Blackness are—nappy hair, being from this neighborhood or that neighborhood, whatever—it's not really as cut and dried as that anymore. It's not as simple a definition as it used to be before when everyone had the expectation that, for example, in New York all the Black people are in Harlem and Bed Stuy and all the Latinos are in East Harlem. Now Harlem has become gentrified and there's Starbucks, and you could go up to Yonkers and find ghettos worse than you could find in Harlem. So it's not as simple to define being Black. You could be the child of two Harvard professors growing up in Cambridge, Massachusetts, having gone to private schools your entire life, have a nanny, summer on the continent—meaning Europe. You're a Black person. You could grow up, you know, in the roughest, toughest part of Boston public schools and you're white. It's not as simple anymore. And consequently the credentials, whatever stripes are supposed to exist that make you Black, are all up in the air."

Stew said, "I want more tolerance of each other within our community. That's really what I want. I think the most controversial thing that's ever come out of my mouth, and I think it's genuinely controversial, is growing up I experienced more oppression from Black people than I did from whites. Because I already knew what white people were all about. I wasn't really looking to them for acceptance. I wanted acceptance in my own community and within my own community I kept getting 'The hair's not right' and 'That music you're listening to isn't right.' I want us to deal with the kid who's reading Camus and playing old rock and going to foreign films and just love him and accept him."

I asked Dr. Marc Lamont Hill how we can best raise the next generation of Black kids to be able to take advantage of modern opportunities. He said, "I think exposing people to different kinds of Blackness early on, so that it becomes taken for granted that Black people are television personalities, politicians, teachers, lawyers, engineers, and ballet dancers. We just have to stretch our imaginations and get people access to those things early so that they become normal. I had to almost superimpose Blackness—I mean, I grew up like a lot of us grew up, admiring permed straight hair. It wasn't until I was in college and joined movements that I fell in love with Black hair. But I had to unlearn a bunch of stuff and when you unlearn that stuff you can be in really good spaces but it's still a process, you're still in recovery. You know, almost always recovering, trying to evict white supremacy from your conscience. You're at war with the world at all moments trying to make that happen, 'cause the world's telling you something different. So that's the active work that we have to do and I think it has to be to some extent devoid of that 'you're just as smart as them' conversation. Kids can read our sort of instinctive obsession with whiteness and measuring ourselves against whiteness. It has to be a conversation about how beautiful Blackness is."

Malcolm Gladwell said many Blacks who enter predominantly white environments, like workplaces or schools, fall into the sort of situation discussed in token studies. "It applies to anyone who's first in the door," he said. "There's three things they talk about: visibility, assimilation, and polarization." "Visibility" refers to tokens receiving a disproportionate share of the group's awareness: They're noticed more. "Assimilation" means tokens are assumed to fit generalizations about their group so they become assimilated with their group identity. "Polarization" refers to differences between tokens and dominants being exaggerated. A study by Rosabeth Moss Kanter concluded, "Visibility generates performance pressures; polarization leads dominants to heighten their group boundaries; and assimilation leads to the tokens' role entrapment."

Gladwell said, "There's all these really interesting, kind of hidden codes about how you have to behave when you're a token. These are certain kinds of rules that they have to follow. For example, with women there's all this really complicated stuff about how they have to, for example, play along because they're treated as the exception. So guys will say, 'You're not like other women, right?' Or they'll say, 'I mean no disrespect to women but I can say this freely 'cause you're so not like other women, they tend to be X.' And the woman is sometimes required to laugh along with the men when they make fun of the other group because she has become an honorary member.

"Visibility is also very interesting. The first woman [or the first Blacks] go through this thing where they're hyper visible, so absolutely everything they do is perceived through a kind of microscope. So even something as simple as the first woman in a sales organization so large that most men didn't know other men's names. But everyone knows the woman's name and who she is. And everything she does everyone knows about. Visibility is this really kind of curious thing because we forget how useful invisibility can be. By 'invisibility' I don't mean that you're being ignored. I mean that you're able to go about your life without everything you do being subjected to all kinds of scrutiny. So implicitly there's something forgiving about environments where you're not highly visible. When you are visible your environment is completely unforgiving. That's a lot of what people, minorities of any stripe, find stressful: that visibility. Visibility doesn't have to be malicious. The mere fact that you are known to all and everything you do is being scrutinized even if it's entirely well intentioned is insanely stressful and by definition screws you up. No one can withstand that kind of scrutiny."

Major Jackson talked about the way race plays out on the sidewalk, among strangers. "I think one of the struggles for many professional Black people is the struggle against, how shall I say it, diminishing their voice and diminishing who they are in the presence of non-Black people. I watched my grandfather, who's a very, very proud Black man, do that. I mean, he didn't go so far as to stoop or anything like that but something changed in his body around white people. He got stiff. Got formal. It's painful for me to bear witness to that. Now, this is a man who was born in 1917 in the South, so that survival technique of kind of adjusting one's body, adjusting one's self, I understood that. But, you know, it was still just painful for me to watch." Jackson finds joy in the different way his generation approaches such moments. "One night I was with my friend Samuel walking in Rittenhouse Square, Philadelphia, and this white woman crossed the street, clearly to get away from us, and Samuel yelled toward her, "Young lady, no need to worry! I speak five languages! I have two degrees! One of them from an Ivy League school!" And there was this acknowledgement of it all that made her even more freaked out. Because he called her on it. So there was this weird vibe. I laughed at it and it was a kind of painful laughter, to think he had to announce his degrees at his schools."


Dr. Melissa Harris-Perry said, "I tend to think Black folks, for the most part, find white people sort of pitiful. Like, almost shadowy in comparison to the substance that is Black life. I think you hear it a lot from Black women around interracial dating—the kind of received response is, well, he can't handle a Black woman because Black women are more . . . pick whatever. Maybe more difficult but also somehow more substantive. So that choosing Blackness is choosing kind of the fullness of humanity that is reflected in Blackness. I think it's part of why womanists love that crazy-ass quote by Alice Walker, 'Womanist is to feminist as purple is to lavender.' I actually think that's how many African-Americans perceive white culture and white America, in precisely that way. Like, they may be lavender but we're purple. I'm sure they have some nice stuff but you know we put more spice in our food, more spice in our life, more, you know, fat on our ass, we're just more. And I'm not sure that constitutes racism—it certainly constitutes stereotyping, a sense that you can collectively determine what a group is—but I think that it's not hostile. It's like we think of them as more sad than bad."

Dr. Blair Kelley said "Black people have a complicated relationship with America. For us, it's a painful love. It has an old history filled with slavery and Jim Crow, so to love America requires a lot more of us. We're a forgiving lover at this point. Because America, for the greater part of its history, hasn't treated Black people well at all and hasn't given much value to Black life at all. So if you come from an abusive relationship and then that person repents and you work it out, you still don't love quite the same way you would have loved had that person never done that to you."

I asked Cornel West what was the most racist thing that ever happened to him. "Probably when I was ten years old, trying to learn how to swim, and my white coach, my dear white coach, took me to his apartment in Sacramento. I jumped in the pool, all the white folks jumped out. They drained the water and said I'd polluted the pool and the place. I just thought, I said, these white brothers and sisters are really sick. I mean, I like to take showers. I have a daily baptism when I take a shower. I know how clean I am and everything and to think that I would be so dirty and poisonous and lethal that I could pollute a pool with my Black body going in . . . ? I said, this is some real sick stuff. I had pity for 'em. It's like, God, these are sick people. They really need help. I can't even swim, I ain't got no stroke or nothing. In fact, I never learned how to swim to this day."

Despite receiving many awards over a long career, Carrie Mae Weems still feels the challenge of survival as an artist. "One of the ways in which I measure whether or not someone is really being successful is to the extent that their work is allowed to really circulate broadly throughout American culture. To that extent it's a very circumspect and very confined territory that Black artists occupy. We're certainly not considered a part of the cannon, the great cannon of American artistic practice. When we look at the great movements in art, whether it's abstract expressionism or modernism or impressionism or cubism or constructivism, we're not a part of those movements. We're not seen as part of those aspects of invention so to that extent, you're always marginalized because you're not considered part of the group of people who really had a hand in the shaping of quote, 'serious artistic practice.' So, you know, when your work comes up for auction, it's not considered a part of the major cannon, it's like this derivative practice. So you might spend a couple hundred thousand for it but you would never spend $10 million for it. Basquiat is in the million-dollar range but he's sort of like the anomaly and he's still not the commodity that Warhol is or any of the other practitioners that came along with Basquiat at that moment right. His auction price sort of tells you how he's really considered in the grand scheme of things next to those people that are considered major. So my great humiliation is that the work is always considered in light of the bigger cannon and in that sense I'm just small potatoes.

"I'm not trying to give up my Blackness so that I can be an artist. I'm interested in my Blackness being considered a part of the greater humanity like whiteness. If we assume that when we talk about de Kooning, we assume that de Kooning is speaking to all of us even though he's painting white people. Why can't my 'Kitchen Table' series stand for more than the Black woman who's in the picture? Why does it have to be considered less than Cindy Sherman's films do? It's still considered less than those things because of this sort of changing same, because it was made by a Black person and Black people still are not completely taken seriously in the same way for their production. And I can't think of the person who's really surpassed that or surmounted that yet in any serious way. And certainly not as a group."


Lorna Simpson said, "A Black figure on the wall in a museum takes up a lot of space. The connotations that are associated with that figure are that it's a Black figure and it's very difficult to elicit a response—and I'm talking about more an art historical response that doesn't just solely focus on race. So therefore if Kiki Smith does a work where it's kind of flailing skin, and there are these shells of Caucasian skin that lay on the floor, there isn't all this reference around race even though in looking at her work it's very specific in that way. But the way that it is looked at is that you can glean a universalist view of humanity in looking at this work about a very specific flailing of a white woman or this white body that is presented. So therefore it expands the interpretation and what you're supposed to come away with but if I were to do that its subject matter becomes circumscribed."

Glenn Ligon said, "I think it has always been there with my work, the reaction. I started working in the early nineties and multiculturalism was the discussion and I distinctly remember reviews of shows where white critics are saying, 'these artists are talking about their identity,' like, period. And that was it. And it was not only an incredible reduction of the work to, like, 'they're just expressing who they are,' as if we had an unmediated direct access to what it means to be Black—you just kind of put it in the painting, or you know make a video out of it, and there it is—but also the sense of territory. That's your territory, that's what you're supposed to be talking about."

Julie Mehretu told me why she likes to work in abstraction. "You can go to the Museum of Modern Art and see my painting and not even know that I'm a Black artist when you look at that painting. I choose the language of abstraction for a reason. For me it's not a denial of wanting to talk about these issues, it's that I feel like so many of these social issues were too complex to talk about with language or with image so I went to abstraction for that reason. Abstraction became so attractive because a lot of the ideas weren't about Black and white, there was all this grayscale that informed my experience and that's why I work within that language. I chose abstraction because of the inability to exactly say what it is you're looking at."

211

Dr. Elizabeth Alexander composed and delivered a poem for the inauguration of President Barack Obama called "Praise Song for the Day." Reading it to the world, she says, was a magical experience. "It was awesome and a profound honor," she said, "but what was really interesting about being up there is that I felt that I was having almost the same experience that I would have been having if I was watching everything and that is to say, [I was] astonished that this day had come and that we had come that far. I was just astonished. And I was with my father, who's seventy-six years old, and with my children and being there with the three generations of our family, that was just overwhelming.

"I was also, as an artist, incredibly, incredibly happy to see that we have a president who values culture, who understands that art can speak in ways that official language cannot, and who believed that that should be a part of the proceedings. I thought that was extraordinary and wonderful. And I really did feel myself very much in the presence of a whole lot of ancestors and I felt that I could see the enslaved Black people who built the Capitol and I could see my ancestor Walt Whitman tending the Civil War dying on the mall and I felt that I could see the slave markets in the distance. All of that was very, very, very present for me in that moment."

Dr. Alvin Poussaint told me the origin of the term "Black." "Adam Clayton Powell Jr. [the legendary Harlem congressman and minister] had used 'Black' and Malcolm X had used 'Black' but it was never used widely until June 1966 when Stokely Carmichael [the legendary leader of the Student Non-Violent Coordinating Committee (SNCC)] was angry as hell after the Meredith March. The marchers had been tear gassed and reporters went up with their TV cameras to get Stokely's reaction to the tear gassing, and he raised his fist to the camera and said, 'Black power, Black power, Black power!' The next Sunday they were on all of the morning talk shows and everyone was asking, 'What's Black power?' He explained that they felt that there was a Civil Rights Act but Black people still had such a sense of inferiority that they had to make 'Black' a positive term to make people feel good about Black and it should no longer be a shameful, derogatory term. It should be something we feel pride in. It caught on immediately, particularly among the young people all over the country, and started the Black is Beautiful movement and I'm Black and I'm Proud. People were ready to get rid of the term 'Negro' because they felt it was put on them by white Europeans. 'Black' caught on with young people right away.

I wrote to Mumia Abu-Jamal: "What does Blackness mean to you?"

He wrote: "I've learned that it's meaning expands, as does time and space itself. That is to say, what it meant to me as a youth, as a member of the Black Panther Party, means completely different things today, for times have changed, and perhaps more importantly, consciousness has changed.

"In the '60s, Black was the byword of a People in struggle, yes—but also in resistance, at all levels of society.

"I remember walking home from the office, and waiting to catch a bus to my Momma's house. It was a hot, sweaty, sticky day, becoming night. Almost every person you passed, youth, elder, man, woman—all either threw up a salute, smiled, gave a 'brutha' greeting, got a 'sista' response. The air was thick with the incense of Black Love—You could see it radiating like heat waves, not off the asphalt, but off the face of the People.

"What makes this experience so memorable, was the negative antithesis of that moment, for, as I was sitting on a bench, waiting for the 42 bus, I spoke to a slightly older dude also on the bench.

"How you doin', brotha?'

'Brutha?' I ain't cho "brutha," nigga! You done fucked up my high!"

"I felt like he sucker-punched me, his words hurt me deeply.

"Part of me recognized that it was the drugs talking, but it was also an insight into something under the drugs: something acrid, hateful, and funky as snakeshit.

"At the anitpodes of Black Love was a niggerness.

"I would look back at that moment, many years later to view the systematic impact of the crack crisis of the '80s. Drugs unleash the worst in us—and it was meant to.

"It atomizes, thus it is the enemy of revolutionary organizing."

I wrote: "Is Blackness in jail different?"

He wrote: "Prison is the dressing room of America, where everybody is naked. The hatreds are more open, unalloyed. So is the repression.

"That's often because the state has immersed two distinct populations together, who would not mix in the exterior world—poor whites (guards) and poor Blacks (prisoners).

"For many Blacks, who don't have historical knowledge, prison is a rude awakening indeed. They are unable to deal with the naked negativity, ignorance, and racism that is the very essence of American prisons."

Reverend Jesse Jackson said, "This generation is unequal and don't know it. We're free now. We're all free now. We're not equal. Today's struggle is for equal. I call it the four stages of freedom: stage one was to end legal slavery. Stage two was to end legal Jim Crow. Stage three was access to the ballot. But you could be out of slavery, Jim Crow, and have the right to vote, but starve to death and face foreclosure. When it comes to the fourth interest, equality, you need access to capital, industry, technology, deal flow, and broadband. You lose allies in that transition. Someone calls you the n-word, you fight back. Someone call you the b-word, you fight back. They foreclose your house . . . ? They don't cut you in on the Wall Street deal . . . ? We're not equipped to fight that fight. That's today's fight. Yesterday's fight was don't call me the n-word. Today's fight is equity and parity: access to capital, industry, technology, deal flow, and broadband. That requires a different kind of analysis and action to go with that action." I asked why he included access to broadband in the list. "Broadband is so key to people who live in the hinterlands," he said. "Without broadband, without access to information, you can't get capital, industry, you can't communicate, you're in a different century. You can't join the computer age. Broadband's a big deal for rural America."

Professor Robert Farris Thompson was not initially a fan of my thesis and sent two timeless emails that showed an intense love for and fascinatingly diasporic perspective on Black culture. "Dear Toure: ini che m ntereke. i would be honored to be interviewed. I am off on research on blacks in Mexico til the last week of March. I must tell you candidly, however, that i am not big on 'post-Blackness' because to me Black culture is forever and therefore never "post". Consider the richness that flows from the great griots, babalawos, iyalorisha, bangudi dya muntu, jazz composers, Sea Island shouters, Afro-Cuban mambo drummers, acute rap minds, inspired black writers like Toni Morrison—at their best all emerge as women and men spiritually aligned. . . . how can you be out-of-date or 'post' when you are spiritually aligned with earth, air, fire and water? or 125th street, for that matter. I remember a Harlem guy saying to me: "oh man, how can anything be post now". if so-called ordinary Black people sense or define the coming of post-Blackness, cool, but until that second coming count me out. kan ben hene, Robert Farris Thompson.

"Dear Toure: Granted if there are 35 million Black people hence 35 million ways of being Black, I would say that those innovating and striking out for something new if they dont know what okra is, never 'signified', have no concept of call-and-response, never say un-un for no, or cool for yes, always smile when they are photographed, wouldn't be caught dead in high affect clashing colors, never double dutched, find rap embarrassing, see no innovations among Black running backs or wide receivers—if they score zero on all of these qualities, well then they may well be post-Black But ol mama culture gonna get their mama. black culture is always evolving, ragtime to jazz to swing to bop to free, or blues into rap, or rumba to son then to mambo—but the basic organizing principles which are weighted differently by every composer of color remain diamond-hard and time resistant, otherwise we wouldnt see relation to Mother Africa. But to rebel or argue against one set of variables—the U.S soul period of the 60's—as 'post-Black' just doesnt work for me against the totality of Black cultures. It ideally should be tested against what was and is happening among all the Black Americas, not just, ahem, the imperial USA. Mother Africa is obviously part of the equation, too, there will always be black eyed peas, suck teeth and cut eye, worship of bunda, signifying tricksters, and, to quote Lisa Jones, style-ways of owning a room that you enter. Cordially, Robert Farris Thompson."

"The funny thing about post-Blackness for me," Greg Tate said, "just cuz I'm so close to Thelma [Golden], is I know that it's a term that was like a clever marketing idea to promote a show of younger Black artists. And in an art world context, the whole notion of Black art carries a pejorative connotation. People thought of it as being limited, restrictive, programmatic. It's a real ideological, provocative kind of neologism she came up with to describe the show. I also know she came up with that name because she didn't wanna describe it as a hiphop show. But the show was called 'Freestyle' so it had a hiphop name. But if you look at the world now, if anything it's becoming post-whiteness. Like whiteness is becoming less relevant as a marker of power, authority, civilization. If you're looking at the places that are looking to be the dominant centers for humanity in the next fifty years or so people are talking about India, China, Singapore."

# Bios

Mumia Abu-Jamal is a death-row inmate in Philadelphia who has been serving time for murder since 1981. He is the best-known death-row inmate in America and his guilt or innocence is widely debated. Before he was arrested he was a member of the Black Panther Party, an activist a journalist, and a broadcaster. During his incarceration he has published several books, including *Live from Death Row.*

Dr. Elizabeth Alexander is a poet, essayist, playwright, professor, and chair of the African American Studies Department at Yale University. She has published five books of poems including *American Sublime* (2005), which was a finalist for the Pulitzer Prize. She has written two collections of essays, *The Black Interior* (2004) and *Power and Possibility* (2007); and a play called *Diva Studies.* She has a PhD in English from the University of Pennsylvania.

Harry Allen is a writer and calls himself a "hiphop activist." He is also the director of the Rhythm Cultural Institute and the host of a Friday afternoon radio show on WBAI-NY/99.5 FM called Nonfiction. He is widely known as the "Media Assassin" for the legendary hiphop group Public Enemy and had a memorable cameo on their 1988 song "Don't Believe the Hype." He responded to Flavor Flav's question, "Yo Harry, you're a writer, are we that type?" by saying, "Don't believe the hype." He is an extraordinary Twitterer and has long been a mentor to me as his manner of thinking is unlike that of anyone I've ever met and consistently inspires me to look at things differently than I normally might. He's the sort of person who reads about physics for fun and brings a scientific approach to almost everything. From talking to him extensively I know he thinks very carefully about every word he utters and is very purposeful about each word choice—which is a powerful and crucial thing for a writer to be reminded of.

Dr. Marcellus Barksdale is a professor of history and the chairman of the African American Studies Program at Morehouse College. He was named Morehouse College Faculty Member of the year for 2010–11. He was one of my professors in college (he also taught at Emory) and a crucial mentor and inspiration.

Keith Boykin is a broadcaster for BET and CNBC, an author, and a commentator. He worked on Bill Clinton's 1992 presidential campaign and then became a special assistant to the president and director of Specialty Media for President Clinton. He was the highest-ranking openly gay person in the Clinton White House and he organized and participated in the nation's first meeting between gay and lesbian leaders and a U.S. president. He also worked on Michael Dukakis's 1988 presidential campaign. He graduated from Harvard Law School. He has written several books, including *Beyond the Down Low: Sex, Lies and Denial in Black America* (2005).

Neal Brennan is a stand-up comedian and the co-creator of "Chappelle's Show." In the Clayton Bigsby sketch you can see his head blowing apart.

He wrote a brilliantly honest joke in which he discusses how white people must have felt on the last day of slavery: "We had a heck of a run, didn't we?" Brennan goes on to tell of a massa saying to a soon-to-be-ex-slave, "You'll be free soon. Please don't murder us. Violence doesn't solve anything." The soon-to-be-ex-slave says, "What about all the times you were whipping us?" Massa says, "Touché, Toby." A moment later Massa says, "If you guys wouldn't mind, can you clear out your stuff? Mexicans should be here to replace you any minute."

Charles Blow is an editorial columnist for the *New York Times*. He graduated magna cum laude from Grambling State University. His 2010 column "Justin Bieber for President" was a classic of political satire.

Jonathan Capehart is an editorial writer for the *Washington Post* who focuses on politics. He was an advisor to Michael Bloomberg in his successful 2000 campaign for mayor of New York City. He's also a regular contributor to MSNBC and is one of the best-dressed men on TV.

Wyatt Cenac is a comedian, actor, and writer who is a correspondent and writer on "The Daily Show with Jon Stewart." He had a lead role in the film *Medicine for Melancholy*. I found out about him while watching the Emmys—when "The Daily Show" won an award many, many people went onstage with Stewart, but only one of them was Black. I tweeted: Who's the Black guy with "The Daily Show?" Within an hour he was told I was asking about him and he tweeted me back.

Dr. Jelani Cobb is an associate professor of history at Spelman College, specializing in post–Civil War African American history, twentieth-century American politics, and the history of the Cold War. He is the author of *To the Break of Dawn: A Freestyle on the Hip Hop Aesthetic* (2007) and *The Devil & Dave Chappelle and Other Essays* (2007).

Cheo Coker is a writer and producer. He wrote the book *Unbelievable: The Life, Death, and Afterlife of the Notorious B.I.G.*, and the screenplay for *Notorious*, the film biography of the Notorious B.I.G. He is also a writer for the TV show *Southland* and executive produced an episode.

Barry Michael Cooper is the screenwriter behind *New Jack City, Above the Rim,* and *Sugar Hill* and the person who coined the term "New Jack Swing" which referred to an eighties and nineties subset of Black music created by Teddy Riley that fused R&B and hiphop.

Brian Copeland is an actor, comedian, radio talk show host, playwright, and author. His one-man show, *Not a Genuine Black Man*, ran for twenty-five months and led to a memoir of the same name (2006). As a singer, Copeland has opened for Ray Charles, Natalie Cole, Aretha Franklin, and Ringo Starr. He is the host of a Sunday morning radio show on San Francisco's KGO. He played Morgan Freeman's son Lee in *The Bucket List* (2006).

Stanley Crouch is one of the great writers of his generation. He is a music and cultural critic, syndicated columnist, and novelist, but is best known for his jazz criticism. He was a noted jazz drummer, a "60 Minutes" essayist, and the recipient of a MacArthur Genius grant. He has written many books, including the novels *Don't the Moon Look Lonesome?* (2000) and the fantastically titled *Ain't No Ambulances for No Nigguhs Tonight* (1972) which is also the title of a 1969 album he wrote. His non-fiction books include *The Artificial White Man: Essays on Authenticity* (2004) and *Notes of a Hanging Judge: Essays and Reviews, 1979–1989* (1991).

His work and his mentoring have had a profound impact on me. He is a writer in the Hemingway and Mailer tradition: masculine, opinionated, egotistical—a fight picker and knockout puncher. Even though I disagree with many of his opinions, I am inspired by the way he expresses himself with his pen and in person.

Rusty Cundieff is a film and television director, actor, and writer. He directed and acted in the legendary hiphop parody *Fear of a Black Hat* and *Tales from the Hood.* He also directed episodes of "The Bernie Mac Show" and "The Wanda Sykes Show," and directed more episodes of "Chappelle's Show" than anyone else.

Chuck D is the lead rapper and founder of Public Enemy, one of the greatest rap groups of all time. At least three of their albums are classics—*It Takes a Nation of Millions to Hold Us Back* (1988), *Fear of a Black Planet* (1990), and *Apocalypse 91 . . . The Enemy Strikes Black* (1991). Chuck's rhymes and persona had a massive impact on my intellectual development, showing me what it meant to be a political and intellectual Black man in the modern world. When I was in college, I arranged for Chuck to come to campus and speak, which led to me spending most of the day with him. I found his example of manhood to be extremely inspiring.

Tananarive Due is an author. She won the American Book Award for her novel *The Living Blood* (2001). She has written many books including *Blood Colony* (2008) and *Joplin's Ghost* (2005) for which she spoke to me about record business minutiae. She teaches creative writing in the MFA program at Antioch University in Los Angeles and has an M.A. in English literature, with an emphasis on Nigerian literature from the University of Leeds in England.

Dr. Michael Eric Dyson is the university professor of sociology at Georgetown University. He is also an ordained Baptist minister and a radio host. He has written sixteen books including *Why I Love Black Women* (2002), *Mercy, Mercy Me: The Art, Loves and Demons of Marvin Gaye* (2005), *Come Hell or High Water: Hurricane Katrina and the Color of Disaster* (2006), *Know What I Mean?: Reflections on Hip Hop* (2007), and *April 4, 1968: Martin Luther King, Jr.'s Death and How It Changed America* (2008). He has a master's and a doctorate in religion from Princeton University. He presided over the 2010 wedding of basketball star Carmelo Anthony and MTV's La La Vasquez.

Okwui Enwezor is a curator, educator, writer, and art critic. He has written several books including *Snap Judgments: New Positions in Contemporary African Photography* (2006).

Lupe Fiasco is an acclaimed MC who's released three studio albums: *Lasers* (2011), *Lupe Fiasco's the Cool* (2007), and *Lupe Fiasco's Food & Liquor* (2006). He won a Grammy in 2008.

Karen Finney is a political consultant with political and corporate clients in the United States and around the globe. She works on political and communication strategy, message development, media training, crisis communications, branding, leadership development, and public affairs. She served in the Clinton White House as deputy press secretary to then First Lady Hillary Clinton and as deputy director of presidential scheduling for President Clinton. She worked as press secretary in Hillary Clinton's successful bid for the U.S. Senate in 2000. I'll never forget sitting beside her on MSNBC during the fallout from the arrest of Skip Gates and feeling her nearly jump through the roof when I said, "What this is really about . . . is white supremacy."

Harold Ford Jr. was a member of the United States House of Representatives from Tennessee's Ninth congressional district centered in Memphis from 1997 to 2007. He was unsuccessful in a bid for the United States Senate in 2006. He is the chairman of the Democratic Leadership Council and the author of *More Davids than Goliaths: A Political Education* (2010). He has a J.D. from the University of Michigan Law School.

Dr. Jeff Gardere is a practicing psychologist who was once the chief psychologist for the Federal Bureau of Prisons. He is the author of *Love Prescription* (2002) and the host of VH1's "Dad Camp," a show about teaching young men how to be good fathers and an excellent example of using TV to change people's lives.

Henry Louis Gates Jr. is the director of the W.E.B. DuBois Institute for African and African American Research at Harvard. He is also the host of the PBS miniseries *African American Lives* and the author of many books including *Finding Oprah's Roots: Finding Your Own* (2007).

Nelson George is an author and filmmaker, and a lifelong Brooklynite. His 2004 HBO film *Everyday People* starred Queen Latifah playing George's HIV-positive activist sister. It's a film of tremendous power. Many think his *The Death of Rhythm and Blues* is a must-read classic of music history. I agree. His *Hip Hop America* is also brilliant: in it he links the history of the Philadelphia 76ers—from Wilt Chamberlain to Charles Barkley to Allen Iverson—to Black music history.

Malcolm Gladwell is one of the great non-fiction writers and thinkers of his generation. He is a longtime *New Yorker* staff writer and the author of four books: *What the Dog Saw* (2009), *Outliers* (2008), *Blink* (2005), and *The Tipping Point* (2000). He is one of my writing heroes.

Dr. Phil Goff is an assistant professor in the Department of Psychology at the University of California, Los Angeles. He has a PhD in social psychology from Stanford University.

Thelma Golden is the director and chief curator of the Studio Museum of Harlem in New York. She is also a guest curator, writer, lecturer, juror, and advisor. In 2008 she was a member of the advisory team of the Whitney Biennial and in 2007 acted as a juror for the UK Turner Prize.

Deborah Grant is an artist. She has had solo exhibitions at Roebling Hall, New York (2006); Dunn and Brown Contemporary, Dallas (2007); and Steve Turner Contemporary, Los Angeles (2007). She has an MFA in painting from Tyler School of Art, Philadelphia.

Vera Grant is executive director of the W. E. B. DuBois Institute for African and African American Research at Harvard.

Dr. Farah Griffin is a professor of English and comparative literature and the director of the Institute for Research in African-American studies at Columbia University. She is the author of several books including *If You Can't Be Free, Be a Mystery: In Search of Billie Holiday* (2001). She has a PhD from Yale.

Dr. Bambi Haggins is an associate professor at Arizona State University who focuses on American film and television. Her book *Laughing Mad: The Black Comic Persona in Post Soul America* (2007) won the Katherine Singer Kovacs Book Award for outstanding book of the year from the Society for Cinema and Media Studies. She has a Ph.D. in television and digital media from the UCLA School of Film.

dream hampton is a writer and filmmaker and the co-author, with Jay-Z, of *Decoded* (2010). She was on *Vibe*'s original staff and produced a peerless documentary about Notorious B.I.G. called *Bigger Than Life*. She has written several timeless pieces about hiphop legends and is one of the best writers of her generation. Her seminal pieces for *The Source* on Snoop (1993) and Tupac (1994) helped shape my understanding of what writing about hiphop should be like.

Kamala Harris is the attorney general of California, the first Black and first woman to hold the office. She is the author of *Smart on Crime: A Career Prosecutor's Plan to Make Us Safer* (2009). She has a JD from University of California, Hastings College of Law.

Michael Harris is an associate professor of African American studies at Emory University and the consulting curator for the Harvey B. Gantt Center for African American Art and Culture in Charlotte, North Carolina. He is the author of *Colored Pictures: Race and Visual Representation* (2003) and the curator of a 1993 exhibit, "Transatlantic Dialogue: Contemporary Art In and Out of Africa," that traveled to the Smithsonian National Museum of African Art. He is an artist with work in the collections of many universities. He has three master's degrees from Yale (philosophy, art history, and African and African American studies and art history) and also a PhD in art history from Yale.

Dr. Melissa Harris-Perry is an associate professor of politics and African American studies at Princeton University. She is the author of *Barbershops, Bibles, and BET: Everyday Talk and Black Political Thought* (2004) and *Sister Citizen: A Text for Colored Girls Who've Considered Politics When Being Strong Wasn't Enough* (2011) as well as a columnist for *The Nation*. I discovered her on MSNBC where her regular appearances on Keith Olbermann's and Rachel Maddow's shows revealed an unusual intelligence and deep understanding of history that made me very comfortable and proud to see her as a Black media figure in those complex conversations. She is also excellent at Twitter.

Christian Haye is a gallerist who ran "The Project" in New York and "MC" in Los Angeles, and represented Julie Mehretu, Barkley Hendricks, Kori Newkirk, Tracy Rose, and Romuald Hazoumé.

Barkley Hendricks is a painter who has been noted for extraordinary portraiture. He is a professor of art at Connecticut College. He earned a master's degree in fine arts from Yale. His work is featured in the National Gallery of Art, the Nasher Museum of Art at Duke University, the Philadelphia Museum of Art, and many other places.

Reverend Dr. Obrey Hendricks Jr. is a professor of biblical interpretation at the New York Theological Seminary and an ordained elder in the African Methodist Episcopal Church. He is a professional musician, a competitive martial artist, and a former Wall Street investment executive. He is a past president of Payne Theological Seminary, the oldest African American seminary in the United States, and is the author of *The Politics of Jesus: Rediscovering the True Revolutionary Nature of Jesus' Teachings and How They Have Been Corrupted* (2006). He has a PhD from Princeton.

Dr. Janet Helms is the Augustus Long Professor in the Department of Counseling, Developmental, and Educational Psychology, and the director of the Institute for the Study and Promotion of Race and Culture at Boston College. Her books include *A Race Is a Nice Thing to Have: A Guide to Being a White Person or Understanding the White Persons in Your Life* (1992).

Dr. Marc Lamont Hill is an associate professor of education and anthropology at Teachers College and an affiliated faculty member in African American Studies at Columbia University. He is the author of *Beats, Rhymes, and Classroom Life: Hip-Hop Pedagogy and the Politics of Identity* (2009) and *Media, Learning, and Sites of Possibility* (2007). He has appeared on Fox News many times, which is admirable for a committed liberal—it's the media equivalent of fighting on enemy territory while using their rules of combat. Despite that, he has always done extremely well. He is now the host of "Our World with *Black Enterprise*."

Reggie Hudlin is the director of *House Party, Boomerang, Servicing Sara*, and other films. He was the president of entertainment at BET from 2005 to 2008. He also had a memorable cameo in Spike Lee's debut film *She's Gotta Have It* as Dog #4. Hudlin is an East St. Louis man who went to Harvard and is part of the firmament of Hollywood, but wears the 'hood and the Harvard in him equally well.

The Reverend Jesse Jackson is a civil rights activist and a Baptist minister, who was an unsuccessful but groundbreaking candidate for the presidency in 1984 and 1988. He also served as the shadow senator for Washington, D.C., from 1991 to 1997.

Dr. John L. Jackson Jr. is the Richard Perry University Professor of Communication and Anthropology at the University of Pennsylvania. He has published three books including *Racial Paranoia: The Unintended Consequences of Political Correctness* (2008), and produced a feature-length film, documentaries, and film-shorts that have screened at film festivals internationally. He has a PhD in anthropology from Columbia University.

Major Jackson is a poet and a professor of English at the University of Vermont. He is the poetry editor of the *Harvard Review* and the author of four collections of poetry including *Hoops* (2006) and *Holding Company* (2011). We met twenty years ago in Philadelphia, his hometown, after I spotted him wearing a T-shirt that said "Back to Africa with a White Woman." My curiosity was piqued. I went up to him and said, "Um, what's that about?" It was the title of a poem of his, and a book of his poems, meant to parody Sixties Black nationalists who exclusively dated Caucasians.

Elon James is a comedian, the founder of the Brooklyn Comedy Company and the Black Comedy Experiment, a part of the comedy troupe Laughing Liberally, and the host of the award-winning web series "This Week in Blackness."

Ben Jealous is the president and CEO of the National Association for the Advancement of Colored People. He has a master's degree in comparative social research from Oxford University where he was a Rhodes Scholar.

Rashid Johnson is a conceptual artist whose work was exhibited in Thelma Golden's landmark 2001 show "Freestyle." He works a lot in photography but also paints and sculpts. He once had an exhibit titled "Chickenbones and Watermelon Seeds: The African American Experience as Abstract Art," in which he gave us photos of black-eyed peas, chicken bones, cotton seeds, and watermelon seeds. That's brilliant. He also once mentioned in the title of his photographs "The New Negro Escapist Social and Athletic Club," which became a bit of an underpinning inspiration for this book.

Dr. Blair Kelley is an associate professor of history at North Carolina State. She is the author of *Right to Ride: African American Citizenship, Identity, and the Protest over Jim Crow Transportation*. I met her via Twitter. She is an excellent twitterer.

Dr. Robin Kelley is a professor of history and American studies and ethnicity at the University of Southern California. He is the author of *Thelonious Monk: The Life and Times of an American Original* (2009), the first book about Monk to include the assistance of the genius pianist's family. Kelley is also the author of the awesomely titled *Yo' Mama's Dis-Funktional!: Fighting the Culture Wars in Urban America* (1997). He has a PhD in history from UCLA.

Dr. Jason King is an associate professor, artistic director, and founding member of the Clive Davis Department of Recorded Music at New York University. He is also a cultural critic, musician, manager, strategist and consultant to artists and labels, and live event producer. His books include *The Michael Jackson Treasures: Celebrating the King of Pop in Photos and Memorabilia* (2009). He has an MA/PhD in performance studies from New York University.

Talib Kweli is one of the greatest MCs of his generation. He has released five solo albums including *Gutter Rainbows* (2010). He first gained fame as part of Black Star, a rap group consisting of Kweli and Mos Def, but I met Kweli when he was working at a great, small Afrocentric bookstore in Brooklyn called Nkiru Books, which is Brooklyn's oldest Black-owned bookstore. Kweli and Mos bought the store and turned it into the Nkiru Center for Education and Culture, a nonprofit organization promoting literacy and multicultural awareness for people of color.

Glenn Ligon is among the most important artists of his generation. He works in many media, including painting, neon, video, photography, and digital. He has had solo shows at the Whitney, the Studio Museum in Harlem, and the Brooklyn Museum of Art and in 2009 President Barack Obama added his piece "Black Like Me No. 2" (1992) to the White House collection.

Wahneema Lubiano is an associate professor and the director of under-graduate studies in African & African American studies at Duke University. She is the author of *The House that Race Built: Black Americans, U.S. Terrain* (1997) and has a PhD from Stanford.

Paula Madison is the former executive vice president of diversity for NBC Universal and a company officer for GE. Madison was the president and general manager of KNBC, NBC's owned and operated station in Los Angeles. She was the first Black woman to be a general manager at a network-owned station in a top five market.

Roland Martin is a journalist, author, and TV personality. He is a CNN political commentator, the host of TV One's "Washington Watch with Roland Martin," and an analyst on the "Tom Joyner Morning Show." He is the author of several books including *The First: President Barack Obama's Road to the White House as Originally Reported by Roland S. Martin* (2010). He has a master's degree in Christian communications from Louisiana Baptist University. He's a great twitterer.

Aaron McGruder is the creator and executive producer of "The Boon-docks," a popular animated show on the Cartoon Network that emerged from a widely syndicated comic strip of the same name.

Julie Mehretu is one of the great artists of her generation. She is an abstract painter who has won the Whitney Museum's American Art Award and the Penny McCall Award. She has had solo exhibits at the Guggenheim Museum in New York and the Guggenheim in Berlin and has work in the permanent collection of the Museum of Modern Art, the San Francisco Museum of Modern Art, the Whitney Museum, the Walker Art Center, the Brooklyn Museum, the Museum of Fine Arts in Boston, and the lobby of the Goldman Sachs tower. She has been honored with a MacArthur Genius Grant. She has an MFA from Rhode Island School of Design.

Paul Miller, a.k.a. DJ Spooky That Subliminal Kid, is a composer, multimedia artist, and writer. He has released many albums including *The Secret Song* (2009), and produced songs on Yoko Ono's *Yes, I'm a Witch* (2007). He's published many books including *Rhythm Science* (2004). He's a professor of music mediated art at the European Graduate School in Switzerland and creator of an iPhone app that lets the device be used as a mixing tool. His film/music/multimedia performance piece "DJ Spooky's Rebirth of a Nation" is a live audio/video remix of D. W. Griffith's *The Birth of a Nation* that includes footage from legendary choreographer Bill T. Jones. It was commissioned by the Lincoln Center Festival and performed around the world.

Dr. Charles Mills is the John Evans Professor of Moral and Intellectual Philosophy at Northwestern University. He is the author of four books including *Blackness Visible: Essays on Philosophy and Race* (1998). He earned his PhD from the University of Toronto.

Paul Mooney is one of America's greatest living comedians. He was part of "The Richard Pryor Show," "In Living Color," and "Chappelle's Show," an incredible triumvirate. He is the author of *Black Is the New*

*White* (2010). Mooney takes the comedian as philosopher and/or social commentator to a new level. One of my favorite jokes of his is about a Black man who moves to an exclusive neighborhood and burns a cross on his own lawn. He yells at his neighbors, "I'm better than all you white people! I don't live next to Black people!" Ah, the delicious irony.

Joan Morgan is the author of *When Chickenheads Come Home to Roost* and a member of the original staff of *Vibe*. She is one of the music journalists I looked up to when I was starting my writing career because she writes with tremendous political passion and doesn't allow her convictions to get swept away by what's popular. Her award-winning 1992 *Village Voice* piece about the rape trial of Mike Tyson is among the best articles I've ever read.

Dr. Carlotta Miles is a child and adolescent psychiatrist and psychoanalyst. We met when I was doing a story about Blacks on Martha's Vineyard, and as with any great psychiatrist, you don't want to stop talking to her.

Dr. Derek Conrad Murray is an assistant professor of the history of art and visual culture department at the University of California at Santa Cruz. He has a PhD in the history of art from Cornell University.

Dr. Mark Anthony Neal is a professor of Black popular culture in the Department of African and African American Studies at Duke University. He is the author of *New Black Man: Rethinking Black Masculinity* (2005) and the co-editor (with Murray Forman) of *That's the Joint!: The Hip-Hop Studies Reader* (2004).

Dr. Angela Neal-Barnett is a psychologist and an associate professor at Kent State University's Department of Psychology. She is the author of *Soothe Your Nerves: The Black Woman's Guide to Understanding and Overcoming Anxiety, Panic, and Fear* (2003). Her work is cited in the surgeon general's report on Mental Health: Culture, Race, and Ethnicity and she is a recipient of the American Psychological Association's Kenneth and Mamie Clark Award for Outstanding Contribution to the Professional Development of Ethnic Minority Graduate Student.

Soledad O'Brien is a CNN anchor who currently hosts the network's "In America" documentaries, for which she recently won the National Association of Black Journalists' award for Journalist of the Year. She is one of my TV heroes because she is classy, intelligent, and an unflappable on-screen presence. I know she's unflappable because when we worked together at CNN I often said things meant to unsettle her, just kinda messing with her, but she always stayed cool.

Abiodun Oyewole is a poet, teacher, and founding member of the legendary spoken-word group The Last Poets which is considered a massive influence on hiphop or possibly, the first hiphop group. The Last Poets delivered politically conscious rhymes in funky rhythms and with an attitude and vibe dervived from the Black Power movement and the Black Arts movement. They, along with Gil Scott-Heron, laid the groundwork for hiphop.

Governor David Paterson was the fifty-fifth governor of New York and the state's first Black governor.

William Pope.L is a visual artist best known for his performance art and interventionist public art, but he also works with painting, photography, and theater. His work was included in the 2002 Whitney Biennial. He is a Guggenheim Fellow. His work is surveyed in the fantastically titled *William Pope.L: The Friendliest Black Artist in America* by Mark H. C. Bessire (2002). He received a Master of Fine Arts in visual arts from the Mason Gross School of the Arts at Rutgers University.

Scott Poulson-Bryant is a writer who's crafted several of the stories that helped me understand what great writing is. He was an early mentor whose thoughtful writing and insightful critique of my writing helped mold me as a writer. He was one of founders of *Vibe* magazine (and the one who suggested the name *Vibe*). His extraordinary profiles of Puff Daddy (1992) and De La Soul (1993) won ASCAP-Deems Taylor Awards for Excellence in Music Journalism. He is working toward a PhD in American studies at Harvard.

Dr. Alvin Poussaint is a professor of psychiatry and faculty associate dean for student affairs at Harvard Medical School. He is one of the premier psychiatrists of his generation and the author of numerous books including *Come On People: On the Path from Victims to Victors*, co-written with Bill Cosby (2007). He was a consultant for "The Cosby Show" and "A Different World."

Sharon Pratt was the mayor of Washington, D.C., from 1991 to 1995. She was the third Black mayor in D.C.'s history, the only woman to have been mayor of D.C., and the first Black woman to be mayor of a major American city.

Questlove is the drummer for and leader of the Grammy Award–winning band The Roots, which has released several classic albums including

*How I Got Over* (2010). The Roots are currently the in-house band for "Late Night with Jimmy Fallon." He is also a DJ and a producer who has worked with Jay-Z, Al Green, D'Angelo, Erykah Badu, and many others. He was the musical director for "Chappelle's Show" and has collaborated with Nike to design the Questlove x Nike World Air Force One. He is a playable character in the basketball video game NBA 2K9. He is also an excellent Twitterer.

Donnell Rawlings is a comedian and actor who had a starring role on "Chappelle's Show." He also had a four-episode air on "The Wire."

Vernon Reid is the guitarist for the Black rock band Living Colour and widely considered one of the best guitarists of his generation. His iconic, incendiary riff on "Cult of Personality" grabbed me the first time I heard it and, thankfully, it is stuck in my head forever.

John Ridley is a comedian, director, actor, and writer who has written several film scripts, including the original script for the film *Three Kings*, and has written for many sitcoms including "The Fresh Prince of Bel-Air" and "Martin."

Dwayne Rodgers is a photographer and a philosopher. He is an excellent twitterer.

Santigold is one the most extraordinary musicians working today. Her 2008 debut album *Santogold* combined New Wave, dub, pop, post-punk, electronica, reggae, and other flavors into an infectious stew. It's still on heavy rotation in my iPod.

The Reverend Al Sharpton is a lifelong Baptist minister, a civil rights activist, and a radio talk show host. He has been a candidate for the U.S. Senate from New York (in 1988, 1992, and 1994), a candidate for mayor of New York City (in 1997), and a candidate for the presidency of the United States in 2004. As a teenager he was a tour manager for James Brown. He has said that was an amazing school for him.

Gary Simmons is a visual artist best known for his erasure drawings in which he uses white chalk that he smudges. He also works as a sculptor. He was part of the 1993 Whitney Biennial and has an MFA from the California Institute of the Arts.

Lorna Simpson is one of the great photographers of her generation. She has won the International Center of Photography Infinity Award and The Whitney Museum of American Art Award. She has had a retrospective at the Whitney and solo shows at the Walker Art Center, The Studio Museum in Harlem, and the Museum of Contemporary Art in Los Angeles. She has an MFA from the University of California, San Diego.

Franklin Sirmans is a curator, writer, and editor. He was the editor of *Flash Art* magazine and the editor-in-chief of *Art AsiaPacific* magazine. He was the co-curator of an exhibit called "Basquiat" and another called "One Planet Under a Groove: Contemporary Art and Hip Hop." He has edited numerous catalogs on contemporary art.

Dr. Claude Steele is the provost of Columbia University and a professor of psychology. He is the author of *Whistling Vivaldi: And Other Clues to How Stereotypes Affect Us* (2010), a great book about stereotype threat.

Dr. Shelby Steele is a writer, documentary filmmaker, and a research fellow at the Hoover Institution at Stanford University. He is the author of many books including *The Content of Our Character* (1991), for which he won the National Book Critics Circle Award in the general non-fiction category. He also won an Emmy for his 1991 "Frontline" documentary "Seven Days in Bensonhurst."

Stew is a singer, songwriter, and playwright. He was the writer and star of the play *Passing Strange*, which won a Tony for Best Book of a Musical. He also wrote and performed "Gary's Song" for "SpongeBob SquarePants."

Stew's play *Passing Strange* is one of the most remarkable plays I have ever seen, documenting the European journey of a young Black man from Los Angeles. It is the classic Black American in Europe story—made famous by Josephine Baker, Richard Wright, and James Baldwin—but where they went to Europe to escape American racism, the main character of *Passing Strange,* who is referred to only as Youth, goes to search for what he calls "the real" and thus figure out who he is. Like Stew, the star of *Passing Strange* goes to Amsterdam and Berlin. Interestingly, the actors who play those with whom Youth interacts in L.A., Amsterdam, and Berlin are all Black—they spend most of the play portraying white people and do so convincingly without relying on masks or makeup, just using actorly gestures and accents.

Greg Tate is one of the greatest writers of his generation and he's on my short list of writing heroes. His work mixes post-structural theory with Black cultural nationalism and his style of writing is, in and of itself, as beautiful and complex as some of what he's written about. I say some only because most of the cultural productions he writes about are less beautiful and complex than his writing style. He is the author of *Flyboy in the Buttermilk* (1992), *Midnight Lightning: Jimi Hendrix and the Black Experience* (2003), and *Everything But the Burden: What White*

*People Are Taking from Black Culture* (2003). He is a founding member of the Black Rock Coalition and a member of the original staff of *Vibe* magazine.

Dr. Beverly Tatum is the current president of Spelman College. She has a PhD in clinical psychology from the University of Michigan, an MA in religious studies from Hartford Seminary, and an LHD from Bates College. She is the author of several books including *Why Are All the Black Kids Sitting Together in the Cafeteria?: A Psychologist Explains the Development of Racial Identity* (2003).

Robert Farris Thompson is the Colonel John Trumbull Professor of the History of Art at Yale University and widely considered America's most prominent scholar of African art. He is the author of several books including the much-lauded *Flash of the Spirit: African and Afro-American Art and Philosophy* (1984).

Baratunde Thurston is a comedian and the web editor at *The Onion*. He is the host of Popular Science's show "Future Of . . ." on the Science Channel and the author of several books including *How to Be Black* (2011). *Thank You Congressional Pages (For Being So Damn Sexy!)* (2006), and *Keep Jerry Falwell Away from My Oreo Cookies* (2005).

Kara Walker is one of the greatest artists of her generation. Her work has often consisted of black cut-paper silhouettes of horrific, nightmarish scenes from slavery that frightened and fascinated viewers, playing with both the historical realism of slavery and the fantastical notions of the romance novel. Her work has been exhibited at the Museum of Modern Art in New York, the San Francisco Museum of Modern Art, the Walker Art Center in Minneapolis, the Modern Art Museum of

Fort Worth, and the Museum of Contemporary Art in Chicago. Walker is the author of several books including *Kara Walker: After the Deluge* (2007), and the subject of several books including *Kara Walker: My Complement, My Enemy, My Oppressor, My Love*. She is the recipient of a MacArthur Genius grant. She has an MFA from the Rhode Island School of Design and is a member of the faculty of the MFA program at Columbia University.

Dr. Dorian Warren is an assistant professor of international and public affairs in Columbia University's Department of Political Science and the School of International and Public Affairs. He is also a faculty affiliate at the Institute for Research in African-American Studies. He specializes in the study of inequality and American politics. He has a PhD from Yale University.

Carrie Mae Weems is one of the most important photographers of her generation. She has been named Photographer of the Year by the Friends of Photography and awarded the Distinguished Photographer's Award in recognition of her significant contributions to the world of photography and the Alpert Award for Visual Arts. She has an MFA from the University of California, San Diego. Her photographs and films have been the subject of solo exhibitions at the Museum of Modern Art, the International Center of Photography, The J. Paul Getty Museum, the Museum of Modern Art in San Francisco, and many others. Her "Kitchen Table" series was an extraordinary portrayal of the Black experience. One photograph I'll never forget from 1990 shows a Black man seated at a table, wearing a jacket and a wide-collared shirt, his face partly obscured by cigarette smoke, sitting directly under a wide-mouthed lamp and looking at a tape recorder. An ashtray and a bottle of wine are off to the side. He could be at home or at a police interrogation, or he could be a spy about to receive his instructions. He's giving the tape recorder a serious face but at the same time he's cool, as if he's being told something heavy and he must weigh how he can accomplish the very difficult and complex task, but he knows he can do it. The caption, printed at the bottom of the photo (which is also the title), takes it to another level: "Jim, if you choose to accept, the mission is to land on your own two feet." Weems is borrowing the language of "Mission: Impossible" to liken the superhuman challenges of being a spy to the challenge of being a Black man trying to get through the day in one piece. Your mission today, my brother, is to survive.

Dr. Cornel West is a philosopher, author, actor, activist, and speaker. He says he has been a champion for racial justice since childhood but he has also told me he was something of a thug and bully as a kid. He is the Class of 1943 University Professor in the Center for African American Studies and the Department of Religion at Princeton University, and his speeches are masterful performances that meld the traditions of the Baptist church and jazz. He acted in both *The Matrix Reloaded* and *The Matrix Revolutions* as Councilor West, serving on the council of Zion. He has released two spoken word albums, including *Street Knowledge* (2004), and many books including *Brother West: Living & Loving Out Loud* (2009) and the acclaimed *Race Matters* (1993). He has a PhD from Princeton.

Mark Whitaker is executive VP and managing editor for CNN Worldwide. He was a senior vice president and Washington bureau chief for NBC News. Before that, he was the editor of *Newsweek*, the first Black American to head a national news magazine, and led them to four National Magazine Awards. He graduated summa cum laude from Harvard, served on the editorial board of *The Harvard Crimson* and went to Oxford University's Balliol College.

Colson Whitehead is among the most respected novelists of his generation and the author of several acclaimed novels including *Sag Harbor*

(2009), *Apex Hides the Hurt* (2006), *John Henry Days* (2001), and the *Intuitionist* (1999). He was awarded the MacArthur genius grant.

Kehinde Wiley is one of the great painters of his generation. He paints contemporary urban Black men in heroic poses that mimic poses from specific old master paintings from centuries ago, thus combining art history and the tropes of hiphop. He has an MFA from Yale. His art is in the permanent collection of the Studio Museum of Harlem, the Brooklyn Museum of Art, the Walker Art Center, and many others.

Juan Williams is a journalist, author, and political commentator for Fox News. He has published several books including *Enough: The Phony Leaders, Dead-End Movements, and Culture of Failure That Are Undermining Black America—and What We Can Do About It* (2007) and the highly regarded *Thurgood Marshall: American Revolutionary* (2000).

Patricia Williams is the James L. Dohr Professor of Law at Columbia Law School and she writes a column for *The Nation* magazine titled "Diary of a Mad Law Professor." She got her JD from Harvard Law. Her 1991 book *The Alchemy of Race and Rights* made the law feel personal.

Saul Williams is a poet, writer, actor, and musician whom I met in the early nineties when he was a star of New York City's spoken word poetry scene. He had a dynamic, passionate style that built on his experience as an actor, musician, and philosopher. He's released several albums, including the awesomely named *The Inevitable Rise and Liberation of NiggyTardust!* (2007). He's published several books including *said the shotgun to the head* (2003). He has acted in many films including a memorable starring role in *Slam* (1998) about a poet who goes to prison.

Terrie Williams is a social worker who has dedicated her career to exposing and battling depression in the Black community. She is also a public relations executive who has represented Miles Davis, Eddie Murphy, and Johnnie Cochran, HBO, and Time Warner. She has published many books including *Black Pain: It Just Looks Like We're Not Hurting* (2008).

Larry Wilmore is a writer, actor, comedian, and producer. He won an Emmy for writing the pilot of "The Bernie Mac Show" and is the author of *I'd Rather We Got Casinos: And Other Black Thoughts* (2009). He is a contributor to Jon Stewart's "The Daily Show," where he is the "senior black correspondent."

Fred Wilson is one of the most important conceptual artists of his time. He was awarded a MacArthur Genius grant and is on the Whitney Museum's board of trustees.

Kevin Wisniewski is an assistant professor of english at Cecil College and the editor of *The Comedy of Dave Chappelle: Critical Essays.*

Kristal Brent Zook is a writer and an associate professor of journalism at Hofstra University and the director of their M.A. journalism program. She has written three books including *I See Black People: The Rise and Fall of African American-Owned Television and Radio* (2008), and has a PhD from the History of Consciousness Program at the University of California, Santa Cruz.

# Acknowledgments

Thanks to my wife Rita for helping me get through the long, intense process of writing a book, and to my kids Hendrix and Fairuz for giving me the motivation that only little ones can supply. But because of my kids I couldn't write at home so thanks to everyone who were generous with space and spirit and loaned me what writers need most, a quiet room: Taryn and Alex Berkett, Alexandra and Phil Broenniman, and Sarah Lazin. Thanks to Sarah, Marty, Amber, Alessandra, and Dom for helping shepherd this from a germ to a book. Thanks to Reggie Hudlin for being a great sounding board. Thanks to Shanta Covington for all your hard work transcribing the tapes. Thanks to all my interviewees for sharing so honestly and to Thelma Golden for helping me connect with so many artists. And a special thanks to the guy who long ago told me to my face, "You ain't Black." You started me down the path that would become this book.

# Index

# Index

# About the Author

Touré is the author of *Never Drank the Kool-Aid*, a collection of essays about hiphop and life, and *Soul City*, a novel, and the *Portable Promised Land*, a collection of short stories. He is an NBC contributor and a regular on MSNBC's *The Dylan Ratigan Show*, and the host of the *Hiphop Shop* and *On the Record* on FuseTV.

He was also CNN's first Pop Culture Correspondent and was the host of MTV2's *Spoke N Heard* and was the host of BET's *The Black Carpet* and the host of several shows on Tennis Channel. Touré remains a Contributing Editor at *Rolling Stone*. His writing has appeared in *The New Yorker*, *The New York Times*, *Artforum*, *Tennis*, *Playboy*, *Vibe*, *Ebony*, *The Best American Essays 1999*, *The Best American Sportswriting 2001*, *The Da Capo Best Music Writing 2004*, and *The Best American Erotica 2004*.

He studied at Columbia University's graduate school of creative writing and lives in Fort Greene, Brooklyn, with his wife and two children.